METAL FATIGUE

American Bosch and the Demise of Metalworking in the Connecticut River Valley

Robert Forrant
University of Massachusetts Lowell

Work, Health, and Environment Series
Series Editors: Charles Levenstein, Robert Forrant, and John Wooding

Routledge
Taylor & Francis Group

LONDON AND NEW YORK

First published 2009 by Baywood Publishing Company, Inc.

Published 2017 by Routledge
2 Park Square, Milton Park, Abingdon, Oxon OX14 4RN
711 Third Avenue, New York, NY 10017, USA

Routledge is an imprint of the Taylor & Francis Group, an informa business

Library of Congress Catalog Number: 2008044326
ISBN 13: 978-0-89503-326-0 (hbk)

Library of Congress Cataloging-in-Publication Data

Forrant, Robert, 1947-
    Metal fatigue : American Bosch and the demise of metalworking in the Connecticut River Valley / Robert Forrant.
        p. cm. -- (Work, health, and environment series)
    Includes bibliographical references and index.
        ISBN 978-0-89503-326-0 (pbk. : alk. paper) 1. American Bosch Corporation (Springfield, Mass.) --History. 2. Metal trade--Connecticut River Valley--History. 3. Plant shutdowns--Connecticut River Valley--History. I. Title.

    HD9506.A64A444 2009
    338.7'66909744--dc22

                                                                            2008044326

Dedication

For my children Leah and Nate, my Dad, and two American Bosch workers,
Tony Fonseca and Donald Staples, who each epitomized everything good
about blue-collar workers, and whose lives remind us of
the quiet dignity found in hard toil.

Table of Contents

Foreword

Metal Fatigue takes this series on to a broader canvas. In previous books our authors explored issues linking working conditions, environmental degradation and sustainability. All these works stress the political and social struggles surrounding the fight for safer work, protection of the environment, and the local and global struggle for a sustainable world. Whether documenting the horrors of cotton dust, the appalling and dangerous conditions in the oil industry, the struggles to link unions and community to fight corporate pollution, or the dangers posed by the petrochemical industry both here and abroad, the books in this series speak directly to the health of workers, community, and the environment. In all these works, the authors, as Forrant does here, keep the politics front and foremost.

As editors, we have always been clear that the analyses presented in this series related to all aspects of work, health, and environment. *Metal Fatigue* takes this further by telling the story of what happened to an industry central not only to the economic core of a manufacturing economy, but also critical to the lives of the workers, their families, and their communities. The impact of what happened here is enormous: jobs and communities destroyed, a whole generation of skilled workers ejected from their jobs and their livelihoods, and a key industry of the U.S. economy essentially eradicated. This is a story of greed, of malfeasance, and of stupidity. It is also the story of the way in which short-term and narrow self-interestedness can leave so many destitute. Similar stories could be told about textiles, boot and shoe manufacture, furniture making, and a host of industries that were the foundations of American industrialization and the livelihood of those who worked in them. There are, however, two important differences distinguishing metal working from many other mass production activities: for the most part, metal workers are highly trained and skilled, and the industry itself makes the equipment that makes the factories.

Forrant writes of this from the heart. He was there, he was a machinist and, later, the business agent for the union. In eight closely argued chapters he unfolds the demise of metal working in the Connecticut River Valley and the consequences not only to the workers and their families but to the region and its economy. When a couple of large companies provide employment to many, and when the secondary industries and tertiary economy are deeply dependent on those companies, their collapse will affect the entire region. And we have seen this movie many times: major manufacturing industry grows up on the natural and human resources a region provides, bringing good jobs and economic growth. As the industry matures, global competition increases, jobs are moved to the un-unionized south and then abroad, local ownership gets bought out (often ownership is transferred to an international conglomerate), wages and jobs are cut to "improve competitiveness" and protect shareholders and, eventually, the industry shuts down leaving massive unemployment, broken families, and shuttered main streets.

To tell this story is to ask a larger question about what we mean by the relationship between work and health and the environment. When a region loses a major employer, such as American Bosch, more than jobs are lost—declining taxes means less money for town and local governments, less is spent on buildings, roads and bridges, on critical social services, and on initiatives to benefit the community. Property values fall and schools lose funding. As families struggle to survive with unemployment or with family members working in low-paying service jobs (if they can find the work), divorce rates go up, domestic violence increases and, perhaps, most tragic of all, suicide becomes more common. As the local economy spirals down, companies supplying the main industry close, recreation centers lock their doors, and everything from pizza joints to clothing stores face bankruptcy. Hospitals lose staff and resources, disease and poor nutrition increase, and the entire panoply of health problems associated with poverty rise. As crime worsens those that can do so flee, tearing the heart from the urban centers. Often, as with the case of Springfield, political corruption blossoms and mismanagement becomes endemic, resulting in the bankruptcy of the city. This is why this story is not just about the collapse of an industry but also about the collapse of a community and a region—the consequences of which link work to health in an all too typical tale.

This is also a book about sustainability. *Metal Fatigue* shows how union leaders, state and local officials, and community leaders in the region failed to both understand what was going on over a 30-year period or build the necessary responses to protect jobs and the community—in short, to *sustain* the social and economic well-being of the region. This story provides many lessons on what can happen when a key industry closes or leaves a region and tells us, ultimately, that we cannot separate work from health both inside and outside the workplace.

John Wooding

Acknowledgments

It is safe to say that this book would not have appeared without the encouragement and support of University of Massachusetts Amherst history professor Bruce Laurie. When my first foray into dissertation work ended with a fire that destroyed a good deal of my research, I left the doctoral program at UMass Amherst and took a series of jobs in a cutlery factory, a plastics factory, and eventually the American Bosch Company in Springfield, Massachusetts. When the Bosch closed in 1986 I had no immediate thoughts of returning to the University, but at Bruce's urging, I did so. He read several chapters in various draft forms and encouraged me to tell the story. Thank you.

I secured a dream job at the University of Massachusetts Lowell in an inter-disciplinary graduate department focused on issues of sustainable social and economic development. There, colleagues were researching, writing, and teaching about how regional economies rise and fall, how policies can have an impact on regions reinventing themselves and reproducing decent jobs for the workers affected by long-term historical processes of deindustrialization. In this regard, I was very much influenced by the important work of two UMass Lowell colleagues, Michael Best and William Lazonick. Had national policymakers heeded their well-crafted words, I am convinced we would not be floundering in the doldrums of global recession at the end of 2008.

I owe a debt as well to two other Lowell colleagues, Professor Chuck Levenstein and Professor John Wooding. Both of them read drafts and offered great suggestions for how to craft the manuscript. In addition, over quite a few lunches and beverages around Lowell and Cambridge, Massachusetts, we plotted and schemed to make our University better and the workplace safer and more sustainable. Both of them, along with Professor Philip Moss and Professor Linda Silka, helped me to see what it is that really good professors do; I only hope that I lived up to their expectations. I also owe John Wooding special thanks for coming up with the book's title. The British do know how to turn a phrase.

Many thanks to the numerous people along the way who read and commented on portions of this work or listened to me discuss it at conferences. A special thanks to students in my labor history and work and technology courses who sat through my lectures on how and why so many-blue-collar regions of the United States were forgotten during one economic bubble after another, all of which were somehow supposed to magically insure wealth and prosperity trickled downward! At the end of 2008, we can see the abject failure of such thinking.

Several librarians at both UMass Amherst and UMass Lowell were extraordinarily helpful in securing obscure books and articles and microfilm rolls of newspapers for me to use throughout my research. In particular, the archivists at UMass Amherst have assembled a terrific collection of trade union documents and other materials that offer a treasure for historians and others interested in the Connecticut River Valley labor story.

Baywood Production Editor Bobbi Olszewski was extraordinarily helpful in keeping me going and carefully editing the manuscript. Without her involvement, the book would still be wallowing in my study. Julie Krempa did a great job helping me with nuts and bolts of getting the manuscript in order. The gifted Mary Lee Dunn provided her great editorial expertise toward the end of the process and improved my words immeasurably. Craig Thomas produced a map of the Connecticut River Valley to help readers spatially locate the story. Two Lowell friends, Jim Higgins and Joan Ross, produced the front and back cover work; lets hope the contents of the book rises to the level of their efforts. Lastly, thanks to another Lowell friend, Andy Jacobson. I did lots of editing and had lots of discussion with people about this book in his café, Brew'd Awakening. If you are ever in Lowell, check it out.

Finally, without appearing too maudlin, this work simply would have been unthinkable absent the time I spent and the friends I made working in what we always referred to as simply "the Bosch."

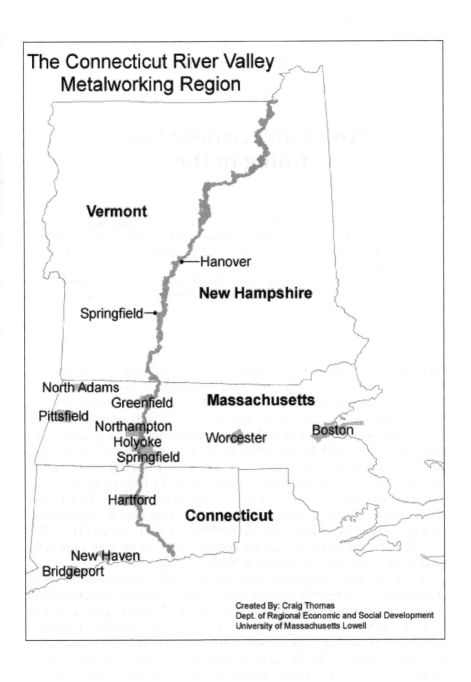

The Connecticut River Valley Metalworking Region

Vermont

Hanover

New Hampshire

Springfield

North Adams

Greenfield

Massachusetts

Pittsfield

Northampton

Holyoke

Springfield

Worcester

Boston

Hartford

Connecticut

New Haven

Bridgeport

Created By: Craig Thomas
Dept. of Regional Economic and Social Development
University of Massachusetts Lowell

CHAPTER 1

"You Don't Believe She is Going to Die"

It's sad. I didn't realize how much it meant to me, till I think about not going back in there. It's a 36-year habit that's going to be hard to break. I can close my eyes and walk through the building, smelling the cutting oil, hearing the machines.

– Donald Staples, 36-year American Bosch machinist,
on hearing the closing announcement on February 4, 1986

On February 4, 1986, at approximately 2 p.m., thousands of workers and their families' lives changed in ways they could only begin to imagine. On that day United Technologies Corporation ordered the closure of the 76-year-old American Bosch manufacturing plant in Springfield, Massachusetts, capping a nearly 32-year history of job loss and work relocation from the sprawling factory. The plant was built in 1911 by the Robert Bosch Magneto Company of Stuttgart, Germany, and in the years before it closed, workers manufactured precision fuel-injection systems for automobiles, trucks, and tanks. Early on, the four-story plant produced electrical starters and other car parts and, for a brief period, radios. Bosch's history represents the quintessence of the story of manufacturing companies in the valley and across the northern tier of the United States. This book describes the profound economic collapse of the region, with a particular focus on the Bosch, as it was known, its workers, and union.

For over 150 years Springfield, Massachusetts, stood at the approximate center of a prosperous two-hundred-mile industrial corridor along the Connecticut River between Bridgeport, Connecticut, and Springfield, Vermont, populated with hundreds of machine-tool and metalworking plants and thousands of workers. Initially, the Springfield Armory, built at the start of the 19th century, propelled the economy forward. By the early 20th century, firms like American Bosch advanced the valley's economy further and provided well-paying work for thousands of people.

1

However, starting in the late 1940s, outside investors and manufacturing conglomerates bought many of the area's leading firms, including Bosch. New owners, intent on securing a rapid and high return on investments, were disinclined to nurture the skill base and felt no obligation to the valley's workers or the rich industrial heritage. The historical account of American Bosch's steady decline and dramatic shutdown is placed in the context of this wider deindustrialization. The Bosch's closure marked the watershed for large-firm metalworking and metalworking unions in the central portion of the Connecticut River Valley, while the crushing collapse of several once-prominent machine-tool builders in Springfield, Vermont, punctuated decline at that end of the river valley.

How I Got in the Middle of Things

In 1974 a house fire cut short my first graduate-school sojourn. After a summer and fall spent planting and weeding countless rows of onions and harvesting pumpkins and squash for local farmers, I took a job in Florence, Massachusetts, in a 75-worker cutlery factory straight from the pages of Charles Dickens. Next, I worked 14 months in a Swedish-owned capital-intensive plastics factory. There, on a single shift, I produced one ton of melamine powder destined for dishes, bowls, cups, and hairbrush and toothbrush handles. After a scrape with the afterlife in an industrial accident, constant exposure to chemicals, and a failed unionization effort focused on health and safety issues, I made my way onto the American Bosch shopfloor. During my early days in the plastics plant, I asked everyone within earshot how they could take the ever-present chemical smells. "You'll get used to it kid," was the common refrain; this proved true, prompting me to get out with my sense of smell still intact.

The Bosch, with its pounding and screaming machinery, heat-treating furnaces, and forklifts careening everywhere was a sprawling and exciting place. There, as badge #4729, I joined over 1,500 men and women who cut, sawed, bent, ground, tapped, milled, and drilled steel. Rising at 5:30 a.m., punching in at 6:30 a.m., clocking out at 3 p.m., I remained for close to 12 years, serving as International Union of Electrical Workers Local 206's elected business agent for 4 of those years. With a grandfather who built machinery for 40 years, a grandmother who stitched baby shoes for some 30 years, a father who cut meat 40 years for the Great Atlantic & Pacific Tea Company, and a working mother who joined the ranks of the mail-order catalog business in its infancy as an order clerk, I made the switch from graduate school to blue-collar work sort of fit.

Having three younger sisters and a brother in a good Catholic household, I joined the working world in 1961 at age 14, bagging groceries and stocking shelves in a small market. I needed to earn money for clothes, the movies, a new Rolling Stones album, Red Sox tickets, or a baseball glove. My dad, active in the Amalgamated Meatcutters union, often took me to his union meetings, sometimes talking during the ride about the importance of sticking together. This concept, lost on me in my preteen years, rushed back when I entered the Bosch. Many workmates reminded me of my Dad: hardworking, dedicated to supporting their families, scrupulously fair, and desperately reliant on their weekly paycheck to "make ends meet," a phrase I heard often at my kitchen table growing up. I recently read a description of how Bruce Springsteen's music "captured the dignity of ordinary work;" this was evident every day I worked at Bosch.[1]

Background to the Closing

United Technologies Corporation (UTC) acquired the Springfield factory in 1978 and a steady diet of layoffs followed. The unionized workforce fell from 1,130 in 1979 to approximately 800 in 1985, well down from the over 3,000 workers who crowded the factory floor during the Vietnam war. Numerous production lines were relocated to UTC facilities in the South and abroad, but despite these cuts, the elected officials and state and national labor leaders we spoke with believed UTC's assurances that the Bosch would never close. Anxiously, we watched friends lose their jobs and read about other plants closing in the region. We did not think we were "crying wolf" or mimicking Chicken Little, shouting "the sky is falling" when we warned anyone who would listen about our fears.

Why the concern? During the 1970s, the Springfield factory's fuel-injection work comprised an ever smaller portion of the corporation's overall business. In 1981 UTC demanded that the union ratify a new incentive plan; without it, spokespersons threatened, the company could not be cost competitive in Springfield. Increasingly unessential and fearful that the factory would close, unionists granted the wage concessions in a vote that bitterly divided workers. Before the vote, management promised a $20 million investment in new equipment for a favorable vote and no new investments should the cuts be rejected. Few investments were made; instead, UTC opened a factory in Columbia, South Carolina, and within three years moved 500 additional jobs there.

The company blamed every round of job cuts on slumping sales, while it continued to ship work customarily done in Springfield to the South Carolina factory. Meanwhile, UTC's order backlog reached $10 billion. Once, after 200 layoffs, management insisted that it was "trying to get its act together," because there was "too much capacity for too little production" in Bosch's manufacturing division.[2] "Yes," we replied, recognizing the "kiss of death" this statement contained, "that's precisely the problem, the excess capacity you developed has made Springfield vulnerable." The union workforce fell below 800 by April

---

[1] Jon Pareles, "His Kind of Heroes, His Kind of Songs," *New York Times* (NYT), 14 July 2002, Section 2, 1.

[2] Arthur Zalkan, "Committee Will Assess Plant's Future," *Springfield Daily News* (SDN), 16 July 1985, 9; Randi Eldredge, "United Says Plans Unchanged," *Holyoke Transcript Telegram* (HTT), 27 June 1985, 10.

1985, and young workers constantly asked me what I thought about their buying a house. "Is my job secure?" "Will we be here at least 10 more years?" "There's plenty of work, right?"

Through plant-gate rallies, a letter-writing campaign, and lobbying efforts with federal, state, and local elected officials, unionists once more warned that the plant's exit strategy was in place. We approached our union's top leaders asking for help in coordinating a summit meeting for all locals in United Technologies plants—nothing much came of this idea. In June 1985 the local newspapers reported unionists at the United Technologies-owned American Bosch plant in Springfield, Massachusetts, had been sounding off for months that United Technologies was going to close the plant.

At a July 1985 briefing for 30 federal, state, and local elected officials, in my capacity as the business agent for International Union of Electrical Workers Local 206, I stated that with their assistance, "We can begin to tackle the difficult problem of keeping a large industrial employer here in the Springfield area, with all the good jobs that the plant presently provides."[3] But UTC's spokespersons issued repeated indignant denials about a possible closing and promised Springfield's mayor and the region's congressional delegation that the Bosch was in the city to stay; nonetheless we remained concerned. I warned everyone not to be taken in:

> We see clearly the impending closing of this plant. All the publicity has been on how Massachusetts is on the rebound. But people are ignoring another reality. The whole industrial base from Greenfield to Springfield is being eroded. There may be jobs available, but they are definitely not good paying ones.[4]

The loss of 200 or 300 jobs should be genuine cause for concern, I noted. However, "these jobs are only the beginning. A clear pattern of mismanagement and disinvestment on the part of United Technologies points toward a phase-out of all operations in Springfield. Repeated management assurances that they have a strong commitment to the city are contradicted by their actions."[5] A little over six months later, oh how I wished I was wrong.

WHY THE STORY MATTERS

For over 150 years along the length of the Connecticut River from just south of Hartford, Connecticut, to White River Junction, Vermont—with Springfield, Massachusetts at its center—thousands of metalworkers and machinists built

---

[3] Local 206 memo, June 2005. "UT Disinvestment Points Toward American Bosch Closing," University of Massachusetts Amherst Labor Archives (UMALA) Local 206 collection.
[4] Local 206 memo, "UTC Disinvestment," June 1985.
[5] *HTT*, June 26, 1985, 8.

machinery and produced components for every critically important industry in the nation. The valley's richly variegated manufacturing base, deeply rooted in a set of industries that required at their core large numbers of skilled workers, produced economic prosperity well into the 20th century. Firms relied on these workers to both submit and exchange their ideas to improve manufacturing processes. Continual skill development is reflected in the widespread recruitment and persistent cultivation of precision machining skills. The arrangement was so successful, according to one account, "that the aggregation of metalworking shops it produced was a model of economic success for 150 years."[6] It would not be hyperbole to call the collection of firms along the river the "Silicon Valley" of its day.

Through the first half of the 20th century, the valley's machinery builders fostered the growth of a range of industrial districts in Massachusetts such as watches in Waltham, footwear in Haverhill, furniture in Gardner, textiles in Lowell, jewelry making in Attleboro, cutting tools and taps in Greenfield, and metalworking and specialist machine making in Worcester and along the Connecticut River. These were the high-technology industries of the 19th and early 20th centuries. The proliferation of industrial sectors, in turn, supported hundreds of small, highly specialized tool-and-die shops and foundries engaged in the production of textile machinery, fixtures, tooling, gauges, and made-to-order components in Massachusetts. Just as the consumer-goods industries created a market for machine-tool makers, the machine makers diffused innovations across the industrial spectrum. Metalworking productivity rose, and workers in the industry enjoyed rising standards of living.

As we will see, the country did not sustain this premier position as manufacturer to the world, nor did the valley's industrial economy change and prosper in the face of global competition. Precision metalworking firms and machinery builders now relocated production to lower wage, nonunion plants. Firms eliminated the formal ways workers engaged in shop-floor problem solving. By the late 1950s and early 1960s, skills development and the diffusion of new production methods lessened while collaborations between firms and between managers and workers on the shop floor that once characterized the valley's history ceased.[7]

For most of the 25 years before the plant closed, managers employed numerous strategies to enhance their profitability and keep the local union off balance. These strategies included expansion to the low-wage southern United States in the 1950s, a flurry of overseas acquisitions in the 1960s, and the construction of production facilities in Italy and Holland in the 1970s and South Carolina

[6]Norman Boucher, "A Natural History of the Connecticut Valley Metal Trade," *Regional Review* (Winter 1994): 6-12, 7.

[7]Wayne Brohel, *Precision Valley: The Machine Tool Companies of Springfield Vermont* (Englewood Cliffs, NJ: Prentice-Hall, 1959).

in 1982. Occasional investments were made in Springfield, but the new products developed in the Bosch's engineering laboratory and experimental machine shop routinely got shipped elsewhere when high volume production was required.

Thus, when the union's negotiating committee met with the company at the West Springfield Sheraton Hotel on February 4, 1986, we anticipated acrimonious negotiations for a three-year labor agreement. With a brand new plant in South Carolina performing what we still called "Springfield work," the negotiating committee worried that the antiquated, four-story Springfield plant could be relegated to the dust heap. We were ready, as one negotiating-committee member described it, "to bargain with the devil for our very working lives." Then, in an instant, the company's chief negotiator, flanked by a quartet of expensively suited top managers devoid of any emotion, handed over a single sheet of paper titled "Plant Closing Memorandum."

At precisely the same moment, several armed security guards entered the plant and the workforce had their world flipped upside down. Retired long-time union president Anthony Fonseca called the announcement a "sucker punch from hell." Fonseca recalled that in 1982 he warned congressional, state, and city officials that UTC would bypass Springfield and produce fuel-injector pumps in South Carolina. "Nobody, nobody wanted to help us despite the letter campaign to stop UTC from selling us out," he noted.[8] Twenty typed lines pulled the rug from under workers and their families and closed the book on the plant's rich history of precision metalworking. For added emphasis, the company called their decision irrevocable. And in a few weeks, union officers received a memorandum titled "PLANT CLOSING: PHASE OUT SCHEDULE." Devoid of human empathy for workers in the plant, it read in part:

> A schedule has now been developed to phase down the Springfield Operation. Starting on March 4, 1986, approximately 85 Springfield employees will be laid off. Subsequently, an average of 60 people will be laid off per week until June. An additional 175 people will be laid off between June and August. . . . More details will be related to you by your supervisor as they become known.[9]

Jobs and a way of life ended. Stunned, we filed out of the hotel, got in our cars, and made the short drive back to the union hall, not knowing that everyone else had been informed of the shutdown. Hundreds of workers sprinted to the hall from the nearby plant and were there to greet us. Angry shouts of "Make them stay or make them pay" reverberated off the buildings.

---

[8]Arthur Zalkan, "'Boiling' Ex-Union Chief Says He Warned of Plant Closing," *SDN*, 5 February 1986.
[9]*Plant Closing Phase Out Schedule*, in possession of author.

A small number of people blamed the union; fortunately, most people directed their anger at the company. One second-shift worker, reporting for work, saw people streaming out of the factory and at first thought he was late for work. "It's an emotional nightmare," he commented. "When I got to work, there were people coming out of the gate crying. The guys on my shift were turning right around and coming out. . . . It was like a funeral in there." Older workers worried about their future and described their jobs in nostalgic and emotional terms. One worker remarked, "I can't picture a company selecting a guy who's 60-years-old to run a machine when they can get someone who is 35 or 40 to do it."

Typical of many long-time employees, Donald Staples spent 36 years in the sprawling factory. Of the 645 union members employed on the day of the closing announcement, 80 had worked at Bosch over 30 years. A union activist, Staples sent two sons to college on the steady wages he earned at Bosch. He planned to work in the plant for one summer after his discharge from the Army in 1945 and then go to college in his home state, New Hampshire, on the G.I. Bill. In a reflective mood he told me:

> It's sad. I didn't realize how much it meant to me, till I think about not going back in there. It's a 36-year habit that's going to be hard to break. I can close my eyes and walk through the building, smelling the cutting oil, hearing the machines. I imagine I will be doing it until the time we close. It's automatic. The only way I got anything in this life is by working for it. And I did. I don't plan on starving to death. There aren't many places that are looking for a 61-year-old ex-machinist, so I don't have any fantasies. But, I definitely want to keep working. You can't live too well if you don't work.

About the closing, he remarked, "It's as if they tell you your mother's sick, but you never believe she is going to die." A skilled machinist and union negotiating committee member, Staples said he once would have been proud if his two sons had followed him into the Bosch; he was very happy they did not.

Bosch veterans worried about their younger colleagues with small children (like me) and large mortgages. Thirty-four-year-old Tom Quinlivan noted right after the closing announcement, "What's the first thing you do? You cut back. I'm starting over at 34. Well, everybody starts over at some point in life. That's all there is to it. I just don't want to go into another shop." With six years in the factory, Bruce Rozell, 33, had been laid off from other metalworking jobs nine times. "I've got a house. I've got two kids. I've got loans. So now I don't know," he said. "I've never had real security. I always expected that little pink slip would be in my pay envelope again, but I never thought she would close for good. What the hell is going on?"[10] Another unionist, 28-year-old Larry Mazza, shared Quinlivan's concerns. With a wife, an 8-year-old child, and a $40,000 mortgage he assumed nine months before the closing, he was concerned about finding a new job. "If I had known for sure they were going to do this, I never would have bought the house," he said. But Mazza was a bit better off than many of his friends, for believing the closing rumors, he took several classes at a local technical training center. "It looks better on a résumé than just working in a shop," he said.

For many people, Bosch was their exclusive employer; so any talk of preparing a résumé was like speaking in tongues. What were they to do? For years, friends arrived at 5:30 a.m., started oil-stained coffee pots, argued about sports and cars, bragged about their children, and offered support when the occasional family crisis disrupted daily life. A rich network of "shop entrepreneurs" peddled donuts and newspapers to raise money for their children's college tuition, a youth baseball or hockey league or a local charity, sold football betting cards in season, and conducted a variety of other small-time gambling enterprises. Company attempts to curtail the coffee pots, newspaper sales, and more questionable practices never succeeded.

For years the union and company-sponsored Athletic Association supported golf, pistol, baseball, softball, and bowling teams in the city's industrial leagues and organized frequent trips to Boston for Red Sox, Bruins, and Celtics games and to New York City for Yankees, Rangers, and Knicks contests. The Boston–New York sports rivalry produced spirited confrontations in the shop; this was the stuff of life. In addition, every fall the Athletic Association rented a local amusement park for a family outing, and it also sponsored a children's Christmas party. Workers wondered how their early-morning get-togethers and the various athletic and family events could ever be replaced.

A local newspaper article titled "The Economy of Indifference" captured the pessimistic mood of most fired workers:

> People who have been earning $11 an hour will now be forced to re-enter the workforce at perhaps half that, requiring many to work two jobs or to depend on a second wage-earner in the family. Too much can be made of this last point, but with all the hand wringing about marital stress, broken families, latch-key children and the range of contemporary domestic ills, it's worth noting that the much vaunted service economy—with its low-paying mall jobs and office satellites—has done nothing to uplift the American family. On the contrary, having a job that is beneath your skill

---

[10] Comments from conversations I had with many workers in the days following the announcement, interviews I conducted several months later and newspaper accounts. Newspaper sources are Marisa Giannetti, "Bitter Pill for Workers at Bosch," *Springfield Morning Union* (SMU), 5 February 1986; Jeanne Mooney, "The Hard Times are Ahead," *HTT,* 7 February 1986, 1.

level, at wages beneath your potential, is degrading. And how does one cost that out?[11]

THE BIG PICTURE: WELL-PAYING JOBS DOWN, INCOME INEQUALITY UP

Less than 50 years ago, the United States accounted for close to half of global manufacturing output, with manufacturing hegemony unchallenged. "According to the Federal Reserve Board's index, manufacturing production doubled between 1945 and 1965 and tripled between 1945 and 1976.[12] Increasing productivity by workers in plants like the Bosch led to rising living standards. Family incomes grew at a spirited rate, enabling Donald Staples to send his boys to college and, later on, making it possible for Larry Mazza to buy a house. However, this premier position eroded as Japan, continental Europe, and several developing Asian nations challenged the country's preeminence in machine tools, precision metalworking, cars, steel, major household appliances, and consumer electronics. The result: between 1973 and 1975 unemployment grew from 4.8 percent to 8.3 percent and from 1979 to 1983 slightly over 2 million jobs (almost 16 percent) were lost in the highly unionized durable-goods production. American industry was "hollowed out."[13] One in five workers' jobs disappeared during the 1980s; the escalation of closings in Greater Springfield was a painful manifestation of this. Among the Fortune 500's largest manufacturers, employment dropped to 12.4 million from 15.9 million in the decade of the 1980s, and among them, General Motors, Ford, Boeing, and General Electric eliminated 208,500 more jobs between 1990 and 1995.[14]

[11] "The Economy of Indifference," *HTT,* March 10, 1986.
[12] Michael A. Bernstein, "Understanding American Economic Decline: The Contours of the Late-Twentieth-Century Experience," in Michael A. Bernstein and David E. Adler, eds., *Understanding American Economic Decline* (New York: Cambridge University Press, 1994): 3-33, 15; David M. Gordon, "Chickens Home to Roost: From Prosperity to Stagnation in the Postwar U.S. Economy," in M. Bernstein and D. Adler, eds., *Understanding American Economic Decline,* 34-76.
[13] In fact, a few weeks after the Bosch closing announcement, in its March 3, 1986 issue, *Business Week* published a special report on what it termed the "hollow corporation." The article quoted Akio Morita, Sony Corporation chairman: "American companies have either shifted output to low-wage countries or come to buy parts and assembled products from countries like Japan that can make quality products at low prices. The result is a hollowing out of American industry. The U.S. is abandoning its status as an industrial power," 57. A framed copy of the cover adorned my office wall until we sold the union hall.
[14] Robert Forrant, "Between a Rock and a Hard Place: U.S. Industrial Unions, Shop Floor Participation and the Lean, Mean Global Economy," *Cambridge Journal of Economics* 24 (2000): 751-769; Michael D. Yates, "Economic Crisis and the Crisis of U.S. Labor," *Monthly Review* 53 (April 2002): 47-55.

This restructuring proved catastrophic for industrial unions, as the percentage of unionized manufacturing jobs declined to approximately 10 percent in the 1990s from almost 50 percent in 1970. In the mid 1950s one in three U.S. workers belonged to a union, compared with one in five in the 1980s and just one in seven in 1999.[15] Over this period very little union-led collective action opposed this massive job loss, nor did labor's political allies in Congress provide relief. Organized labor's ranks thinned as manufacturing declined, while communities scrambled to save jobs and attract new ones by offering companies financial inducements to stay put or move in. Corporations sought "tribute" where they could find it and eager to command what Jefferson Cowie called "the spatial relations" of production firms routinely threatened work removal to quash organizing campaigns and further blunt labor's bargaining-table demands.[16] The river valley's unions failed to develop what geographer Andrew Herod described as "networks of solidarity across space," which might have slowed the outflow of jobs.[17] For example, Bosch unionists could have appealed to their counterparts in Springfield, Vermont, who, as we will see, were also faced with threats to their livelihoods. However, Vermont workers had remained members of the United Electrical Workers, unlike their Bosch neighbors who left the U.E. in the early 1950s. The Bosch case reveals how futile workers' situations were when they traversed the slippery slope of concessions.

By 1996 about three-quarters of employed workers labored in service industries, up from two-thirds in 1979, and the manufacturing powerhouse General Electric generated over half its revenues from financial and business services. Pharmaceutical companies making pain-killing drugs, ulcer medications, and anti-depressants comprised four of the ten largest corporations in the United States, an intriguing commentary and on our psyche. Giant retailer Wal-Mart—in 1998 the nation's fourth-largest corporation measured by revenues—created over 500,000 jobs in the late 1980s and early 1990s. Now, what's good for the United States is no longer what's good for General Motors but what's good for Sam

[15] Harley Shaiken, *Automation and Global Production: Automobile Engine Production in Mexico, the United States, and Canada* (San Diego: University of California, Center for U.S. Mexican Studies, 1987); Barry Bluestone and Bennet Harrison, *The Great U-Turn: Corporate Restructuring and the Polarizing of America* (New York: Basic Books, 1988); Robyn Meredith, "The Brave New World of General Motors," *NYT*, 26 October 1997, C1; L. Belsey, "Labor's Place in the New Economy," *Christian Science Monitor*, 27 March 2000, 1.

[16] Jefferson Cowie, *Capital Moves: RCA's 70-Year Question for Cheap Labor* (Ithaca: Cornell University Press, 1999), 185.

[17] Andrew Herod, *Labor Geographies: Workers and the Landscapes of Capitalism* (New York: The Guilford Press, 2001), 259.

Walton![18] In a sharp reversal of positive socioeconomic trends in the 20 years after the Second World War, the loss of well-paying industrial jobs caused a national wage depression and increased income inequality.[19]

This downward trend persisted in the last two decades of the 20th century; between 1987 and 1996, average compensation grew 1.1 percent, compared with 4 percent between 1977 and 1986 (including the 1983 recession). Inflation-adjusted median income in the mid-1990s was roughly 5 percent lower than in the late 1970s, and household wealth was highly concentrated, with the top 5 percent of households, those making $133,000 or more, holding 21.4 percent of all income compared with the bottom 60 percent, with 27.6 percent of household income. As the 20th century ended, nearly 20 percent of households had a zero or negative net worth (greater debts than assets). The growth of low wage, nonunion service employment and part-time employment contributed to these trends, and the global capacity glut in steel, autos, computer-chip fabrication, and aircraft production guarantees that these trends will persist.[20]

David Harvey and Erik Swyngedouw documented a similar phenomenon in discussing massive layoffs at a Rover assembly plant in Cowley, an industrial suburb of Oxford. Restructuring "meant not only the loss of many of those secure jobs which secured community affluence for many, but a transition in the qualities of the jobs that remained (through speed-up, deskilling, and the like) so that the

---

[18] For union membership see L. Belsey, "Labor's Place in the New Economy." For a discussion of the global aspects of capital flight, see William Greider, *One World Ready or Not: The Manic Logic of Global Capitalism* (New York, 1997), esp. chs. 5 and 7; International Labour Organization, *The Impact of Flexible Labour Market Arrangements in the Machinery, Electrical and Electronic Industries* (Geneva, 1997); William Lazonick and Mary O'Sullivan (eds), *Corporate Governance and Sustainable Prosperity* (New York: Palgrave, 2002); John Tagliabue, "Buona note, guten tag: Europe's New Workdays," *NYT,* 20 October (1997), D1; Louis Uchitelle, "Global Good Times Meet the Global Glut," *NYT,* 16 November (1997), D1. For important theoretical work on deindustrialization see Andrew Herod, *Labor Geographies;* Andrew Herod, *Organizing the Landscape: Geographical Perspectives on Labor Unionism* (Minneapolis: University of Minnesota Press, 1998); Teresa Hayter and David Harvey (eds), *The Factory & The City: The Story of the Cowley Automobile Works in Oxford* (London: Mansell, 1993); Andre Lipietz, *Mirages and Miracles: The Crisis of Global Fordism* (London: Verso, 1987); Doreen Massey and Richard Meegan, *The Anatomy of Job Loss: The How, Why and Where of Employment Decline* (New York: Methuen & Co., Ltd., 1982).

[19] A good deal of the material in this section relies on Suzanne Konzelmann and Robert Forrant, "Creative Work Systems in Destructive Markets," in Brendan Burchell, Simon Deakin, Jonathan Michie, and Jill Rubery, eds., *Business Organisation and Productive Systems* (London: Routledge, 2002). Chuck Collins, Betty Leonard-Wright and Holly Sklar, *Shifting Fortunes: The Perils of the Growing American Wealth Gap* (Boston: United for a Fair Economy, 1999); David Weinberg, "A Brief Look at Postwar U.S. Income Inequality," *Current Population Reports* (1996): 60-191; F. Hansen, "Compensation in the New Economy," *Compensation and Benefits Review* (January/February 1998): 7-15.

[20] C. Collins et.al., *Shifting Fortunes,* 1999.

difference between the marginalized and the employed became less rather than more marked."[21]

In Massachusetts during the 1940s and 1950s, several cities dominated the manufacturing economy: Lawrence, Lowell, Fall River, and New Bedford in textiles and apparel; Brockton, Haverhill, Lynn, and Peabody in footwear; and Springfield, Greenfield, and Worcester in precision metalworking and machinery building. From the 1960s to the 1990s, close to one-third of the jobs in several manufacturing categories disappeared, including apparel, electrical equipment, industrial machinery, and textiles. From the late 1980s to 1997, total manufacturing establishments declined almost 14 percent, and employment fell nearly 25 percent. Where there was manufacturing growth, concentrated in the production of goods for the computer and telecommunications industries, none of the state's old-line industrial cities shared in the growth and prosperity. None of the 22 Massachusetts communities with at least 10 high-tech manufacturing firms were in the Connecticut River Valley. In other words, many of Massachusetts' older industrial centers failed to benefit from the 1990s economic boom and became mired in a severe downturn, one with historical roots in the loss of precision manufacturing and industrial production.[22]

In 2004 the City of Springfield's financial plight became so severe that it fell under the control of a five-member Finance Control Board set up by the state legislature and named by Republican Governor Mitt Romney. The Board was to work for three years to administer a badly needed bail-out loan from the Commonwealth and to put the City's muddled financial affairs in order. The price of the loan was the end of democratic decision making for the city of 152,000. In 2007, because not enough progress had been made, the life of the Control Board was extended through 2009. Some parts of the city run better, but many essential services have been cut, bitter labor relations exist with teachers and most other municipal unions, and there was no concerted effort to rebuild the city's, and by extension the region's, economies. Poverty increased, and the neighborhoods

[21] David Harvey and Erik Swyngedouw, "Industrial Restructuring, Community Disempowerment and Grass-Roots Resistance," in T. Hayter and D. Harvey (eds), *The Factory & The City*, 11-25, 16; United States Department of Housing and Urban Development, *The State of the Cities 2000* (Washington, DC: GPO, 2000).

[22] Robert Forrant and Shawn Barry, "Winners and Losers: High-Tech Employment Deals an Uneven Hand," *Massachusetts Benchmarks*, Summer 2001, 12-16; Sue Kirchhoff and Bill Dedman, "90s Boom Bypassed many Mass. Regions, Census Shows," *BG*, 22 May 2002, 1. Massachusetts figures, www.boston.com/census. Marcella Bombardieri, "Richer, Poorer: For Many in Mass., 90s Boom was Just a Bust," *BG*, 5 May 2002, B1.

Median household income adjusted for inflation fell in major cities including New Bedford, Pittsfield, Springfield, and Worcester, and median household income in former metalworking cities in the Connecticut River Valley dropped well below the state average ($50,502). The numbers are Greenfield, $33,110; Holyoke, $30,441; Springfield, $30,417. Just outside the valley, the former industrial cities of North Adams ($27,601) and Pittsfield ($35,655) fared no better.

were neglected as city leaders attempted to jump-start the moribund downtown. Finally, the Control Board's failure to build broad-based consensus around any of its actions meant that between 2004 and 2007 little was accomplished to revitalize the civic engagement required to get Springfield off of life support.

WHAT'S INSIDE

The next chapter traces the growth of machinery building and metalworking along the Connecticut River during the 19th and early 20th centuries by examining events in Springfield, Massachusetts, and the central role that the Springfield Armory played in developing and diffusing precision-machining skills and collaborative relationships among firms in the region. Indeed, the river valley's prosperity emanated from its highly diversified industrial economy. The third chapter details the history of the American Bosch plant from its construction in 1911 through the early 1950s, and includes a discussion of successful efforts to unionize the plant in 1937, the 1948 sale of the firm to a Wall Street investment company, and the internecine labor battles in the plant in the early 1950s, which culminated in the replacement of the plant's original union, the United Electrical Workers, with the International Union of Electrical Workers. The next three chapters consider the collapse of metalworking and machinery building in the Connecticut River Valley from 1950 to approximately 1990. Chapter 4 follows Bosch jobs to Mississippi during the early 1950s and analyzes workers' reactions to the loss of hundreds of jobs and the first inkling of permanent employment insecurity. I detail the elaborate steps managers took to cultivate alternative production sites in the 1950s and early 1960s. Chapter 5 describes events in the Bosch from the 1960s to its closure in 1986. In Chapter 6 a wider lens is utilized to consider what happened to many of the region's precision-metalworking and machine-tool firms as the United States went from being the world's leading exporter of machine tools to its leading importer. This story is told through several case studies of firms in Springfield, Massachusetts, and Springfield, Vermont. Chapter 7 moves to the southern end of the Connecticut River Valley and considers union–company dynamics between Pratt & Whitney Aircraft and the International Associations of Aerospace Workers. For most of the 1980s and 1990s workers there suffered through several rounds of deep layoffs and the occasional threat by Pratt to cease jet engine manufacturing in the state. The final chapter returns to Springfield, Massachusetts, and discusses the city's current financial situation and how its crushing debt is linked to the entire region's massive job loss. Numerous failed economic development schemes, gross mismanagement, and political corruption exacerbated the slump caused by the disappearance of thousands of jobs.

In 1954, just after Bosch managers announced they would build a factory in Mississippi, an unsigned letter appeared in the union's *Labor Bulletin* from a unionist who asked and answered: "Is Bosch doomed in Springfield?"

The working class may succeed in postponing its final breakdown; they cannot avert it whichever way they turn, whatever remedy they resort to, they cannot overcome the fatal contradictions that gnaw ceaselessly at the workers' vitals. . . . The moving to Mississippi plan is one of the desperate schemes to which stockholders have turned to increase their dividends.[23]

A short time later a worker expressed everyone's anxiousness over job loss and falling living standards in a poem that lampooned Charles Perelle, then the company's top boss.

Perelle Psalm
Perelle is our shepherd. We are in want
He maketh many to lie on park benches
He leadeth many beside his still factory
He restoreth our doubt in his administration
(Yea, though we walk through the valley of unemployment)
We will always remain hungry.
He clobbers our rates with new methods
Our expenses over-runneth our income.
Surely poverty and hard living shall follow us, all the days
Of the Perelle administration.
And we shall dwell in a rented house forever.[24]

The poet's bitterness is a sharp contrast to the company's sentiments in a 1927 newspaper advertisement titled "Gaining Worldwide Recognition of Springfield Craftsmanship." The company boasted,

The Bosch craftsman finds a joy in his work. It leaves his hands to make the world better—to make it more livable and to make life happier. He is a substantial citizen. He spends over three million dollars yearly, and mostly in the city of Springfield. He buys homes, motor cars, and everything else a happy, healthy home-loving citizen needs.[25]

So much had changed in 30 years; so much more would change in the 28 years after the poem was written, for by then Bosch would be closed.

Finally, a symposium in the June 2002 issue of *The Journal of American History* on how historians' lives can enter their work raised interesting questions for me. I have never been too far from the memories of the Bosch's closing. One does not forget the experience of watching hundreds of workers lose their jobs. I wondered about my family's economic future while I listened to older workers express their fears for the future. John Demos made the point that the historian's selection of subject is inextricably rooted in self. "Far from being a matter of serendipity . . .

---

[23] *Labor Bulletin* (LB), April, 1953, 2.
[24] "Perelle Psalm," *LB,* February, 1958, 2.
[25] *SMU,* 26 June 1927, 23H.

such choice is powerfully, and personally, determined."[26] In what follows, I punctuate the historical narrative with my experiences as a machinist and a union leader in the Bosch, and my experiences as a 30-year resident of the Connecticut River Valley, who participated in struggles to maintain and promote sustainable livelihoods for working people. I believe I did justice to the historian's craft, so as not to bring shame on my academic mentors. At the same time, I hope I did justice to the story of co-workers like Donald Staples, who confided to me that the Bosch closing "felt like a death in the family." In telling significant portions of this story from a worker's vantage point, I wanted to convey the larger story of the thousands of machinists and metalworkers who, though they were almost always smarter about their work than their bosses acknowledged, and who were more principled than the corporate officers who dismantled the regional economy, were unable to use their knowledge to reconstitute that economy in a way that was friendly to the working class.

[26] John Demos, "Using Self, Using History . . . ," *The Journal of American History* 89 (2002): 37-42.

CHAPTER 2

"A Breeding Ground for Inventors and Skilled Labor": The Valley Flourishes

THE INDUSTRIAL BEEHIVE

In his comprehensive 1930 history of Massachusetts industry, Orra Stone referred to Springfield as "a beehive of diversified production," with 24 large factories, having annual production in excess of $1 million and numerous smaller supporting specialty shops.[1] Internationally and nationally recognized, the city's and larger valley's skill base drew England's Rolls Royce, Inc. to the region in 1919 after an exhaustive search for potential sites for a new manufacturing facility. Access to an expansive supply of highly skilled machinists and easy access to quality drop forgings and other precision parts dictated the decision. "The artisans of Springfield—from long experience in fine precision work—were found to possess the same pride in workmanship as the craftsmen of England," Rolls Royce concluded. In the early 1920s the Springfield Rolls Royce factory employed 1,400 workers and built automobiles costing $20,000.[2] Henry Ford too praised the city's metalworkers noting, "The skill of Springfield's engineers and workers is traditional. . . . (I)n its world-wide search for never ending improvements, the Ford Motor Company has found in Springfield dependable sources for a substantial portion of its equipment and parts used in building Ford cars."[3] The American Bosch, one of Stone's 24 large factories, was a big part of this vibrant metalworking region.

Built in 1911 by the Robert Bosch Magneto Company of Stuttgart, Germany, and unionized by the United Electrical Workers in 1936, the plant

---

[1] Orra Stone, *History of Massachusetts Industries: Their Inception, Growth, and Success* (Boston: S. C. Clarke Publishing Co., 1930) Vol. 1, ch. 26, "Springfield: The Industrial Beehive of Massachusetts and the Habitat of Almost Four Hundred Manufacturing Enterprises," 481-574. By 2002, just two of Stone's "Big 24" remained.

[2] O. Stone, *History*, 550. "The Rolls Royce in Springfield," *Vanity Fair* (June 1926). The Springfield Rolls Royce plant ceased production in the early 1930s as the customer base shrank with the onset of the Depression.

[3] *Springfield Republican* (SR), 21 November 1936, 13.

specialized in the design and manufacture of precision fuel-injection systems for automobiles, trucks, and tanks in the 1960s. Earlier, the four-story plant produced electrical starter parts for cars and for a time radios. Factory photos from the 1930s show toolmakers with lab coats and ties plying their honorable trade. At the onset of the Second World War, over 200 greater Springfield specialty machine shops and metalworking firms produced precision components and machine tools. According to a 1941 Work Projects Administration study,

> Springfield's products have been for the most part the essentials of other industries, the machines, the tools, and units that turn the wheels of industry the world over. Because of this inter-relationship and the diversification of her industries, Springfield has suffered less from economic upheaval than single-industry cities of New England.[4]

For a time after the Second World War, manufacturing jobs in the region expanded. In Hampden County, Massachusetts—which contained the region's largest cities of Springfield and Holyoke—nearly 60 percent of employment was in manufacturing; but from this high-water mark, employment dropped continually for the rest of the 20th century. There remain in the valley an infrastructure of old mills and factories extremely expensive to modernize, an aging precision metalworking skill base, and a large number of small and medium-size (10-100 employees) contract machine shops, whose current growth, ironically, is constrained by the profound absence of skilled metalworkers. In this chapter, I review the valley's 19th-century industrial history, followed by sections on the development of several firms, including the Armory. Springfield's industrial development and workforce structures are compared with those of Holyoke, Lowell, and Worcester, Massachusetts.

THE SKILL BASE FORMS

For over 150 years Springfield, Massachusetts, was at the approximate center of a prosperous two hundred-mile industrial corridor along the Connecticut River between Bridgeport, Connecticut, and Windsor, Vermont. The city benefited from a 1794 decision by the United States Congress to locate a federal armory there. Described by one British visitor as "beautifully situated on an eminence overlooking the town,"[5] the Armory diffused numerous production techniques to other firms that built tools, fixtures, machinery, molds, rifles,

---

[4]Writers' Program of the Work Projects Administration, *Springfield, Massachusetts* (Springfield: City of Springfield, 1941). 57.
[5]The description is in Nathan Rosenberg, ed., *The American System of Manufactures: The Report of the Committee on the Machinery of the United States 1855 and the Special Reports of George Wallis and Joseph Whitworth* (Edinburgh: Edinburgh University Press, 1969): 364.

carriages, rail cars, and eventually automobiles.[6] The Armory functioned as the hub of this industrial district. According to historian Merrit Roe Smith, Springfield became a "magnet for skilled mechanics and inventors and the center of a thriving gun trade in the Connecticut Valley." Hundreds of skilled mechanics and machine designers took a stint at the Armory before traveling to other clusters of machine-tool and metalworking companies throughout New England.[7] The Springfield region enjoyed a comparative technological advantage over many other regions of the country due to the diffusion of Armory manufacturing techniques, such as the utilization of gauges, fixtures, jigs and dies, and the availability of large numbers of skilled metalworkers. According to David Hounshell, "The Armory acted both as a clearing house for technical information and a training ground for mechanics who later worked for private arms makers or for manufacturers of other goods."[8] Economist Norman Boucher describes how everyone benefited from this arrangement: "The Armory got its desired technology, the local economy prospered, and the small-arms manufacturers developed both a reliable customer and the expertise they needed to tackle new markets." Glynnis Trainer described New England as a "breeding ground for inventors and skilled labor." In his 1916 account of the machine-tool industry, Joseph Wickham Roe noted, "If New England no longer holds all the good mechanics in the United States, there was a time when she came so near it that the term 'New England mechanics' had a very definite meaning over the whole country."[9] Economist Michael Best contends:

[6]Michael Frisch, *Town into City: Springfield, Massachusetts and the Meaning of Community, 1840-1880* (Cambridge: Harvard University Press, 1972); Nathan Rosenberg, ed., *The American System of Manufactures.*

[7]M. Frisch, *Town into City.* The quote is in Nathan Rosenberg, ed., *The American System of Manufactures,* 364; Merrit Roe Smith, "The Military Roots of Mass Production: Firearms and American Industrialization, 1815-1913," unpublished paper, Massachusetts Institute of Technology Science, Technology and Society Program (1995) quoted in Erin K. Flynn, "Expediting Organizational Transformation in the Small Firm Sector: Lessons from the Metalworking Industry," Ph.D. diss., Massachusetts Institute of Technology, 2001, 41. For a historical analysis of industrial growth in pre-Civil War New England, see François Weil, "Capitalism and Industrialization in New England, 1815-1845," *The Journal of American History* 84 (1998): 1334-1354. For a historical overview of the British industry in the late 19th and early 20th centuries, see A. J. Arnold, "Innovation, Deskilling and Profitability in the British Machine-Tools Industry: Albert Herbert 1887-1927," *Journal of Industrial History* 2 (1999): 50-71.

[8]David Hounshell, *From the American System to Mass Production* (Baltimore: The Johns Hopkins University Press, 1984).

[9]Norman Boucher, "A Natural History of the Connecticut Valley Metal Trades," *Regional Review* 4 (Winter 1994): 6-12, 7; Glynnis A. Trainer, "The Metalworking Machinery Industry in New England: An Analysis of Investment Behavior," master's thesis, Massachusetts Institute of Technology, 1979, 30; Joseph Wickham Roe, *English and American Tool Builders* (New Haven: Yale University Press, 1916), 109.

Inadvertently, New England became the site of a regional technology management capability. The world's first precision machine tool industry, created in the wake of applying interchangability, facilitated the integration and mutual development of production and technology. But it also diffused the new principle to the whole region and other parts of the country and, by so doing, created a vehicle for transferring technology cross sectors.[10]

Hounshell offers that the keys to the Armory's success were its early reliance on private arms contractors as a source for reciprocal innovation and the perfecting of parts inspection. Felicia Deyrup detected collaboration's importance for skill and technology diffusion in her study of the region's gun-making industry. Deyrup uncovered a rich contracting system among firms promoting a "spirit of cooperation and mutual aid" that had much to do "with the rapid development of the industry in the first thirty years of the nineteenth century." The Armory and collaborating machine shops engaged in the purposeful cross-fertilization of machine-tool designs. The techniques they perfected dispersed widely among goods producers along the Connecticut River. A clearinghouse for new machines, materials, and manufacturing processes, the Armory greatly enhanced the region's reputation for precision and quality work and the "aggregation of metalworking shops it produced was a model of economic success for 150 years."[11]

By the mid-1840s, 73 machine shops, 6 cotton factories, 3 paper mills, 4 printing concerns, 2 tool factories, a saw factory, saw and grist mills, 2 brass foundries, 2 plow manufactories, and 8 firms involved in the production of railroad cars and coaches dominated Greater Springfield's and the river valley's economy. The city's prime Connecticut River location provided easy transportation to Hartford, Connecticut, and New York City's markets, and in the late 1840s and early 1850s, rail connections to Boston and Worcester, Massachusetts; Hartford, Connecticut; and Albany, New York, stimulated additional growth. The population climbed to 18,000 in 1850 from 1,500 in 1790, with the sharpest growth—400 percent—between 1820 and 1850 as manufacturers expanded their shops. Fifteen miles north, Northampton's thriving cutlery and

[10] Michael Best, *The New Competitive Advantage: The Renewal of American Industry* (New York: Oxford University Press, 2001), 26.

[11] D. Hounshell, *From the American System to Mass Production*, 33-34, 44; M. Best, *The New Competitive Advantage*. Hounshell cites Felicia Deyrup's Arms Makers of the Connecticut Valley (Northampton, MA: Smith College Studies in History Series, 1948) for its documentation of instances when the Armory's patternmakers and skilled foundrymen made machine casting for many area machine-tool builders without the internal capacity to do so. N. Boucher, "A Natural History," 7. Boucher adds, "Indeed, the Connecticut River style of regional clustering—characterized by the presence of many neighboring firms from the same industry providing complementary and competing products and services—is often promoted today as a strategy for economic growth. Recent examples range from the high-tech clustering of eastern Massachusetts and Silicon Valley, California, to the textile and ceramics industries of north-central Italy," 7.

hand-tool industries found customers in the burgeoning markets for agricultural implements. Continuing up the valley, firms in the Greenfield area specialized in the manufacture of cutting tools, machinists' hand tools, and measuring devices. Still farther north, 25 metalworking establishments in Windsor, Vermont, population 2,800 in the 1840s, produced rifles, sewing machines, and machine tools.

In the 1820s and 1830s the lack of all-around skilled workers became an obstacle to long-term growth. Master mechanics banded together in 1824 and started the Springfield Mechanics Association. Along with apprentice education and training, the Association maintained a technical library and held quarterly meetings with lectures on such topics as Chemistry Connected with Metals, The Mechanic Arts, and Duties of Masters to Their Apprentices. The organization's bylaws contained a hard-and-fast rule against any member employing another's apprentice, should that apprentice have run away or broken an arrangement with his master. Encouraging serious devotion to the metal trades, the Association offered a 10-dollar gold medal to apprentices who served their full term without resorting to "strong drink." To further ease the skill shortage, Northampton's cutlery firms recruited workers from Sheffield, England.[12] Finally, a late 1840s upsurge of skilled labor from Germany boosted the labor pool.[13] By the Civil War, metalworking expertise diffused widely as mechanics and machine designers worked in the Armory and other Greater Springfield shops and then traveled to clusters of metalworking companies in Providence, Rhode Island; Worcester, Massachusetts; Hartford, Connecticut; and Windsor, Vermont.[14] David Meyer notes that Greater Springfield's firearms industry capitalized on "the technical skills already in the region, embedded in small forges, foundries, and mechanical workshops that provided diverse metal goods for the prosperous economy."[15]

---

[12] Mason A. Green, *Springfield Memories: Odds and Ends of Anecdote and Early Doings* (Springfield: Whitney and Adams, 1876), 54-55. The 10-dollar gold piece offer proved so successful that it was abandoned when in one year 32 apprentices were eligible and the association's treasury was not large enough to make the promised payout.

[13] M. Frisch, *Town into City*, 15; Martha Van Hosen Taber, *A History of the Cutlery Industry in the Connecticut Valley* (Northampton, MA: Smith College Studies in History, XLI, 1955).

[14] See Joseph Wickham Roe, *English and American Tool Builders* (New York: McGraw-Hill Book Company, 1916). Roe produced several genealogies of industries tracing the 19th-century movement of key personnel from plant to plant. For the interconnections in the Connecticut River Valley, 139; and for Worcester, Massachusetts, 223.

[15] M. Frisch, *Town into City*, 74; Dermit Whittlesey, *The Springfield Armory: A Study in Institutional Development* (Ph.D. diss., University of Chicago, 1920), 265; David Meyer, "Formation of Advanced Technology Districts: New England Textile Machinery and Firearms," *Economic Geography*, Extra Issue (1998): 31-45, 42. John G. Palfrey, *Statistics of the Condition and Products of Certain Branches of Industry in Massachusetts For the Year Ending April 1, 1845 (1846).*

Challenged by the national government to produce weapons faster and cheaper, the Armory relied on its mechanics to improve plant efficiencies. Precision gauges and fixtures greatly enhanced internal quality, while the rigorously maintained production standards it established for its growing legion of subcontractors also improved local firms. The owners of small metalworking shops benefited from the careful study of Armory techniques and organizational methods, and over time its problem-solving approach sank deep roots in the Connecticut River Valley. The Armory manufacturing system's potential crystallized at the outset of the Civil War, when nearly a tenfold increase in arms production occurred. In 1861 over 3,000 workers produced guns, compared with approximately 250 workers in late 1859. Rail cars carried hundreds of metalworkers and would-be metalworkers to jobs in Springfield from the surrounding hill towns of western Massachusetts. At war's end, many commuters became permanent residents of the city.

Civil War-induced demand strengthened collaborations among companies.[16] Bruce Tull states,

> If there was still any question on how to produce precision components in the North, the Civil War was a period of massive diffusion of "armory practice." Hundreds of firms subcontracted to produce either complete arms or components, and the Armory continued its practice of openly sharing its machinery patterns with virtually every contractor, subcontractor or machine builder in the northern states.[17]

An 1861 letter from Springfield mayor Daniel Harris to Armory Director Ripley highlights the collaboration. The James T. Ames Company, along with being one of the largest suppliers of large cannon to the government during the war, produced some of the Armory's machinery. Mayor Harris learned of a contract that the Ames Company had to produce barrels for several large cannon for the Armory, and urged the Armory's Ripley to procure the carriages for the cannon locally. Harris informed Ripley that the Wason Works was just the place "to get that work well and expeditiously done." Ripley agreed, and the Wason Works received the contract for the gun carriages. This type of joint manufacturing project strengthened the regional economy and helped to establish the river valley as a national manufacturing center in the years after the Civil War.[18]

---

[16] Moses King, *King's Handbook of Springfield, Massachusetts: A Series of Monographs Historical and Descriptive* (Springfield: James D. Gill, 1884), 35-37.

[17] F. Deyrup, *Arms Makers,* 66; Bruce Tull, "The Springfield Armory as Industrial Policy: Interchangable Parts and the Precision Corridor," Ph.D. diss., University of Massachusetts Amherst, 2000.

[18] M. Frisch, *Town into City,* 15, 79. Roe's *English and American Toolbuilders* contains numerous genealogies of firms that reveal the movement of key personnel from plant to plant in the Connecticut River Valley. Deyrup uncovered a contracting system that promoted a "spirit of cooperation and mutual aid" which had much to do "with the rapid development of the industry in the first thirty years of the nineteenth century," *Arms Makers,* 66; M. Van Hosen Taber, *A History of the Cutlery Industry.*

INNOVATION SPREADS

Innovations most often spread among firms through the linked personal histories of mechanics and engineers. In the 1830s Worcester, Massachusetts-born brothers Loring and Aury G. Coes operated a woodworking-machinery and spinning-machinery firm in Worcester's Court Mill complex, one of several sites in Worcester offering manufacturing space and steam-engine-derived power for small companies engaged in mechanical pursuits.[19] An October 1839 fire destroyed the Court Mill and without insurance, the brothers left Worcester for jobs as patternmakers in a small Springfield, Massachusetts, foundry that did work for the Armory. There they produced patterns for a new-style wrench that could be opened and closed with the thumb of the hand that held it. The Coes' returned to the rebuilt Court Mill in 1841 with their patterns and little else. They sold their spinning-machine patterns and used the proceeds to obtain a patent for their wrench design. Eventually a local hardware dealer financed the brothers, and in the mid-1840s with 15 men, they were making 500 to 600 wrenches a month.[20]

Pratt & Whitney Machine Tool was established in 1869 under the direction of Francis Pratt and Amos Whitney. Pratt served an apprenticeship in the machine shop of a Lowell, Massachusetts, textile mill, while Whitney served his at the Essex Machine Company in nearby Lawrence, building textile machinery. Both men moved to Hartford, Connecticut, in the late 1850s and met for the first time in the Colt Firearms Company toolroom. After a brief stint there, they spent one year at the Phoenix Iron Works in Hartford and then started up Pratt & Whitney, building planers, spindle drills, gang drills, jig borers, thread millers, and surface grinders. Drawing on their gun-making expertise, the two established a gauge division at Pratt & Whitney to insure the accuracy and the interchangeability of the parts being produced for their machine tools. On the roof of the fast-growing Hartford plant, 15-foot-high letters spelled out the word ACCURACY, the firm's marketing credo.[21]

Born in rural Uxbridge, Massachusetts, Edward Bullard founded the Bullard Machine Tool Company in Bridgeport, Connecticut, in 1894. Bullard's parents died when he was 7 years old, and he eventually lived with a family who arranged an apprenticeship for him at the Whitin Machine Works. He moved to Hartford to live with his sister and worked for several years in the toolrooms of Colt Firearms and Pratt & Whitney. After several failed efforts over almost 30 years, he opened the Bullard Machine Tool Company and maintained a prestigious list of

[19] Charles G. Washburn, *Industrial Worcester* (Worcester: The Davis Press, 1917), 136-138; *Massachusetts Spy,* 15 May 1839, 2; 26 September 1839, 2.

[20] Manuscript pertaining to Industrial Worcester, Charles G. Washburn Papers, Box 7, folder 1, American Antiquarian Society.

[21] For Pratt & Whitney's early history, R. F. V. Stanton, *Accuracy For Seventy Years 1860-1930* (Hartford, CT, 1930).

customers, including Carnegie Steel, American Locomotive, National Cash Register, Elgin Watch, and Westinghouse. The company's sales breakthrough came in 1913 after months of collaboration between Bullard's son and engineers at the Ford Motor Company. This effort produced a multispindle drilling machine capable of machining an automobile flywheel in under 2 minutes, a feat that had previously taken 18 minutes on a series of conventional machines.[22] Further north, L. S. Starret's career began as an apprentice at the Athol Machine Works in Massachusetts. He received patents for a quick-adjustable wrench and a combination square. Starret moved out on his own to make the wrench and the combination square and several additional machinists' tools, including thread gauges and the quick-adjusting micrometer.[23]

The "Industrial Beehive" Prospers: 1880-1930

Metalworking establishments along the Connecticut River grew dramatically in scope and variety after 1850, influenced first by the highly specialized skills developed in the Armory. Machinists came to the valley from the eastern part of Massachusetts to be trained. By 1860 shops in Franklin County, along the Massachusetts–Vermont border, turned out 49 percent of the nation's cutlery. After the Civil War, the valley's machinery makers built specialized equipment for New England's pulp and paper and shoe industries, textile companies, watchmakers, furniture manufacturers, munitions makers, typewriter and bicycle builders, and jewelry makers. Massachusetts machinery output rose a spectacular 158 percent between 1885 and 1890. When the 20th century opened, the state's machinery builders ranked second in the nation in sales ($2.6M) behind Ohio ($6.4M), with Connecticut ($1.8M) and Vermont ($284,000) ranked fourth and ninth respectively.[24] In 1910, of the 743 firms in the nation producing automobiles, auto bodies, and parts, 100 were in Connecticut, Massachusetts, and Vermont, the majority in the river valley; by comparison, 113 such firms were in Michigan. In 1920, 25 percent of the nation's machine tools were shipped from Massachusetts, Connecticut, and Rhode Island; one-fifth of the nation's machine-tool firms with more than 100 workers were located along the Connecticut River.[25]

---

[22] Irwin Robinson, *Yankee Toolmaker* (Bridgeport, CT: The Bullard Company, 1955).

[23] Kenneth Cope, *Makers of American Machinists' Tools* (Mendham, NJ: Astragal Press, 1994).

[24] M. Van Hosen Taber, "A History of the Cutlery Industry in the Connecticut Valley," 3-10.

[25] *Thirteenth Census of the United States Vol. 10, Manufacturers* (Washington, DC: GPO, 1913); *Fourteenth Census of the United States Vol. 10, Manufacturers* (Washington, DC: GPO, 1923); Commonwealth of Massachusetts, *A Directory of Massachusetts Manufacturers* (Boston, MA, 1913).

In the early 20th century, Central Vermont machinery firms received 200 patents.[26] Not to be outdone, in the opening decades of the 20th century, mechanics and engineers at Springfield, Massachusetts-based Stacy Machine Works invented an upright drill, the Bauch Machine Tool Company produced threading machines, and Hampden Grinding Wheel produced a new style grinding wheel. Elsewhere, Moore Drop Forging's 1,400 foundrymen and machinists turned out machine beds for the midwest's huge auto plants, Storms Drop Forge's 1,000 workers and Perkins Gear and Machine's 350 pattern makers and skilled machinists crafted parts for global export. Nationally, in 1920, Massachusetts and Connecticut ranked no less than third in total output of an array of machines, including engine lathes, turret lathes, bench lathes, milling machines, grinding machines, boring machines, and planers. Persistent reciprocal relationships among tool builders, their customers, and the hundreds of small, specialized tool-and-die shops and foundries that machined fixtures, tooling, gauges and made-to-order components, enhanced the valley's competitiveness.[27]

Metalworking and machine-making firms behaved like a "transmission agency," spreading innovations to final goods producers in different industries.[28] The *American Machinist* noted that in the Armory "many good ideas are gathered from the rank and file and it is to the foreman's best interests to bring out the best that is in his men." Armory historian Patrick Malone concluded, "Successful foremen at Springfield always followed this practice; most of them had risen from the rank and file in the production shop or had served an apprenticeship under a skilled machinist." The Armory's shop culture placed great value on workers' practical experience, promoted shop-floor participation in machine design and incremental innovation and, in Malone's words, "encouraged respect for the ideas of practical men" in machine design and incremental innovation.[29]

Springfield, Massachusetts, led the region. In 1880, 437 firms employed over 7,000 workers producing envelopes, fine writing paper, sewing machines, church organs, ice skates, paint and chemicals, steam boilers, and fine watches. In 1910 manufacturers employed 12,361 workers, with foundries, machine shops, machine-tool builders, and electrical machinery firms leading the way. Precision-metalworking firms supported the diverse needs of these manufacturers for such things as molds, tools, fixtures, slitting knives, machinery attachments, and

[26] Arthur F. Stone, *The Vermont of Today* (New York: Lewis Historical Publishing Company, 1929), ch. 23.
[27] *Fourteenth Census of the United States Vol. 10;* R. Forrant, "'Neither a Sleepy Village Nor a Coarse Factory Town': Skill in the Greater Springfield Massachusetts Industrial Economy 1800-1900," *Journal of Industrial History,* 4, 24-47; O. Stone, *History of Massachusetts Industries,* 539.
[28] Nathan Rosenberg, "Technological Change in the Machine Tool Industry, 1840-1910," *Journal of Economic History* 23 (1963): 414-446.
[29] Patrick Malone, "Little Kinks and Devices at the Springfield Armory, 1892-1918," *Journal of the Society of Industrial Archeology* 14 (1988): 59-76, 64.

entire specialty machines. Taylor and Tapley Manufacturing was typical of such firms. Formed by the consolidation of several smaller firms, the company owned valuable patents, molds, dies, and patterns for the paper collar and cuff industry. Taylor and Tapley had two very distinct workforces. In one part of its five-story brick factory, young women produced shirt collars and cuffs as well as rolls of raw material for other collar and cuff manufacturers, while elsewhere skilled machinists built machinery and machinery attachments.[30] The R. F. Hawkin's Iron Works, established in the 1840s, built railroad engine-houses and rail bridges. After the Civil War, Hawkin's employed a "large corps of tried and experienced mechanics" in its extensive iron foundry, boiler works, and machine shops to manufacture bridges, boilers, bolts, and forgings for railroads and manufacturers across the Eastern United States.[31]

A 1913 state manufacturers directory identified 40 Springfield firms producing machine tools and precision machine-shop products.[32] As trolley lines extended from the downtown in the early 1900s, new homes were built on streets that carried the names of well-known period automobiles like Chalmers, Packard, Ford, and Duryea.[33] Manufacturing clustered in two distinct locations: one, in East Springfield, became home to a massive Westinghouse plant and the Stevens-Duryea Car Company, the first automobile factory in the country; the other was in the city's North End. The North End contained dozens of metalworking firms and specialized tool-and-die shops and foundries engaged in the production of fixtures, tools, and spare parts for larger companies. Big or small, firms employed mainly skilled machinists and precision assemblers.[34]

The Wason Car Manufacturing Company, a prominent North End firm established in 1846, drew upon the city's rich skills in the production of railroad coaches for virtually every major rail line in the United States, and it exported rail cars to China, Brazil, Venezuela, and Canada. In the 1870s Wason occupied some 16 acres, and there, several hundred skilled workers in metalworking, carpentry, and cabinetry produced hundreds of rail coaches a year; 1875 sales

---

[30] M. King, *King's Handbook*, 333-334.

[31] M. King, *King's Handbook*, 336-337.

[32] Commonwealth of Massachusetts, *A Directory of Massachusetts Manufacturers* (Boston, MA, 1913). The automobile builders included Knox Automobile, Atlas Motor Car, Sultan Motor Company and Springfield Metal Body Company and the Wason Manufacturing Company. Very little is written about what became of these firms. Firms engaged in the manufacture of electrical machinery included the Bosch Magneto Company. Machine-tool firms included Bausch Machine Tool, Chapman Valve, and Van Norman Machine Tool. By 1930 greater Springfield manufacturers accounted for 75 percent ($308 million) of the total sale of all manufactured products produced in the Connecticut River Valley, see K. Lumpkin, *Shutdowns in the Connecticut River Valley* (Northampton: Smith College Studies in History Series, 19, April 1934), 150-151.

[33] For photographs of early Springfield factories, see Donald J. D'Amato, *Springfield—350 Years: A Pictorial History* (Virginia: The Donning Company, 1985).

[34] D. J. D'Amato, *Springfield—350 Years*, 139.

exceeded $1.5 million. The firm had one multiyear contract worth $1.5 million with the Central Railroad of New Jersey for 240 passenger, mail, and baggage cars. The North End housed several other carriage companies, including Smith Carriage, which in 1892 produced the body for the nation's first gasoline-powered automobile. Also in the North End, in 1895 the Duryea Motor Wagon Company, the country's first major automobile builder, assembled its first cars.[35]

Machine-tool companies transmitted innovations because they worked closely with goods producers to resolve production problems. Without such collaborations, Springfield likely would have been a commercial and transportation center. Instead, according to Armory historian Derwent Whittlesey, Springfield developed an economy with "fewer drawbacks than that of most manufacturing cities. . . . As a consequence, Springfield is neither a sleepy village resting on its past glories, nor is it a coarse factory town, conspicuous for its slums and tired workers."[36] Integral to this success were two historical continuities: the region's ability to design and build machine tools and related accessories, and the large number of skilled machinists attracted to the area. Firms relied on skilled workers to both submit and exchange their ideas on how to improve machinery performance. They recruited and persistently cultivated precision machining skills through their sponsorship of apprentices and vocational–technical education.[37]

WORKING IN SPRINGFIELD

What did Springfield's occupational structure look like? A comparison of the occupational structure there with nearby Holyoke, Massachusetts, and other mill cities demonstrates this skill base, as well as the distinction between Springfield's workforce and that of textile-mill communities across Massachusetts.[38] As Table 2.1 shows, Holyoke lacked a significant number of metalworkers. Thus, the city could not look to a pool of innovative metalworking firms and workers when the textile and paper mills began exiting Holyoke after World War I. By comparison, Springfield's diversified industrial base remained a source of innovation and renewal during the first half of the 20th century.

[35] For a discussion of 18 prominent Springfield manufacturers, see M. King, *King's Handbook*, 319-370.
[36] N. Rosenberg, "Technological Change"; D. Hounshell, *From the American System*, 33-34, 44; D. Whittlesey, *The Springfield Armory*, 265.
[37] For a discussion of the cultivation of skills, see Michael Best and Robert Forrant, "Community-Based Careers and Economic Virtue: Arming, Disarming, and Rearming the Springfield, Western Massachusetts, Metalworking Region," in Michael Arthur and Denise Rousseau, eds., *The Boundaryless Career: A New Employment Principle for a New Organizational Era* (New York: Oxford University Press, 1996): 314-330. Planning Services Group, *The Regional Economy; Federal Population Census, 1920, 1930, 1940.*
[38] Figures from the 1885 Massachusetts Census for occupations employing 100 or more workers show the following: *Massachusetts Census, 1885.*

Table 2.1. Occupations in Springfield
and Holyoke, 1885

	Springfield	Holyoke
Gun makers	250	—
Machinists	219	225
Iron workers	154	—
Steam car builders	174	—
Woolen mill operatives	—	1,125
Cotton mill operatives	—	2,205
Paper mill operatives	—	2,820

By the late 1930s almost 20 percent of Springfield manufacturers and 57 percent of the manufacturing workforce engaged in some form of machinery building or precision metalworking. By comparison, Worcester, Massachusetts, a large and well-diversified manufacturing center approximately 50 miles from Springfield, had 28 percent of its firms and 46 percent of its manufacturing workforce so employed. There remained, from 1930 through the 1950s, a higher ratio of skilled machinists, toolmakers, and millwrights to semiskilled metalworkers in Springfield than in other Massachusetts cities. Springfield employment grew slowly in the 1920s and early 1930s, but in mid-1936 employers reported shortages of skilled metalworkers and scrambled to establish training programs.

Distinctions exist in a comparative analysis of the principal occupations in mill cities like Holyoke and Lowell with Springfield. In 1880, 63 percent of Holyoke workers labored as operatives in woolen, paper, and cotton mills; 57 percent of those workers were born in Ireland and British Canada. By contrast, in the same year, only 13 percent of Springfield workers were mill operatives.[39] Two distinct employment patterns existed through the first three decades of the 20th century (Table 2.2). Springfield and Worcester represented one path, Holyoke and Lowell the other. In 1930, 23 percent of Worcester's and 13 percent of Springfield's manufacturing employment was in iron and steel, metals and electrical machinery; for Holyoke and Lowell, the figures were 8 percent and 6 percent respectively. Mill occupations comprised 6 percent of Springfield and 11 percent of Worcester's workforce, compared with 45 percent in Holyoke and 35 percent in Lowell.[40]

[39] *Massachusetts Population Census, 1880.*
[40] *Massachusetts Population Census, 1930.*

Table 2.2. Industry Employment in 1930

	Holyoke	Springfield	Worcester	Lowell
All industry	22,245	66,521	82,993	40,662
Iron and steel	1,547	5,117	15,932	1,969
Metals	78	962	445	95
Electrical machining	154	2,710	2,366	252
Clothing	176	1,202	1,888	493
Shoes	7	27	2,130	2,880
Paper	4,966	1,179	1,385	227
Cotton mills	751	424	183	5,274
Woolen mills	1,736	34	1,320	2,268
Other textiles	2,465	1,285	2,360	3,324

The concentration of metalworking helped the state offset the sharp reduction in mill work between the two world wars and again in the first few years after World War II. But the location of firms provided benefits to a handful of cities. Table 2.3 traces production-worker levels in four Massachusetts cities from 1900 to 1987. With its precision metalworking, Springfield grew and prospered from the 1930s into the late 1950s, long after mill cities Holyoke and Lowell slumped. Employment gains in Springfield between 1939 and 1947 were twice the state average; Holyoke, Worcester, and Lowell reached their employment pinnacles in 1919.

Well into the 20th century Springfield machinery builders and their small-shop allies crafted machine tools for national and international customers. Van Norman Machine Tool, Chapman Valve, and Package Machinery were three Springfield companies with rapidly expanding international markets. Van Norman manufactured specialty grinding and milling machines; Chapman Valve operated three large foundries and produced the castings for hydrants, pipefittings, sluice gates, and valves ranging from one-quarter inch to nine feet in diameter. Package Machinery, formed in 1912 by the merger of several smaller companies based in Springfield; Milwaukee, Wisconsin; Louisville, Kentucky; Chicago, Illinois; and New York City and Brooklyn, New York, manufactured automatic package wrapping equipment. First year sales were $140,000; by 1930 they approached $2 million.[41]

[41] O. Stone, *History,* 539.

Table 2.3. Production Workers in the State and
Selected Cities 1900-1987

Year	State	Holyoke	Springfield	Worcester	Lowell
1900	438,200	12,519	8,152	22,593	29,254
1905	488,399	14,685	10,523	22,796	29,303
1914	606,698	17,493	14,240	29,452	29,904
1919	713,836	18,904	18,429	44,831	31,154
1929	547,509	13,770	17,414	31,636	17,097
1933		10,646	12,490	23,160	13,308
1939	460,674	8,539	13,846	31,659	13,828
1947	601,603	12,532	22,426	37,834	16,053
1958	498,612	8,606	18,811	26,548	13,045
1967	507,900	8,100	17,200	24,800	13,000
1972	416,000	6,800	13,200	19,700	11,700
1977	407,000	5,800	12,900	17,600	10,700
1982	397.000	5,500	11,300	14,500	13,300
1987	348,300	5,000	7,700	11,100	11,300

1939-1947 increase wkrs.	30 percent	46 percent	62 percent	19 percent	16 percent
1947-1977 decline wkrs.	32 percent	53 percent	42 percent	53 percent	33 percent
1947-1987 decline wkrs.	42 percent	60 percent	66 percent	71 percent	30 percent

A 1930 survey of 5,000 New England final-goods producers conducted by the U.S. Department of Commerce found that in Springfield "the large number of successful firms, including Van Norman, Chapman Valve, Westinghouse, and Bosch relied on worker skills to design and build new equipment and products." The richly detailed analyses of New England manufacturing concluded that the shop-floor skill base and innovative and forward-looking employers provided the region with its so-called competitive advantage.[42]

[42] William Cooper, Forward to Charles Artman's, *The Industrial Structure of New England* (Washington, DC: GPO, 1930), xi.

Springfield's employment base grew at twice the state average from the late 1930s to the late 1940s, and there were frequent shortages of machinists. In 1936 Westinghouse, Van Norman, and American Bosch established a collaborative apprenticeship program that consisted of classroom instruction in shop mathematics and blueprint reading, and hands-on training in the setup and operation of machine tools. The Springfield Armory enrolled 500 employees in evening skills courses in 1940 and 1,000 more in 1941. Despite these efforts, one plant manger lamented, "Skilled mechanics who understand their machines have this year been at a premium. Specialization over a period of many years has led to a large group of just machine operators. They could pull a lever, but that was about it."[43]

As we will see in subsequent chapters, soon after the Second World War, deep-seated structural weaknesses befell the river valley's metalworking and machine-tool firms.[44] Where just 20 years earlier the region's strengths were lauded, in 1951 President Truman's Council of Economic Advisors highlighted several signs of decay in a survey of the New England economy. No longer were the river valley's firms adapting to changing production technologies, nor were its machine-tool builders sufficiently engaged in new-product development to lead in innovation as they once did. Firms deemphasized skill and "turned their attention away from industrial progress and have shown, too often, a greater interest in the preservation of the status quo."[45] The Council noted,

> To some extent manufacturing success in the 19th century and the early part of the 20th century seems to have bred lethargy and complacency among New England industrialists, which handicapped the region it its competition with newer regions. The gap between ownership policies motivated by short-run financial considerations and the need for long-run modernization, research and product development has also intensified manufacturing problems in New England.[46]

This changed behavior reverberated up and down the Connecticut River Valley as precision-metalworking firms and machinery builders passed out of local control and new production technologies emerged as cudgels to beat down skilled labor. Expanded manufacturing opportunities overseas and in the southern United States, combined with skill-enhancing machinery, allowed firms to make serial moves into places that offered lower-wage workers, a union-free environment, and tax breaks and other incentives designed to induce plant

---

[43] *SR*, 25 October 1936, 11.

[44] R. Forrant, Plant Closings; U.S. Department of Commerce, *Manufacturing Censuses,* selected years.

[45] Council of Economic Advisers, *The New England Economy: A Report to the President* (Washington, DC: GPO, 1951), xxii.

[46] Council of Economic Advisers, *The New England Economy,* 26.

relocations. Springfield and the wider valley hemorrhaged jobs at an alarming rate as during the 1970s and 1980s, 45 percent of the city's manufacturers closed. Skill counted for very little and even the slightest semblance of shop-floor cooperation all but vanished.

In 1951 the president's Council called for the region to refocus on its industrial heritage—technological innovation and workforce skills—to revive a slumping economy, but this did not happen. For a time the Korean War rearmament boom acted like a pressure-release valve, allowing workers and firms to ignore their problems. But a wartime production spike could not stimulate sustainable growth or fend off the plant closings that eventually rocked the valley.

CHAPTER 3

American Bosch and Its Workers: A Historical Overview

From its 1911 start-up on farmland along the banks of the Connecticut River, American Bosch contributed to the valley's industrial vibrancy. But we will see that in the late 1940s financial forces from outside the river valley began purchasing the valley's leading firms, the Bosch included. In the 1950s the Bosch's new owners, a Wall Street financial holding company, commenced an aggressive international search for nonunion skilled and semiskilled labor, which resulted in the piecemeal relocation of Bosch work for some 35 years before its ultimate closure in 1986. The Bosch's demise by "hundreds of small cuts" is symbolic of old-line manufacturing's decline in the industrial northeastern United States. This chapter tells the story of the company's early history, including its unionization in the 1930s. Subsequent chapters document its closure and the collapse of the metalworking sector in the Connecticut River Valley.

American Bosch: 1911-1945

Founded in 1886 in Stuttgart, Germany, Robert Bosch A.G. built its U.S. factory in 1911 on farmland in Springfield's North End. The German firm sought a region with workers capable of producing complex electrical products. Early photographs show hundreds of lab-coated machinists producing parts for the emerging automobile and truck industry (Figure 3.1). A serious place to work, employees were dismissed for offenses like the improper use of cuspidors and singing or whistling while on the job.[1] Seized during World War I for security reasons by the federal Alien Property Custodian, it was purchased by a group of Springfield-area investors and renamed the American Bosch Magneto Company (Figure 3.2). By 1920 the four-story plant turned out 50 percent of the electrical starter parts required by the U.S. vehicle industry and employed 3,000 workers.

---

[1]"Walking Down Memory Lane at Bosch," *SMU*, 2 January 1958, 7; *Progress*, 27 December 1957, 2.

Figure 3.1. Photo of Bosch workers.

Figure 3.2   Historical photo from 1910 of the Bosch Magneto Company.

At war's end, German-based Bosch opened a U.S. factory and engaged in almost a decade of patent-rights litigation with its U.S. competitor, and they unsuccessfully sued Attorney General A. Mitchell Palmer and the Federal Government for wrongful seizure, claiming damages of more than $1 million. Robert Bosch also fought the American Bosch Magneto Company's various legal efforts to block the German company from selling products under the name "Original Bosch." Out-of-court agreements in 1929 and 1930 resulted in American Bosch acquiring Robert Bosch's U.S. subsidiary. In return, Robert Bosch received 70,000 common shares of the newly named United American Bosch Corporation and options for the purchase of an additional 50,000 shares. During the years of litigation, Robert Bosch had secretly bought thousands of its rival's shares on the open market, so the 70,000 additional shares gave it ownership of over 50 percent of the company's stock. With court proceedings concluded, the Springfield company changed its name to the American Bosch Corporation (AB). In 1938 the company started manufacturing fuel-injection equipment and other products for the aircraft and automotive industries, markets that would constitute the company's core business for the next 30 years. Even in the depths of the Depression, American Bosch sales increased to $7.5 million from $6.1 million between 1935 and 1936.[2]

Bosch Unionizes

In 1933, when production workers attempted to organize the Chapman Valve Company, the Springfield Central Labor Union—an American Federation of Labor affiliate—cautioned workers "that the word strike be removed from their thoughts at the present time. The intelligence of the workers and employers in this territory was adequate to cope with labor difficulties."[3] Until the early 1930s fairly peaceful labor relations existed between owners and the valley's metalworkers, fueled in part by the relatively high wages they received. Average pay in Springfield remained in the top five in Massachusetts during the 1920s and early 1930s. In the late 1920s average weekly manufacturing wages in Springfield stood at $25.42, while Holyoke's and Lowell's were $21.79 and $19.13, respectively. Worcester, another metalworking center, was the highest

[2]Orra Stone, *History of Massachusetts Industries* (Boston: S. J. Clarke Publishing Co., 1930), 543; Robert Bosch Magneto Company, Inc., Press Release, 16 July 1925, copy in author's possession; Office of Alien Property Custodian, *Annual Report for the Fiscal Year Ending June 30, 1944* (Washington, DC: Alien Property Custodian), 62-63.
[3]The statement was made to Chapman Valve workers by Kenneth Taylor, president of the Springfield Typographical Union. Taylor urged workers to form two separate unions, one for skilled pattern and moldmakers and the other for machine operators and foundry hands (*SDN*, 23 August 1933).

at $26.38.[4] But despite the higher-than-average pay, between 1936 and 1941 the United Electrical, Radio and Machine Workers organized thousands of workers across the northeast who were responsible for 80 percent of all U.S. production of electrical goods, from the smallest appliances like toasters and fans to the world's largest electrical generators. Many of these workers were in Springfield.[5]

First Steps

From its opening until the early 1930s there was no labor organization in the Bosch plant, nor were there regular raises or paid holidays. Who worked and at what job was left to management's discretion, with the majority of workers never knowing from one day to the next whether they had wages coming in. Apart from a core of highly skilled tool-and-die makers and machine set-up specialists, men and women lined up at the factory gates at 5 a.m. hoping to be let inside. Historian Maynard Seider describes what a worker at a nearby North Adams, Massachusetts, plant faced daily. "I had to walk two miles to work, and I could not punch in until the work came down my line," he recalled. "Sometimes I wouldn't even work at all and they'd send me back home. Then, I would no more than get back home and they would send for me again." Ronald Schatz, in his history of General Electric and Westinghouse union organizing, uncovered a similar situation. Machine operator Art McCollough reported, "The company had the god damned thing so unequal you know, that a foreman's favorite would be making a hell of a lot more money than somebody else, and this other guy might be doing more, better, a higher rated job than the foreman would admit it was. . . ."[6]

An account of the Bosch local's history prepared for its 25th anniversary celebration noted, "Many of the workers at the American Bosch plant had been members of guilds in Europe," but that in the 1920s it was "unheard of to mention the forming of a guild or anything resembling the likes of a union."[7] Aware of the discontent among workers, in 1933 Bosch superintendent Donald Murray established a company union in an attempt to short-circuit independent

[4]Massachusetts Department of Labor and Industries (MDLI), *Annual Report for 1938*, 49.
[5]*UEN*, 7 January 1939, 4-5. By 1939, the UE union represented workers at the following: Emerson Electric, General Electric, Westinghouse, Delco-Frigidaire, Edison Storage Battery, Phelps Dodge, Allis Chalmers, Singer Sewing Machine, and Pratt & Whitney. Gross sales of the top 26 corporations UE had at least one local in were almost $1 billion.
[6]Maynard Seider, "The CIO in Rural Massachusetts: Sprague Electric and North Adams, 1937-1944," *Historical Journal of Massachusetts* 22 (1994): 51-73, 55; Ronald Schatz, "American Electrical Workers: Work, Struggles, Aspirations 1930-1950," (Ph.D. diss., University of Pittsburgh, 1977), 68.
[7]*LB*, September 1963, 2.

organization. But he rejected all requests from the in-house union for improvements in wages, benefits, and working conditions. After three years, workers realized, "A stronger and more effective means must be used to show the Company that the workers at the Bosch really meant they wanted improved working conditions."[8]

In April 1936 Matthew Campbell, president of United Electrical Workers Westinghouse Local 202, began a series of secret house meetings with Bosch workers. Born in Scotland in 1890, Campbell, a disabled World War I veteran, arrived in Springfield just before his twentieth birthday. Married, with three children, Campbell owned a home in a neighborhood of skilled industrial workers and white-collar employees and was employed for 15 years as a toolmaker at Westinghouse before leading the city's industrial union movement. His labor and political views were shaped by events in Scotland. Springfield attracted machinists from the British Isles between 1900 and 1925 because there was a high demand for their skills. Workers carried stories about the Labour Party's growth, the increase in trade-union membership in the United Kingdom, and the bloody wave of strikes and mass protests for a shorter workweek.

At Westinghouse, Campbell and other skilled immigrant workers organized a similar movement. After a series of work stoppages against Westinghouse during 1933 and 1934, the company recognized UE and Local 202. Campbell became a UE regional vice president in 1935, and a year later he led Local 202 out of Springfield's American Federation of Labor-affiliated Central Labor Union and into the nascent Congress of Industrial Organizations. In 1938 he became a state vice president of the CIO. Elected the Westinghouse local's president in 1934, Campbell held the position until, at age 51, he suffered a fatal heart attack in June 1941. With the Westinghouse local as a base of support, and assisted by other Westinghouse machinists, Campbell organized several western Massachusetts companies, including Milton Bradley, Van Norman Machine, Package Machinery, Worthington Pump, and the Bosch.[9]

[8]"Our History," *LB*, September 1963, 2. For a discussion of similar conditions at Ford, see Stephen Meyer's *The Five Dollar Day: Labor Management and Social Control in the Ford Motor Company, 1908-1921* (Albany: State University of New York Press, 1981); Daniel Raff, "Ford Welfare Capitalism in its Economic Context," in Sanford Jacoby, ed., *Masters to Managers* (New York: Columbia University Press, 1991).
[9]*Springfield City Directory*, 1934. Copies of directories are found in the Pioneer Valley Historical Museum, Springfield, MA. Directories were useful in determining the occupations of union organizers and early in-plant activists. Campbell's obituary appeared in the *SDN*, 2 June 1941, 8 and in the *United Electrical Workers News* (UEN), 7 June 1941, 1.

Labor's Electoral Strategy

Along with union organizing, Campbell coordinated labor's electoral strategy in Springfield, becoming the United Labor Party's (ULP) 1935 candidate for mayor. The party pledged to "always give preference to local products in its purchases, provided prices and labor conditions are up to our local standards." According to a party spokesperson, "The organization of this labor party is a logical step accompanying the development of labor unions whose voting strength is now so great it demands true representation." Workers from many of the city's large metalworking factories sought endorsements from clubs, civic organizations, and other unions. During the mayoral campaign, Campbell met with large numbers of workers from nonunion plants.[10]

The ULP appealed to a broad coalition of small-home owners, office employees, professionals, the unemployed, as well as factory workers. It supported public ownership of the city utilities, state and national legislation to reduce the work week and secure old age pensions, cash relief or public work at prevailing union wages for the unemployed, and it wanted the city's tax burden shifted from small-home owners to more equitable taxation of large industries.[11] The occupations of ULP candidates for other offices reveal the significant role of skilled workers during the campaign. These included a plater and assembler from Chapman Valve; a toolmaker from Fiberloid Corporation; a machinist from Spaulding; and a machinist, mechanic, tool grinder, final inspector, pattern maker, and production supervisor from Westinghouse.[12]

The ULP appealed to workers, stating, "We believe that the rank and file, now that they have the opportunity will vote the way they strike, shoulder to shoulder, united in a tremendous vote for themselves at last."[13] But, despite Campbell's candidacy, the ULP failed to garner much of the labor vote, for in a blow to unity the AFL-affiliated Central Labor Union (CLU), consisting of building-trades unions and a small number of die makers and toolmakers at a few metalworking plants, endorsed the Democratic Party candidate. The CLU stated that it would not "be swayed or swerved into any political action by a mixed group of members and non-members, affiliated and non-affiliated unions, and by some individuals not members of any union." They characterized Campbell as "self-anointed, self-appointed, and self-seeking," and warned that his efforts would "lead the people of Springfield to judge the strength of labor by the sorry results you are about to achieve." Only the president of the Painters Union broke

[10] *SMU*, 5 September 1935, 1; 10 September 1935, 6; 11 September 1935, 6.
[11] *SMU*, 24 September 1935, 6.
[12] *SMU*, 24 September 1935, 6. The September 13 *Springfield Morning Union* reported the signatures and addresses of residents who signed Campbell's nomination papers. Using the 1934 city directory, it was possible to determine place of employment and occupation for ULP candidates and many who signed nomination papers.
[13] *SMU*, 1 October 1935, 4; 7 October 1935, 3.

CLU ranks and supported Campbell, arguing that the strategy of "defeating our enemies by electing our friends needed to be updated to defeat our enemies— elect our own."[14]

By wide margins, Republicans swept every office, with Campbell a distant third with 2,152 votes; the Republican winner and his Democratic challenger received 22,762 and 17,565 respectively. But the loss did not deter Campbell from politics or union organizing, and in an ironic twist, he played a pivotal roll in the 1937 successful mayoral campaign of one of Springfield's leading industrialists, Democrat William Putnam. Putnam had earlier embraced Campbell and the UE as a badly needed voice for labor during the UE's organizing campaign at his Package Machinery Corporation.[15]

Bosch Local 206

A few months after this electoral defeat, Campbell and other Westinghouse workers played an integral part in UE's national campaign to organize Westinghouse and General Electric. By 1936 locals were successfully established at GE's electrical-transformer plants in Schenectady, New York; Lynn and Pittsfield, Massachusetts; and at Westinghouse's radio and appliance plants in Springfield, Massachusetts and Buffalo, New York. In 1936 UE represented only 15,000 workers out of the 300,000 men and women in the electrical, radio and home-appliance industries, three years later nearly 80 percent were UE members.[16]

In April 1936 the UE's national president, James Carey, urged Campbell to organize Bosch, and organizers began to distribute the union's newspaper, the *Peoples Press,* at the plant during the spring and summer. Reading the newspaper, Bosch workers learned that the Local 202 Westinghouse contract guaranteed pay increases linked to company profits. Workers were to receive automatic 1 percent wage increases for every $60,000 a month the company made over a base figure of $600,000. As a result, workers received wage boosts of between 9 percent and 13 percent every month from May to October 1936.[17]

A 1932 study commissioned by the Massachusetts legislature revealed that despite Springfield's comparatively high earnings, as early as 1927 average annual income for the majority of metalworkers had fallen below $1,568, the amount the legislature estimated that a family of four needed to be adequately

[14] *SMU,* 8 October 1935 4; 24 October 1935, 1; 1 November 1935, 14; 4 November 1935, 1.
[15] *SMU,* 6 November 1935, 1.
[16] R. Schatz, "American Electrical Workers." Figures in Jules Backman, *The Economics of the Electrical Manufacturing Industry* (New York: New York University Press, 1962), 328.
[17] *Springfield Republican* (SR), 14 October 1936, 12. Carey to Campbell, 24 April 1936, UE District 2 Archives.

maintained. Thus, Bosch workers who had not received pay raises since 1930 jealously eyed the Westinghouse labor agreement.[18] By fall 1936, 52 percent had signed membership cards to affiliate with the UE, and an election for UE Local 206 officers was scheduled for October 16.

In a challenge to the as-yet-unrecognized and fledgling local, on the afternoon of October 15 management fired Leo Goulet, a 14-year employee and toolroom group leader running for union vice president, and Viola Theriaque, an assembler, with a dozen years in the factory, running for recording secretary. Goulet allegedly allowed workers to smoke on the job, a violation of company rules, while Theriaque was let go for a "lack of work." Despite or perhaps to spite the terminations, Goulet and Theriaque were elected to union positions the next day and two of the day-old local's officers were out on the street. Campbell demanded their reinstatement, but Bosch management refused to recognize Local 206 or meet with him. The union warned the company that both workers needed to be rehired by October 23 but did not indicate what might occur should this not take place, and the deadline passed with newly elected Local 206 president Robert Shields expressing his hope for an amicable end to the conflict.[19]

In the midst of these efforts to gain union recognition, Bosch workers read in the local newspapers that sales were increasing for the valley's machine-tool builders. "Plants Run Full Tilt Under Heavy Unfilled Orders" read a newspaper headline. Van Norman's milling and ball bearing grinding machines were in heavy demand by car makers, and Pratt & Whitney Machine Tool in nearby Hartford, Connecticut, could not produce its lathes, shapers, and vertical grinders fast enough to meet domestic and foreign demand. Several companies were working double shifts for the first time since 1930, causing metalworking employment in Greater Springfield to exceed 20,000 in September 1936, an increase of 4,000 jobs from the start of the year.[20] Increased work caused a shortage of skilled machinists, and several companies initiated state-funded training programs for the unemployed in conjunction with the Springfield School Department. Classes ran seven hours a day, five days a week, for eight weeks on blueprint reading, shop mathematics, and the operation of several

---

[18] MDLI, *Annual Reports for 1938,* 40 and *1939,* 43; Special Commission on Stability of Employment, *Final Report* (Boston, 1933), 61, 105, 125.
[19] *SR,* 12 October 1936, 7; *SR,* 19 October 1936, 1. *SDN,* 24 October 1936, 4.
[20] *SMU,* 6 October 1936, 1; 11 October 1936, 18; 14 October 1936, 5; *SDN,* 16 November 1936, 1, 16; 17 November 1936, 4; 18 November 1936, 11; 21 November 1936, 1; 29 November 1936, 17; 22 November 1936, 18a. At the end of 1936 the *Springfield Republican* reported that the output of local manufacturers was still strong. Gilbert and Barker, Greenfield Tap and Die, and Van Norman were running at full capacity, and there was increased activity in Holyoke's Fall Alpaca woolen mills. See *SR,* 27 December 1936, 14a.

machines. Of 65 workers in the program over the summer of 1936, 61 got job offers before they completed the program.[21]

Bosch workers believed that the expansive business climate put them in an excellent bargaining position and escalated their demands that the fired unionists be hired and Local 206 be recognized. But UE president Carey cautioned Campbell to wait for the National Labor Relations Labor Board to rule on the terminations.[22]

Management escalated the conflict by scheduling a vote of its own to determine whether workers wanted the UE to represent them. The local's leaders protested; in response, the company fired 200 workers a few days before the scheduled vote. Angry workers wanted to walk off the job, but once again caution ruled and representatives were sent to Boston to file another NLRB protest. Campbell warned the company that a walkout was unavoidable, and management countered that orders would fall and layoffs increase should the local become too strong.[23] Before the board ruled, the company and union met at the behest of the chair of the New England NLRB and, after a day-long session, management agreed to reinstate the fired union officers, call back the 200 recently dismissed workers, and recognize Local 206. The union immediately opened a storefront office a short walk from the plant and monthly dues of $1 for men and 50¢ for women were soon collected.[24]

The company dragged its feet on contract talks and then decided to hold in-plant elections for officers for its four-year-old company-sponsored union. This prompted a carefully orchestrated in-plant work stoppage.[25] On Monday, February 15, 1937, unionists turned their machines off, stood or sat silently next to them for 59 minutes, and then resumed work. President Shields stated, "We simply knocked off work at one o'clock and resumed again at 2 o'clock. Everything about the demonstration was orderly. They know our attitude and it now rests with them whether any more labor trouble develops."[26] Shortly after the protest, management returned to the bargaining table. "There is no question that the majority of the employees at the plant are members of the Electrical

---

[21] "Making Skilled Mechanics Out of Unemployed Fills Local Employment Needs," *SR*, 25 October 1936, 2E; "Report Machine Tool Demand is Holding Strong," *SR*, 11 October 1936, 18.

[22] *Carey to Campbell*, 24 November 1936, UE District 2 Archives. Campbell's letter to Carey could not be found, but it appears from Carey's tone that Campbell had some misgivings over not having adopted a more militant strategy to gain recognition.

[23] "Rumors of Trouble at Bosch Factory Become Ominous," *SR*, 10 December 1936, 1.

[24] *SR*, 12 December 1936, 5; *SDN*, 4 December 1936, 5; 6 December 1936, 1. *M. Campbell to James Carey*, 17 December 1936, District 2 Archives.

[25] "Dispute About Bosch Plan Headed for Showdown," *SMU*, 16 February 1937, 1.

[26] "Any More Labor Trouble Up to Bosch, Union Says," *SMU*, 17 February 1937, 1.

workers union," Shields asserted. "Any more labor trouble is up to them."[27] Local 206 became the workers' legitimate voice without resorting to a walkout or a lengthy sit-down strike. The 59-minute stoppage had convinced management to discontinue the company union and reach a contract agreement. Only one other local attended UE's 1938 national convention with a signed labor agreement.

Bosch workers received an initial 2.2 percent raise and Labor Day became their first paid holiday. In 1938 workers won a 10¢ base-rate increase and time-and-a-half pay for hours worked in excess of 8 during the day, 40 for the week, and all Sunday work. In 1940 grievance and arbitration procedures were put in place and six paid holidays and a vacation schedule based on years of service were obtained. In addition, seniority rights were defined, with all future layoffs and recalls to work based on plantwide seniority. A job classification book became part of the contract in 1941. Steady per-hour wage gains of 8¢ in 1938 and 10¢ in 1939 were achieved; in five years hourly base-pay rates increased from a range of 20¢ to 50¢ to a range from 60¢ to $1.21. By comparison, only after numerous work stoppages and sporadic sit-down strikes throughout the early months of 1941, did the UAW and Ford agree to a 10¢-per-hour pay increase, the first raise for Ford workers in three years.[28]

Local 206 contracts were more elaborate than most other agreements reached during the late 1930s and early 1940s. David Brody characterizes early agreements as "thin affairs, largely codifying existing conditions and limited to wages, hours, vacations, and weakly drawn grievance and seniority provisions." The 1940 Bosch agreement established the important principle of plantwide seniority. The contract contained strong maintenance of membership language, stating that employees "will be required as a condition of employment with the Company to maintain their membership in good standing during the life of this Agreement."[29] The UAW did not get a similar agreement with General Motors until 1950. And in 1941, the local gained the right to represent the plant's office workers, excluding engineers and supervisors.[30]

[27] SR, 17 February 1937, 1; 18 February 1936, 1. Campbell pointed out that events in the plant should not be interpreted as a sit-down strike. SDN, 16 February 1937, 2.
[28] LB, September 1963. Nelson Lichtenstein, Labor's War at Home: The CIO and World War II (New York: Cambridge University Press, 1982), 46-47. U.S. Steel, General Motors, General Electric, and other corporations similarly increased wages. For a survey of collective bargaining agreements in the late 1930s, see Emily Clark Brown, "The New Collective Bargaining in Mass Production: Methods, Results, Problems," Journal of Political Economy 47 (1939): 30-66. Brown points out that a section on management's rights, which occurs in the basic steel agreements, was taken almost verbatim from earlier company-sponsored employee representation plants. The clause read in part, "The management of the works and the direction of the working forces. . . is vested exclusively in the Corporation" quoted in Brown, 35.
[29] David Brody, Workers in Industrial America (New York: Oxford University Press, 1980), 178. Local 206 Contract, 1942, 30.
[30] Local 206 Contract (1942), 26, 33.

SKILLED WORKERS AND UNION ORGANIZATION

Matthew Campbell's union career fits a pattern revealed in several studies of industrial union formation in the 1930s and 1940s. Several Westinghouse local officers, including tool grinder and business agent Wallace Kennedy, along with vice president Leonard Wade and negotiating committee member John O'Connell, both machinists, worked closely with Campbell. Two of Bosch's first officers were highly skilled: diemaker Leo Goulet and tool designer Robert Shields. Among 10 other Bosch union officers, 7 held skilled jobs, while at Westinghouse, several toolmakers, final inspectors, and set-up men were early union officers.[31] Schatz discovered that a majority of the 28 organizers and officers in UE plants in Erie and East Pittsburgh, Pennsylvania; Lynn, Massachusetts; and Schenectady, New York, were highly skilled. And among them, 23 were Northern European immigrants or their children, with 14 of Scottish, Irish or English descent.[32]

Campbell and activists like him offered a clear alternative to the petty tyranny of individual foremen in dispensing work. In Ronald Schatz's study of the electrical industry, worker William Winn told how "People bring farm baskets and get good jobs, overtime, privileges. And you couldn't do nothing about it. What could you do?"[33] During the company–union era, long-time Bosch workers recalled that "if you were called to work on Monday morning and no work was available, you could spend the next forty hours in the plant and go home with the large sum of $1.40—for you may have gotten one small job during those forty hours of hanging around." High-seniority workers bristled under a system that allowed foremen to decide who would work, and this surely helped many of them see the value of organization.[34] In *Piper Tompkins*, a fictionalized 1946 account of a Connecticut metalworking factory by Ben Field, the issue of work distribution figures prominently. Field, a machinist and former UE member, described how workers provided foremen with food from their home gardens to be placed on well-paying jobs and receive overtime.[35]

According to historians Steve Babson and John Barnard, skilled workers played a dynamic role in the formation of the United Auto Workers. Babson notes that "tool and die makers were the cutting edge of auto unionism in Detroit. Production workers provided the critical mass that pushed the UAW forward, but

[31] Occupations found using *Springfield City Directories*, 1925-1935.
[32] R. Schatz, *American Electrical Workers*, 90-100. Schatz states that these men resembled the "labor aristocrats" of 19th century England, 110. See also Ronald Schatz, "Union Pioneers: The Founders of Local Unions at GE and Westinghouse, 1933-1937," *Journal of American History* 66 (1979): 586-602.
[33] Quoted in R. Schatz, *American Electrical Workers*, 68. Both workers were machine operators in Pennsylvania Westinghouse plants.
[34] "Our History," *LB*, September 1963, 2.
[35] Ben Field, *Piper Tompkins* (New York: Doubleday & Co., Inc., 1946).

as they stormed the walls of open-shop Detroit, they moved through breaches opened by the tool and die makers. . . ." Barnard, in his study of the 1939 General Motors tool-and-die-makers strike, highlights that the strike "secured the UAW's position in GM, and therefore in the auto industry." Auto plants required two types of highly skilled workers: those who prepared the tools and dies needed to manufacture automobile parts and those who set up and maintained the thousands of pieces of equipment in an assembly-line-paced production plant. When a 1939 strike at the Detroit Fischer Body plant escalated to 12 plants and 7,600 workers, GM conceded that preparations to bring out its 1940 cars were at a standstill. GM explored getting dies produced at area job shops, but machinists refused to touch the work. Rebuffed, the company negotiated a settlement with the strike's leader, Walter Reuther.[36] Able to turn out precision work to exacting requirements, these industrial craftsmen were levelheaded and systematic in their approach to factory work, and these traits carried over to union organizing.[37]

War Work Boost and Post-War Decline

Benefiting from the surge in war-based production, Bosch expanded during the Second World War and union membership grew. War production achieved what the New Deal could not, accelerated job growth. Sixty-nine thousand workers labored in the aircraft and related parts industries in 1939; this increased more than tenfold by 1945. As plants expanded, the valley's machinery builders boomed. Historian David Noble found that, "In 1940, only 28 percent of machine tools in use were less than ten years old; in 1945 the ratio had risen to 62 percent.[38] Sales climbed to $50 million in 1943 from $13 million in 1941, and employment rose to 6,700 from slightly under 1,000. Sales and employment peaked in 1944 at $61.2 million and 7,300 respectively. As back orders mounted, a 600-worker production facility opened in Providence, Rhode Island.[39]

In 1941, because of concerns that German-based Robert Bosch was in possession of too much company stock, the United States Treasury took over day-to-day operations of the Main Street plant, while the Alien Property Custodian's office (APC) seized control of 77 percent of the company's voting

[36] Steve Babson, *Building the Union: Skilled Workers and Anglo-Gaelic Immigrants in the Rise of the UAW* (New Brunswick: Rutgers University Press, 1991), esp. chs. 4 and 5; John Barnard, "Rebirth of the United Automobile Workers: The General Motors Tool and Diemakers' Strike of 1939," *Labor History* 27 (1986): 165-187.

[37] The skill issue is important to consider in analyzing national events that would overtake UE in the late 1940s and early 1950s.

[38] Ann Markusen and Joel Yudken, *Dismantling the Cold War Economy* (New York: Basic Books, 1992), 42-43; David Noble, *Forces of Production* (New York: Oxford University Press, 1986), 5-8; Wayne Broehl, *Precision Valley: The Machine Tool Companies of Springfield Vermont*, esp. ch. 8, "Arsenal of Democracy."

[39] *SDN*, 27 March, 7 May 1942; *SMU*, 27 March, 22 June 1942; Office of Alien Property Custodian, *Annual Report for the Fiscal Year Ending June 30, 1944*, 63.

stock. This stock, ostensibly owned by Swedish interests, was controlled by a group of German industrialists closely associated with the Robert Bosch Corporation. The APC's Leo Crowley managed the stock and could sell it at his discretion.[40] In March 1942 the Treasury Department ordered 23 employees, all non-U.S. citizens, fired as security risks. This happened even though a statement by top management noted, "The termination of the services of these employees should not be construed as any indication that they have been found to have been engaged in subversive activities." Twelve of the 23 employees, including the vice president for product development, worked in the Engineering department.[41]

By the middle of the war, Bosch magnetos powered most military airplanes, including those produced by Boeing, Gruman, Vultee, and Sikorsky Aircraft. Battleships, aircraft carriers, destroyers, and submarines sported engines with Bosch fuel injectors. A 1945 issue of the industry trade publication *Steel Horizon* praised Bosch. There, "In the manufacture of diesel fuel injection equipment tolerances are measured not just in thousandths of an inch, which is generally accepted as precision manufacture, but in hundred-thousandths, a degree of accuracy not found in the finest of watches. . . ."[42]

In May 1943 Bosch produced the greatest volume of war material in its history, contradicting rumors that organized sabotage existed in the plant.[43] To keep output high, many skilled workers received draft deferments.[44] Bosch even employed men and women confined to a nearby military hospital. Bedridden patients packaged gaskets for diesel fuel injectors and checked production time-study figures, while ambulatory men operated drill presses and sanding belts in the hospital's small repair shop. According to the 1945 Alien Property Custodian's report, "The exercise, the satisfaction of earning wages at useful work, and the distraction from pain have improved the spirits and hastened the recovery of lightly injured as well as gravely stricken men."[45]

In a move reminiscent of the Armory's Civil War behavior, Bosch established a wide-ranging network of subcontractors. Participants included Whitin Machine Works in Whitinsville, Massachusetts, normally a textile-machinery builder; Rogers, Lunt and Bowlen, a Greenfield, Massachusetts, silversmith; and the Sacco-Lowell Shops in Biddeford, Maine. Like the Armory before it, Bosch's

---

[40] *SMU,* 14 February 1941; "Twenty-three Employees Are Removed at Bosch on Federal order," 27 March 1942, 1.

[41] *SDN,* 15 March 1942; *SMU,* 27 March 1942, 1.

[42] "Top Notchers in Production" quoted in *SMU,* 6 April 1945; *SMU,* 7 June 1944.

[43] *SMU,* "Bosch Sabotage Reports Are Denied," 9 June 1943, 3.

[44] *SMU,* "Bosch Corp. Products Taking Important Part in Invasion," 7 June 1944, 6.

[45] *SMU,* 14 February 1941; *SDN,* 15 March 1942; Office of Alien Property Custodian, *Annual Report for the Fiscal Year Ending June 30, 1945,* 60.

engineers established quality-control programs at each site.[46] Local 206 members agreed not to strike for the duration of the conflict, and they helped to establish a Labor-Management War Production Committee in 1942 to eliminate scrap and costly production delays. At one point, 27 workers stayed in the plant around the clock for four days producing fuel-injection equipment for several battleships damaged in the battle of Midway, and in August 1944 the union local received the Army and Navy "E" award for production excellence.[47]

Small stock dividends were paid to investors by the APC between 1942 and 1944. The APC also set aside nearly $5 million in profits to assist it in what it anticipated would be a costly adjustment to peacetime production. The cash reserve soon figured prominently in the plant's return to civilian ownership.[48] Bosch emerged from the war as part of the electrical-machinery and vehicle-components sector of the nation's burgeoning manufacturing economy, with its principal peacetime products diesel fuel-injection equipment and automotive electrical equipment, including generators, windshield-wiper motors, and voltage regulators. Aircraft-engine magnetos, half of net sales during the war, accounted for less than 5 percent of sales by 1946.[49] Net sales from July 1, 1945, to June 30, 1946, fell to $26.5 million, just 43 percent of 1944 sales. Nonetheless, it was reasonable in late 1945 for Bosch workers to assume that the high concentration of UE locals in the valley and labor's steadfast support for the war effort—there were no work stoppages during the war—would provide a strong bargaining position and allow them to maintain their shop floor.

But at war's end the Federal Government declared surplus: the close to 300,000 machine tools it had purchased to support war production, dumping the equipment on the market at bargain-basement prices. New England machine-tool builders were forced to layoff thousands of their workers as orders disappeared.[50] From late July to mid-August the Navy canceled just over $7 billion in orders and the business press predicted that 5 million workers would lose their jobs. In western Massachusetts and Connecticut 100,000 jobs were at risk due to the government's cancellation of $250 million in contracts. Hartford, Connecticut-based jet-engine maker Pratt & Whitney terminated 1,200 workers when it closed its East Longmeadow, Massachusetts, plant, and it idled its massive

---

[46] American Bosch Company, *A Story of Teamwork* (unpublished paper, 1977, PVHM).

[47] *LB*, September, 1963.

[48] *LB*, 23 March 1943; 2 June 1943, 9. Profits in 1943 were almost $4 million, however the APC held on to $2.5 million of it. *LB*, 5 April 1944; 21 March 1945.

[49] Office of Alien Property Custodian, *Annual Report for the Fiscal Year Ending June 30, 1946*, 63.

[50] A. Markusen and J. Yudken, *Dismantling the Cold War Economy*, 42-43; D. Noble, *Forces of Production*, 5, 8.

east Hartford factory for two weeks, a move that affected 25,000 workers. In Springfield, Perkins Machine and Westinghouse each laid off 1,500 workers.[51]

At Bosch, employment plummeted from 7,300 workers in early September 1945 to fewer than 2,000 at the start of the new year. For much of 1946 the APC debated what to do with the Springfield factory, as nearly $20 million in orders were cancelled. The hope was for a speedy return to automotive-parts production along with a sales boost from several new products under development in the plant's research and engineering laboratory, called "the most complete of its kind for any company of its size in the country."[52] However, the lingering ownership muddle hampered long-term planning. Roger Putnam, the lone Springfield manufacturer on the APC's board of directors, wanted the firm to be sold to local manufacturers. Unhappy with the delay in figuring out what new ownership might look like, one local newspaper chided, "In as much as Bosch is a manufacturer of metal products rather than legal briefs it might be well to get more persons familiar with the former production on the board."[53]

In July 1948 the APC sold its 77 percent block of Bosch shares in a sealed bid auction that attracted several investors, including the Detroit diesel-pump manufacturer Excello Corporation; Electric Auto Lite of Toledo, Ohio; and Lehman Brothers. The two-year-old New York-based financial holding company AMRA made the top bid of $6 million, $11.28 a share. AMRA's managing partners included individuals from several Wall Street law firms and the presidents of the American Securities Corporation and the American Overseas Development Corporation. The $6 million purchase price was well under the plant's April 1948 valuation of $13.5 million, or $13.64 a share. Just two weeks after the sale, the public learned that AMRA had put up less than $1.5 million of its own cash for the company. In fact, the cash reserves the APC had accumulated during the war of close to $5 million, augmented by a retooling fund of $500,000, made the purchase nearly a gift. This prompted the *Springfield Union* to question the sale: "The cash figure is of particular interest because it is contended in some quarters that ownership of the American Bosch could have been brought to Springfield if there had been 10 men willing to put up $150,000 each."[54]

Concerned that a local buyer had not come forward, the paper's business editor noted, "that the days are apparently gone when that amount of money could be raised locally because of what seems to be a present lack of interest in

[51] Office of Alien Property Custodian, *Annual Report for the Fiscal Year Ending June 30, 1946,* 63; *SR,* 3 August 1945, 19; 15 August 1945, 1; 16 August 1945, 1; 17 August 1945, 1; 20 August 1945, 1. Layoffs were abrupt, for as late as August 3rd local newspapers were running help-wanted advertisements for area metalworking firms.
[52] *Springfield Evening News* (SEN), 19 September 1945, 1.
[53] *SDN,* 19 September 1945; *SMU,* 7 April 1948.
[54] *SMU,* 22 July and 26 July, 1948.

such ventures."[55] The concern was prompted by the fact that in the 1930s, AMRA's principal investor, Charles Allen, had gained control of the locally based Wickwire Spencer Steel Company, merged it with the Colorado Fuel and Iron Company, and soon thereafter shuttered Wickwire. When asked about this, Allen stated a Bosch move from Springfield was "unthinkable."[56]

AMRA also owned the Brooklyn and Garden City, New York-based ARMA Corporation, which manufactured gyroscopes and precision electrical measuring equipment. Like Bosch, ARMA lost defense contracts at the war's end, and its workforce fell to 1,800 in 1946, from 9,000 in mid-1945. ARMA relied on Navy and Air Force research contracts for its new products, including guidance-control systems, computer devices, searchlights, and gun-control technology.

AMRA intended to operate the factories as separate divisions of a merged 2,000-worker corporation.[57] Brooklyn's production work moved to Springfield so that the Brooklyn facility could focus on military research and efforts to market a new computer-controlled lathe called the Arma-Matic. In part, the Bosch purchase was made to get access to the machine-tool market and the high-skilled precision machinists needed to produce the lathe, which was designed by Massachusetts Institute of Technology-trained physicist Frederick Cunningham.[58] The machine could be "converted quickly from one job to another. It was intended to take only seconds to change a piece of stock and the control tape, and only a few minutes to prepare the tape." Running a traditional lathe required a worker's two hands and undivided attention; the tape-controlled Arma-Matic lathe freed up the worker to operate more than one machine. Thus, *Business Week* pointed out, the considerable value of Cunningham's machine is, "A man doesn't have to be skilled to run it," and "he could run up to four machines simultaneously."[59]

In 1949 Bosch and ARMA merged, and the holding company changed its name to American Bosch-ARMA (ABA). Donald Hess, Bosch's president since 1938, became the company's managing director and also maintained his title as Bosch president. Herbert Guterman, an electrical engineer with considerable manufacturing experience at General Electric and Raytheon, was named to run ARMA. Under the reorganization, Bosch owned ARMA and gained control of its $7 million cash reserve. The reserve grew in 1946 and 1947 when, despite showing a profit, no dividends were paid out. The merger statement revealed

[55] *SMU*, 22 July and 26 July, 1948.
[56] *SMU*, 10 July 1948.
[57] *SMU*, 10 July 1948. AMRA's principal investor Charles Allen had done business previously in Western Massachusetts.
[58] *SMU*, 10 July 1948. D. Noble, *Forces of Production*, 88-89. When job loss in both companies is analyzed, the merged firm went from a combined 16,300 to 3,800 employees. At the time of the merger, employment was 23 percent of what it had been at the height of wartime production.
[59] *Business Week* quoted in D. Noble, *Forces of Production*, 90.

that $6.5 million from the reserve was to be used to pay off AMRA's outstanding bank loans, including the $3.5 million it had borrowed in 1948 to buy Bosch.[60]

LABOR SPLITS

While several corporations merged after the Second World War, the opposite occurred in the house of labor. Springfield metalworkers gained a strong union voice and wage, benefit, and seniority language improvements in the 1940s, however unionists' collective strength dissipated in the early 1950s. Just as management's power solidified and many corporations began the global hunt in earnest for nonunion labor, union locals were caught up in an internecine battle between the United Electrical, Radio and Machine Workers (UE) and the upstart, anticommunist International Union of Electrical Workers (IUE) for control over the valley's existing union locals. These events culminated in two tumultuous weeks in November 1949 when the IUE gained control over locals at American Bosch, Westinghouse, and four other large Springfield plants and the nearby General Electric plant in Pittsfield. The mean-spirited fight left trade unionists bitterly divided at the precise moment when unity was essential.

In 1954 unionists "threw in the towel" in the fight against permanent job loss. An editorial in the local's *Labor Bulletin* stated that permanent layoffs were inescapable. "It will be hard for us to stand by and watch our living move from under our noses," the column lamented, "and what hurts most is that we can't do anything to stop the flow of work from going out the door."[61] A majority of the Westinghouse rank and file sent a similar message to its officeholders when they soundly defeated William Lieberman's 1958 bid for a seventh successive one-year term as Local 202 president. Lieberman had held elected union office since the local's founding in 1933, and repeatedly in 1956 and 1957 had called on the state AFL-CIO to support a boycott of Westinghouse products because of persistent rumors that the Springfield facility would be closed. By then, 2,000 Springfield jobs already had been shifted to Columbus, Ohio. Workers believed that his activities alienated the company and caused the layoffs.[62]

---

[60] Ronald Schatz, *The Electrical Workers: A History of Labor at General Electric and Westinghouse, 1923-1960*, Urbana, Ill, University of Illinois Press, 8. Workforce levels are found in Local 206 membership and seniority lists, UMass Archives. Manufacturing value added in the industry rose from $941M on the eve of World War II to almost $4B in 1949 and $10.6B.

[61] *LB*, May 1954, 4.

[62] *SDN*, 21 October, 28 February 1958, 1; 21 October 1958, 27; 27 February 1959, 1. Joan Reilly, *A History of the Westinghouse Electric Company in Springfield, 1915-1970: The Demise of a Giant* (1986) unpublished paper in the Pioneer Valley Historical Society Westinghouse Papers. Westinghouse closed in 1970 after layoffs brought the once 5,000-member union local down to 200 members.

United Electrical Workers Under Attack

In 1936 three distinct groups coalesced to form the UE.[63] One group was headed by James Carey, leader of the Philadelphia-based Radio and Allied Trades National Labor Council; a second group was led by James Matles, who brought in locals affiliated with the Machine Tool and Foundry Workers along with 14 International Association of Machinist lodges. The third group comprised workers from several General Electric facilities, including plants in Lynn, Massachusetts, and Schenectady, New York, identified with Julius Emspak. Carey became union president at the UE's first national meeting and Emspak, Secretary-Treasurer. When Matles and the machinist locals came into the UE in 1937, he became director of organizing. In 1941 Carey lost his bid for reelection to the UE presidency, defeated by Al Fitzgerald of the Lynn, Massachusetts GE. Described in a *Saturday Evening Post* profile as a "Small dark young man boiling with nervous energy," and the "best kind of fighting Irishman," Carey remained secretary-treasurer of the CIO. From there he stayed in contact with the radio-plant locals he originally brought into the UE. Allied with the Association of Catholic Trade Unionists (ACTU), in 1948 Carey began a campaign to turn UE locals against their national leadership.[64] Established in 1937 by New York priests, labor organizers, and social reformers, ACTU was concerned with what it perceived were the dangers communists in the labor movement posed for Catholic workers. The group paid particular attention to the UE because half of its members were Catholic.[65]

The UE faced external pressures during 1946 and 1947 as Congressional subcommittees investigated the union, and at the same time it faced a challenge from Harry Block, who organized UE Members for Democratic Action

---

[63] There are several histories of the United Electrical Workers and studies of anti-communism in the labor movement that analyze the UE-IUE split including: Michael Bonislawski, *The Anti-Communist Movement and Industrial Unionism: IUE vs. UE* (University of Massachusetts Boston Master of Arts Thesis, 1992); Martin Halpern, *UAW Politics in the Cold War Era* (Albany: State University of New York Press, 1988); Stephen Meyer, *Stalin Over Wisconsin: The Making and Unmaking of Militant Unionism, 1900-1950* (New Brunswick: Rutgers University Press, 1992); Steve Rosswurm, ed., *The CIO's Left-Led Unions* (New Brunswick: Rutgers University Press, 1992); R. Schatz, *The Electrical Workers.*

[64] Block, founder in 1933 of the Philadelphia Philco radio, attended the UE's founding convention, and was president of the Philadelphia district of UE. R. Filippelli, *The United Electrical, Radio and Machine Workers,* 53; the Carey sketch appeared in the *Saturday Evening Post,* 1 March 1947, 27.

[65] R. Schatz, *The Electrical Workers,* 181.

(UEMDA).[66] But despite the intensive public scrutiny, between January 1946 and September 1947, UE won 86 percent of the 571 representation elections it participated in at new shops or in shops where there was a challenge by another union. At a Pulaski, Virginia, RCA plant, merchants took out a full-page newspaper advertisement urging workers to vote for the UE based on its record of achievement and its ability "to support its members in their effort to win the things that they are entitled to as Americans;" UE won 739-3. UE's staffers were also visible on the political front where, for example, they led an important fight in the Massachusetts legislature for passage of a law guaranteeing strikers unemployment pay.[67]

The Rise of the International Union of Electrical Workers in Springfield

In October 1947 the *Springfield Union* printed an open letter from Anthony Cimino, the former president of Westinghouse UE Local 202, to Ralph Forsstrom, then president of Bosch UE Local 206. He repeated the allegations made by Joseph Alsop in the *Saturday Evening Post* that several UE national and district officers were Communist Party members and then urged Bosch unionists to join a local chapter of Harry Block's UE Members for Democratic Action.[68] Forsstrom's defense of the UE against communist-baiting from UEMDA members and his votes at the just-concluded UE national convention had earned him Cimino's attention.[69] At the convention, against Local 206's unified ballot directive, Forsstrom voted for Matles, Emspak, and Fitzgerald for national office, while the two other UE delegates to the convention, James Manning and William Slattery, voted against the three as instructed by the union's Executive Board.

---

[66] According to Block, local unionists who resisted what he termed "communist dictation," were relegated to second-class membership in their locals. R. Filippelli, *The United Electrical, Radio and Machine Workers*, esp. 68-88, 201. In 1948 three key issues divided CIO unions: the Henry Wallace presidential campaign, membership in what was argued was the communist-dominated World Federation of Trade Unions, and support for the Marshall Plan. See F. S. O'Brien, "The 'Communist Dominated' Unions in the United States Since 1950," *Labor History* 9 (1968): 174-190, esp. 185-186. Block's role in establishing the UEMDA is discussed in R. Schatz, *The Electrical Workers,* 180-181.
[67] *UEN,* 9 November 1946, 4; *UEN,* 2 August 1947, 7; *UEN,* 9 August 1947, 1; Election figures are in *UEN,* 27 September 1947, 8.
[68] *SMU,* 29 October 1947; Joseph S. Alsop, "Will the CIO Shake the Communists Loose?" *Saturday Evening Post,* 22 February 1947, 15 and 1 March 1947, 26.
[69] *Ralph Forsstrom to James Matles,* September 22, 1946 (UE Archives District-Local Series, ff. 247x). The 1946 Milwaukee convention marked the first time an open electoral challenge to UE national leadership took place. By eight-to-one majorities each attempt failed. Local 206 was now identified by its votes at this convention as in the Carey-Block camp (R. Schatz, *The Electrical Workers,* 184).

Upon his return from the convention, Manning, an All-American football player and graduate of Jesuit-run Fordham University in New York City, actively opposed UE local leaders. While I uncovered no direct evidence linking Manning to Carey and ACTU, it appears likely that Manning was exposed to their perspectives on trade-union issues while attending college in New York City, which was an ACTU stronghold. However, despite being the focus of UEMDA's and ACTU's attention, the rank and file reelected Forsstrom local president over Manning in November 1947, and in November 1948 they elected him business agent with 71 percent of the vote, 1096-438, over William Slattery, the UEMDA's hand-picked candidate.[70] Manning and several other UEMDA members worked as stock handlers, positions that gave them a great deal of in-plant mobility, and they used their positions to agitate against Forsstrom. In 1948 and 1949 UEMDA regularly leafleted Bosch workers at shift changes, informing them that if "Communism is an issue in any of your unions throw it to hell out and throw the advocates out along with it."[71]

In 1949, to shift attention from internal union politics, the UE mounted a national campaign against high unemployment and stagnating wages. A national Executive Board resolution blamed big business and Congress for 5 million jobless workers. However, in an indication that the nation's anticommunism was affecting UE members, Carey received three times more delegate votes for president in September 1949 than in 1948. On November 1, 1949, the UE resigned from the CIO before they could be expelled at the CIO's upcoming national convention. But the Westinghouse, Chapman Valve, Van Norman, and Monsanto UE locals broke with their national leadership, proclaiming, "We're staying in the CIO. We don't know yet how this is to be done, but we'll find a way. Between the UE and the CIO the choice is clear—it's CIO every time." The next day Herman Greenberg, president of the western Massachusetts CIO Council, announced that the CIO had formed a national 10-person committee charged with setting up a CIO-affiliated labor organization in Springfield for workers interested in quitting the UE. Former Westinghouse local president Cimino was Springfield's representative on the board. At the same time, the CIO issued a national charter to the International Union of Electrical Workers and named James Carey the union's first national president. The IUE sent telegrams to the 1,500 manufacturing plants where UE represented workers, calling on management to break off their dealings with the union.[72]

---

[70] Election results for this period are contained in the Local 206 papers, UMALA; "All American James Manning Honored," *SR,* 12 June 1966.

[71] *SDN,* 9 September 1947. The "throw them out" statement was first made by Philip Murray, president of the Steelworkers. The *News* reported that "A number of delegates from the Springfield area have expressed their growing distrust of the left-wing elements in the UE union." Leaflet quoted in *SDN* article titled "Bosch Workers Urged to Battle Reds in UE," 18 September 1948.

[72] *SDN,* 1 November 1949, 1, 4; 2 November 1949, 12; 3 November 1949, 1, 5.

While all of this was going on, the Bosch local held its elections. A plant-gate, election-eve rally hosted by the western Massachusetts CIO attracted over 1,000 workers, who heard several speakers urge them to dump Forsstrom. Forsstrom was running for business agent against Ralph Chicketti, a union steward and stock handler with 30 years seniority and a staunch anti-UE leader. At a postrally press conference arranged by Chicketti's supporters, retiree Ben Toppe, one of the plant's very first union officers, returned a plaque given to him by Forsstrom recognizing his years of service to the labor movement. "It (the plaque) was one of my most prized possessions," Toppe offered, "until some of the signatories became associated with the left wing." He accused Forsstrom and the rest of Local 206's present officers of selling workers down the Volga River. Forsstrom lost in a close vote, 690-670, and in the same election, Frank Broderick, another anti-UE leader, became local president. The day after the election, the *Daily News* headline read "Bosch UE Defeats Forsstrom: Leftists Lose Last Hope of Major Influence Here."[73]

In less than one week workers at Van Norman, Westinghouse, Chapman Valve, and Monsanto exited the UE for the IUE. In nearby Pittsfield, on Sunday, November 20, members of General Electric UE Local 255 voted to join the IUE. Right before the vote, unionists rallied at St. Mary's Roman Catholic Church, where they heard the parish priest equate the choice between UE and the IUE with the choice between "Washington and Moscow and ultimately Christ and Stalin."[74]

Local 206 remained affiliated with the UE until the end of November, but management refused to negotiate with the union or turn over the union dues it collected from workers' pay. The plant's industrial-relations manager informed the UE and the IUE that dues would be placed in escrow "until the affiliation status of Local 206 is definitely established." The move gained national attention as it marked the first time a company refused to recognize the UE absent a new, legally sanctioned representation vote. In a few weeks time the amount withheld grew to close to $15,000, money the UE sorely needed to mount an effective challenge to the IUE.[75]

On November 9 Forsstrom, the union's lame-duck business agent, chaired a Steward's Council meeting, which affirmed its support for the UE. Stewards then sent a telegram to the IUE's Carey, demanding, "He keep his nose out of our business and stop interfering with our current contract negotiations." But the next afternoon the union's Executive Board—composed of top officers and a much smaller number of stewards—refused to endorse the UE. At the union's regularly scheduled, Sunday, November 19 monthly membership meeting,

---

[73] *SDN,* 5 November 1949, 1. In a related story Herman Greenberg praised Bosch workers for defeating Forsstrom.
[74] *SDN,* 21 November 1949, 32.
[75] *SDN,* 4 November 1949, 1; 8 November 1949, 1, 32.

Forsstrom made a motion that "We must unite all members of Local 206 to force the company to live up to the contract in every respect and postpone all talks on leaving the UE until the legal expiration of our contract on June 23, 1950." Chicketti, the business-agent-in-waiting, walked to the front of the packed hall and waved petitions he claimed contained over 600 signatures from Bosch workers demanding immediate action on the affiliation issue. By a procedural vote, Chicketti's motion "ordering all officers to withdraw immediately from the UE and sign IUE membership cards" replaced Forsstrom's motion and then easily passed in a voice vote. A second motion directed Broderick and Chicketti to attend an IUE organizing meeting in Philadelphia the last week of November.[76]

Broderick and Chicketti then called for a special Executive Board meeting for Saturday, November 25. At the meeting, Forsstrom, second-shift vice president Theodore Gagnon, trustee Donald Bergeron, and three negotiating-committee members were expelled from office for their refusal to comply with the membership directive that they disaffiliate from UE and sign IUE membership cards. These six local officers and 25 other workers signed an open letter of support for the UE right after the November 19 membership meeting. In stark contrast to the "UE 31," by the end of November, 1200 workers had signed IUE membership cards.[77]

For the first half of 1950 the union remained divided while everyone awaited a National Labor Relations Board representation election scheduled for June 2nd. Anthony Cimino, now an IUE international representative, worked closely with Bosch's IUE supporters and the IUE national office and loaned the Bosch–IUE group nearly $10,000 over the first half of 1950 to print flyers and pay for other preelection activities. On June 2 workers voted 964-724 to end their affiliation with the United Electrical Workers.[78] The UE made one attempt to reestablish itself in the Bosch in 1952 when Forsstrom led a brief campaign to represent workers in the maintenance department, experimental machine shop, and tool-and-die and gauge area; workers voted 127-78 to remain in the IUE.[79]

---

[76] General membership meeting minutes, 19 November 1949, UMALA Local 206 files.

[77] Executive Board minutes, 14 November 1949; General membership meeting minutes, 19 November 1949; Special Executive Board meeting minutes, 25 November 1949, UMALA Local 206 files.

[78] IUE correspondence files contain several letters from Frank Broderick to Cimino like this one dated 28 February 1950. "Our court case is still pending. We will have enough money to pay expenses trough Friday March 3rd, after that, our cash on hand will be exhausted" (UMALA Local 206 Correspondence Series II). *SMU,* 3 June 1950, 1.

[79] *SDN,* 20 and 22 August 1958.

Skill Mattered: Who Supported the UE and the IUE?

An analysis of the individuals associated with the UE and IUE from 1947 to 1950 indicates why Forsstrom attempted to reassert the UE among skilled workers. Only 21 of the occupations of the 31 workers who signed the open letter to stay in the UE could be determined. Skilled positions were held by 18, with 5 of them toolmakers and 4 all-around machinists. Among the IUE's 10 most highly visible supporters, there was only one skilled worker, with the rest machine operators, stock handlers, and storeroom clerks. At Westinghouse, where workers signed a public statement opposing the IUE, the occupations of 7 members could be determined. Five were skilled machinists and millwrights and two were assemblers.[80] A similar pattern existed among UE and IUE supporters in East Pittsburgh Westinghouse UE Local 601. Ronald Schatz writes, "Although exceptions can be noted, the UE generally captured majorities in those sections of the bargaining unit in which a high proportion of the workers were either skilled, well paid, or both. The IUE won those sections of the unit in which the proportion of skilled or well-paid work was lower."[81]

Remarkably, the new IUE Local 206 dated its history from 1936, celebrating its 25th anniversary in 1961 without any mention of UE's founding role. At the celebration, the workers who led the anti-UE fight were canonized as the true pioneers of the Bosch union. After the split, three men dominated IUE Local 206: James Parker, a stock clerk served as president from 1952 to 1958; Jim Manning, a work expediter, was business agent from 1952 to 1958; and Ralph Chicketti, another work expediter, served as president and served on several negotiating committees.[82] The social and political bedrock of UE Local 206 during the 1930s and 1940s—tool-and-die makers, machinists, and mechanics—held no office above union steward in the 1950s and through most of the 1960s.[83]

---

[80] For Westinghouse see *SDN*, 18 November 1949, 1. The 14 signed noncommunist affidavits to conform to Taft-Hartley guidelines, established themselves as UE Local 202 and petitioned the NLRB for what ended up being an ill-fated certification election. For an account of the 25th anniversary celebration, see *LB*, September 1963, 3.

[81] R. Schatz, *The Electrical Workers*.

[82] Names were gathered from meeting minutes and newspaper articles. Occupations were determined using city directories and union newspapers. Employment records for the period could not be found. IUE officers were determined from election files in UMALA Local 206 files.

[83] While beyond the scope of this research, it would be interesting to determine if any UE skilled workers left the large plants in the early 1950s to start smaller firms of their own. There is evidence that in parts of Europe, and particularly northern Italy, workers expelled from large firms for their communist political views established new plants. In *Labor Radical* Len De Caux reports on visits with several labor organizers and officers affected by the attacks on alleged communists in the labor movement. Besides eliminating communists, De Caux contends, the move also eliminated "most earlier labor idealism." See Len De Caux, *Labor Radical* (Boston: Beacon Press, 1970), 504-506.

The UE had negotiated a series of national agreements with two of the largest corporations in the country—General Electric and Westinghouse—during the late 1930s and 1940s. In the 1940s close to 80 percent of the workers in the electrical-goods industry belonged to UE. But, as a result of the internecine battle with IUE and raiding by other unions, in 1957 UE's membership was 71,000, down from almost one-half million in 1945. Meanwhile, General Electric and Westinghouse were "freed from the constraint of a powerful nationwide union" as they redesigned jobs and expanded their national and international manufacturing capabilities.[84]

Up and down the Connecticut River Valley, no systematic anticapital flight campaign materialized, nor was there a concerted communitywide effort made to bring new jobs to the valley. With such a free hand, Bosch and other valley corporations eagerly established multiple manufacturing sites in the low-wage and nonunion southern United States and overseas. The next chapter chronicles Bosch's move to Mississippi, a script that Westinghouse, Van Norman, and other employers followed between the mid-1950s and late 1980s. For the region's metalworkers and skilled machinists, there was to be no happy ending.[85]

---

[84] R. Schatz, *The Electrical Workers,* 232-233.
[85] R. Schatz, *The Electrical Workers,* 226. By 1963, in terms of membership numbers UE only represented 10,000 GE workers. Other unions with a sizable presence in GE were: IUE – 68,000; IAM – 9,000; UAW – 5,500.

CHAPTER 4

Work Moves Out:
Bosch Doomed in Springfield?

According to the Springfield Free Press, the American Bosch Co., a permanent fixture in Springfield, is leaving its location in that city for a free plant, free taxes for ten years, and low-wage labor in Columbus, Mississippi.
— Senator John F. Kennedy
from the floor of the United States Senate, 1953

American industry was undamaged by the Second World War and soon accounted for close to half of the world's manufacturing output; Connecticut River Valley firms and workers shared in the prosperity. After a downturn in the late 1940s, primarily caused by defense cuts, Springfield firms like Bosch added workers. Productivity rose, and workers enjoyed rising standards of living. Precision metalworking helped Greater Springfield and much of the river valley prosper long after textile and paper cities like Lowell and Holyoke struggled with job loss. Between 1939 and 1947 Springfield's production workforce growth of 62 percent doubled the statewide average.[1] However, the country and the valley were unable to sustain their positions as "manufacturer to the world" and in the mid-1950s Bosch and other firms began their exodus. As firms fled the region, Massachusetts Senator John F. Kennedy made several speeches on the dangers of runaway companies. He warned that defense contracts in the aircraft and electrical-machinery industries and inflated government payrolls masked the static behavior in civilian companies.

Up and down the river valley firms passed out of local control and, in a remarkable downturn, half of Springfield manufacturing facilities closed between

---

[1] *SR*, 25 October 1936.

1950 and 1987.[2] Across the country over 2 million well-paying jobs in the highly unionized durable-goods sector disappeared between 1979 and 1983 alone.[3] The process of deindustrialization is discernible through a review of events at Bosch, which became part of a large corporation in the late 1940s. Just a few years after its acquisition, the new owners relocated hundreds of jobs to Mississippi in a pattern that continued over the next 30 years. The switch from localized ownership—with its primary concern on the well-being of the Springfield plant—to ownership with the capacity to play off the interests of factories, workers, and communities, one against the other, poisoned the Bosch's labor relations and led to bitter strikes in the 1970s and 1980s.

A SOUTHERN STRATEGY EMERGES

The first big move came in 1953 with the opening of a production facility in Columbus, Mississippi, a city of approximately 20,000 people (46 percent African American) located 125 miles west of the steel center of Birmingham, Alabama. Columbus, the largest city in Lowndes County, population 37,852, had a 6 percent unemployment rate in 1950, with 21 percent of citizens engaged in manufacturing. In *Capital Moves,* Jefferson Cowie describes the South's demand for job-creating investment from the North as "reaching fever pitch in the 1960s." Bosch's relocation of several hundred jobs to Columbus was a small element in the state's comprehensive factory-attraction campaign, and it foreshadowed the serious challenges to the now-fragile underpinnings of the Connecticut River Valley economy.

[2]Robert Forrant, *Metalworking Plant Closings and Major Layoffs in Hampden County, 1967-1986* (Springfield: Machine Action Project, 1987); U.S. Department of Commerce, *Manufacturing Censuses.* For the Holyoke story, see William Hartford, *Working People of Holyoke* (New Brunswick: Rutgers University Press, 1990), esp. ch. 8.
[3]For a discussion of these trends, see Stephen Herzenberg, J. Alic, and H. Wial, *New Rules for a New Economy: Employment and Opportunity in Postindustrial America* (Ithaca: Cornell University Press, 1998); Harley Shaiken, *Automation and Global Production: Automobile Engine Production in Mexico, the United States, and Canada* (San Diego: University of California Center for U.S. Mexican Studies, 1987); Kim Moody, *Workers in a Lean World: Unions in the International Economy* (New York: Verso, 1997); Max H. Kirsch, *In the Wake of the Giant: Multinational Restructuring and Uneven Development in a New England Community* (New York: State University of New York Press, 1998); John T. Cumbler, *A Social History of Economic Decline: Business, Politics, and Work in Trenton* (New Brunswick: Rutgers University Press, 1989). Kirsch examines the impact on Pittsfield, Massachusetts as General Electric eliminated 3,000 jobs there between 1974 and 1982, while Cumbler traces industrial decline in Trenton, New Jersey. On the decline of union power, see Barry Bluestone and Bennett Harrison, *The Deindustrialization of America: Plant Closings, Community Abandonment and the Dismantling of Basic Industry* (New York: Basic Books, 1982). Kirsch notes that unions in New England were successful in 70 percent of their organizing campaigns in the 1950s, a figure that fell under 50 percent by the early 1970s, 29.

Between 1940 and 1950 Mississippi issued $5,360,000 in industrial bonds through its Balance Agriculture With Industry (BAWI) initiatives, and the program paid off. Plants constructed with these bonds accounted for 76 percent of the state's increased employment and 34 percent of its earnings between 1940 and 1958. In 1959 bond-built factories provided 36,000 jobs and $100 million in wages across Mississippi.[4]

Historian James Cobb writes that

> The all-out devotion to the cause of growth and the unexamined faith in growth as a panacea for all that ailed the South formed the basis of a consensus broad enough to span the region's ideological spectrum. An indelible belief in the ameliorating potential of economic growth led a number of the South's small cadre of moderates and liberals to accept low wages, discriminatory hiring, blatant anti-unionism, tax exemptions, and worker exploitation as unpleasant means to an ultimately redemptive end.[5]

In the 1930s, in an effort to end their long-standing dependence on agriculture, several southern states established their own BAWI programs, and hundreds of cities and several states competed for manufacturers. A 1937 *Springfield Daily News* story described the establishment by nine southern states, Mississippi among them, of a $500,000 fund for a national marketing campaign extolling the region's cheap power and pliant labor. L. W. Roberts, Jr., former secretary of the Democratic Party's National Committee, was hired to coordinate activities.[6]

During the Depression several Mississippi cities were found guilty of illegally dangling Works Progress Administration (WPA) funds as bait to attract northern factories. In one highly publicized case, Ellisville, Mississippi, spent $26,000 of the funds ostensibly for the construction of a vocational education center. Instead, a hosiery company fleeing Pennsylvania in the middle of a strike bought knitting machines with the funds and employed vocational center trainees for $4.00 a week making its finished goods.[7] Elsewhere, Clanton, Alabama, boasted "no hostile unions here and none desired," while in South Carolina there were no unions or union activity of any kind, thus "workers give a day's work for a day's pay."

In 1951 Mississippi Governor Fielding Wright informed the Whirlpool Company, "The particular area you have in mind has an abundance of

---

[4]United States Bureau of Census, *Census of Population 1950*, vol. 2, part 24, Mississippi (Washington, DC: GPO, 1952); Jefferson Cowie, *Capital Moves: RCA's 70-Year Quest for Cheap Labor* (Ithaca: Cornell University Press, 2000), 79. For an excellent account of the BAWI program, James Cobb, *The Selling of the South: The Southern Crusade for Industrial Development* (Urbana: University of Illinois Press, 1993), 29-30.

[5]James C. Cobb, "Beyond Planters and Industrialists: A New Perspective on the New South," *The Journal of Southern History* 54 (1988): 45-68, 59.

[6]"South to Spend Half Million to Seek Industries,"*SDN,* October 1, 1937, 16.

[7]See J. Cobb's *The Selling of the South.*

intelligent native labor and is entirely free of those conditions that tend to impair employer–employee relations." One Mississippi city described its "wonderful labor, 98 percent native born, mostly high school graduates," who will "lower average hourly industrial wage rates 5 cents to 49 cents below other southern states and from 50 cents to 95 cents below Northern states."[8]

With wages a substantial fixed cost, manufacturers became enamored of a move south, and in unionized factories, managers dangled the specter of relocation in an effort to hold down wage demands. General Electric adopted its southern strategy after the Second World War, breaking apart its concentration in the industrial Northeast in hopes of gaining leverage over its mostly unionized workforce. Textron combined its southern strategy with a global one as it shifted metalworking and apparel production from Massachusetts to Puerto Rico and textile production from New Hampshire to the South. Bosch was to follow a similar path as it sent work to Mississippi in the 1950s and 1960s and built factories and entered joint production ventures in South America.[9]

Before being torn apart by the "red scare" in the late 1940s and early 1950s, the United Electrical, Radio, and Machine Workers Union (UE) issued a report on the increase in plant relocations. The South, UE warned, needed greater trade-union organization to help end racial discrimination and to blunt what it labeled the low-wage "sword of Damocles" hanging over all workers. As companies shifted work from the Northeast and decentralized production in smaller shops, unions needed an organizing strategy that took these changes into account. Unions also needed to cultivate broad-based community support to oppose work relocations.[10]

Northern companies had built plants in the South before, so the escalation of activity in the 1950s should not have been a big surprise. United States Steel built two coke ovens, two cold-rolling mills, a continuous strip mill, and a turning mill there in the early 1930s.[11] A 1951 *Business Week* article, "Plant Transfers Irk Unions," described the United Auto Workers' futile attempt to block Ford Motor Company from shifting production out of Detroit. Since 1945 Rouge Local 600 alone had lost 20,000 jobs by work transfers. "In expanding times such plants are additions, not replacements," *Business Week* pointed out. "What bothers the unions is that ultimately they may result in diminished operations at earlier sites. This is a greater concern to local unions than internationals."[12]

In a 1962 book, economist Victor Fuchs analyzed plant relocations and employment shifts from 1929 to 1954. He uncovered the large-scale movement of skilled work in aircraft engines and related components. His findings

[8] J. Cobb, *The Selling of the South*, 97-98, 100.
[9] *UE News*, 25 December 1948, 6-7.
[10] *UE News*, 14 September 1946, 7.
[11] *SR*, 17 October 1936, 18.
[12] *Business Week*, "Plant Transfers Irk Unions," 1 December 1951, 36.

challenged the conventional wisdom that only New England's labor-intensive jobs were at risk.[13] In dies, tools, and attachments, machinery, and electrical machinery—the river valley's stock-in-trade—New England and the Middle Atlantic states lost out to the West, South Central, Pacific Coast, and South Atlantic states, a worrisome trend for Springfield's skilled metalworkers.[14]

BOSCH TAKES THE BAIT:
COLUMBUS HOOKS A BIG ONE

Several northern manufacturers built plants in Mississippi in the early 1950s. In 1952 the Oldbury Electro-Chemical Company of Niagara Fall, New York, constructed a $3.5 million factory in Columbus, and Westinghouse opened a 600-worker multimillion dollar factory in Vicksburg.[15] The Columbus Industrial Development Committee agreed to purchase the land for a Bosch factory and to pay for the construction of an access road, water main, and sewer and power lines, at a total cost to the city of $750,000. When Bosch president Donald Hess announced the start of Mississippi construction, he said in part, "When one or more companies start producing in an area where operating costs are much lower, other competitive companies in the same field also have to move in order to survive. It is either move or quit." Referring to Mississippi development officials Hess gushed,

> They will help find a plant site; they will build a building and rent it to you at a very reasonable rate. They will arrange to put in railroad sidings; provide good roads to the plant; run in water and sewers and do everything else you need to make the proposition attractive.

The city's *Commercial Dispatch* lauded the factory as "Part of Columbus' road to progress, with more jobs and more money for our people."[16]

While Bosch management was deciding whether to move, they assured unionists and Springfield's elected officials that, "It is absolutely out of the question that we would ever think of leaving Springfield." From his Florida home, ABA's Chairman of the Board Joseph Ridder stated, "We intend to keep American

---

[13] Victor Fuchs, *Changes in the Location of Manufacturing in the United States Since 1929* (New Haven: Yale University Press, 1962). Data in Fuchs, 128-137.

[14] *Ibid.*, 240.

[15] *Commercial Dispatch* (CD), "Work to Begin Clearing Site for Plant," 22 October 1952, 1; "Westinghouse Multimillion Dollar Plant Built," 16 November 1952, 1.

[16] *CD*, "What is a New Industry Worth to You?" 3 April 1953, 4; "City Council Agrees to Call Industrial Bond Issue," 18 August 1953, 1; "Am. Bosch to Build Large Plant Employing About 800," 14 April 1953, 1.

Bosch Corp. in Springfield fully occupied."[17] In a letter to their 3,200 Springfield employees, management promised the "highly specialized, low volume work" would stay put. Yet the letter carried a not-so-thinly veiled warning: "American Bosch is essentially following the trend of other manufacturers in the highly competitive automotive components business who have found the operation of branch plants to be advantageous." The company concluded that the present transition would be made "with a minimum of cutbacks."[18]

For Bosch, the move was about more than cost savings. Hess and Ridder were aware that the wage benefits gained by the move would quickly erode. According to a well-publicized study by McKinsey & Company, early movers "capitalized in years past upon the economic immaturity of the South" and profited handsomely, but the wage gap had closed considerably since the end of the Second World War. Tightening labor markets, and a lack of skilled workers and managers limited the potential gain of Southern investments. "Even when labor costs are low now there is always the possibility to be taken into account that the advantage may be lost by the time a new plant is built or an old one bought and remodeled, for in many areas the cost is moving upward."[19] Disciplining labor entered into the equation.

Bosch's management searched for a southern base of operations long before the Columbus move became public. In 1952, after the loss of a lucrative Ford Motor Company parts contract to a southern transplant, the company focused on a handful of sites, including the eventual "winner," Columbus, Mississippi. Communities were encouraged to conduct a labor-market survey designed to determine the number of women between the ages of 18 and 40 who would be interested in factory employment. During the survey process, there were concerns in Columbus that there weren't enough women interested in the jobs. The local newspaper reported, "The situation on the male registration appears good with the goal in sight. But on the other side of the picture it is not good. The number of white women has barely reached the halfway mark."[20]

[17] SMU, "Expansion of Bosch into South Not to Cut Jobs Here," 2 March 1953, 1.

[18] SMU, "Bosch Corp. Announces New Mississippi Plant,"15 April 1953, 1. For contemporary discussions of plant relocation strategies see for example Robert M Atkins, "A Program for Relocating the New Plant," Harvard Business Review 30 (November-December 1952): 113-118; William Doty, "The Southern Picture," The Spectator (August 1952): 44-45; National Industrial Conference Board, Techniques of Plant Location, Studies in Business Policy, No. 61 (New York, 1953); U.S. Bureau of Labor Statistics, Wage Differentials and Rate Structures Among 40 Labor Markets (Washington, DC: GPO, 1953); Joe S. Floyd, Jr., Effects of Taxation on Industrial Location (Chapel Hill: The University of North Carolina Press, 1952).

[19] John O. Tomb, "Should Industry Move South," Harvard Business Review 31 (September-October 1953): 83-90, 86.

[20] CD, "Labor Survey on Proposed New Industry Begins Tuesday," 2 March 1953, 1; Ibid., "Labor Survey Climax Seen on Saturday," 6 March 1953, 1; Ibid., "Labor Survey Slow Despite Tub Thumping," 7 March 1953, 1; Ibid., "Labor Survey Passes Goal," 15 March 1953, 1.

At the time of the survey, Lowndes County, where Columbus was located, ranked tenth poorest among Mississippi's 55 urban areas. Almost half of Lowndes County's 38,000 residents were African American, yet the survey focused strictly on finding white female workers. Bosch managers were intent on keeping the new plant's workforce white to further divide the region's workers and lessen the chances of a successful union drive. The city extended the survey to 17 surrounding communities and 1,083 women and 923 men completed the questionnaire.[21] On April 14, 1953, Korean War peace talks disappeared from the local newspaper's front page, supplanted by the announcement that Bosch would locate their $1 million factory in Columbus. Eight hundred workers, mostly white women, soon began assembling small electrical motors that powered automobile windows, windshield wipers, seat lifts, and convertible tops.[22]

During the Mississippi move, Charles Perelle became president of American Bosch/ARMA; the search for lower operating costs became his central preoccupation. Viscerally antiunion, Perelle had worked his way up from part-time employment at a Seattle, Washington, Boeing plant during the early 1930s to become manager of Boeing's entire Canadian operation. A top manager at Vultee Aircraft during the Second World War, Perelle moved to Gar Wood, a manufacturer of speedboats and truck bodies, and after a brief stay there, he managed production at ACF Brill, a bus manufacturer. In late 1954, Charles Allen's financial holding company, which owned Brill, liquidated it and Allen named Perelle president of the American Bosch Corporation, with Hess becoming chairman of the board.[23]

UNIONISTS RESPOND

In mid-April 1953, as rumors swirled that work was going to Mississippi, Local 206 business agent Jim Manning urged unionists to oppose the move, referring to it as the "Mississippi Muddle" (Figure 4.1). According to Manning, "Now we are facing a bitter fight to maintain a Bosch plant in Springfield and we mean just that." He accused Donald Hess of betraying local workers "in a manner as the Japanese Ambassador did just before Pearl Harbor," blasting the move as a transparent attempt "to get away from paid holidays; three weeks vacations; cost

[21] United States Bureau of the Census, *Census of Population 1950*, Vol. II, part 24 Mississippi (Washington, DC, 1952). *CD* "Labor Survey on Proposed New Industry Begins Tuesday," 2 March 1953, 1; *CD*, "Labor Survey Climax Seen on Saturday," 6 March 1953, 1; *CD*, "Labor Survey Slow Despite Tub Thumping," 7 March 1953, 1; *CD*, "Labor Survey Passes Goal," 15 March 1953, 1.
[22] *CD*, "Am. Bosch Co. to Build Large Plant Employing About 800," 14 April 1953, 1. Bosch officials surely were aware that the work survey was being given to only white women and there is no evidence that they urged Columbus officials to do otherwise.
[23] *SDN*, "Hess Named Chairman of Bosch Board," 1 May 1954, 8; a description of Perelle appeared in Fortune, 1959, 115.

Figure 4.1. Cartoon "Mississippi Movement" from *IUE Local 206 Bulletin*, April 1954.

of living increases; pensions; paid insurance; and seniority."[24] Local 206 president Jim Parker stated, "This one time all of you must get into the battle, for though the North won the Civil War, the Union Army better organize and really win this one. When they open the gates of their new plant in Columbus, they will find themselves surrounded by IUE-CIO organizers."[25] In an unsigned letter in the *Bulletin*, a rank-and-file unionist asked, "Is Bosch doomed in Springfield?"[26]

Parker, Manning, and several other union officers traveled to Washington, DC in October 1954 for meetings with the Massachusetts Congressional delegation. They wanted to gain the delegation's support for national legislation eliminating a provision in the Taft-Hartley law that allowed manufacturers bringing new industry to a community to receive a six-month exemption on payment of the legal minimum wage. And they wanted support for a law denying defense contracts to corporations that moved production during a strike or to escape an existing labor agreement. The Congressional delegation rejected both requests.[27]

IUE also mounted a campaign to organize the Mississippi factory. Questioned by a local reporter about organizing, Perelle remarked, "We are not afraid of this (union) election. Let's go right ahead with it. Why delay?"[28] Perelle had recent history on his side; since 1952, unions in Greater Columbus factories lost 20 campaigns and the CIO abandoned their once-concerted effort to organize the South. Undaunted, the IUE seized on Perelle's braggadocio and descended on Columbus.

Parker provided organizers with information on wages, benefits, and seniority protection for a series of prounion newspaper advertisements during the three-month campaign.[29] IUE distributed an article outlining the international's position on southern industrial growth. It described how plants were abandoned in Trenton, New Jersey; White Plains, New York; Bridgeport, Connecticut; Pittsfield, Massachusetts; Philadelphia, Pennsylvania; and how production started in Louisville, Kentucky; Tyler, Texas; Rome, Georgia; and Ashville, North Carolina. It noted, "There is a considerable difference between an expansion of production; part of which is to take place in non-industrial areas, which we

[24] *LB*, April 1953; Hess letter to workers, 15 April 1953, UMALA Local 206 files.
[25] *LB*, 15 April 1953, 1.
[26] *LB*, 15 April 1953, 2. For a portion of the letter see p. 14.
[27] *LB*, October and November, 1954.
[28] *CD*, "Union Election Set for October 22," 8 October 1954, 1. For examples of failed organizing campaigns see *CD*, "The Garment Plant Situation," 30 October 1953, 1; *CD*, "Here is What the Union Can Do To You," 19 November 1953, 9; *CD*, "Union Defeated By Plant Ballot," 16 September 1954, 1; *CD*, "Beneke Workers Reject Union 2-1," 17 September 1954, 1.
[29] 'Dear Friends' Letter, 19 October 1954, in UMALA Local 206, Correspondence File, Series 2.

favor, and simply changing existing production from one area to another." It was fine for corporations to relocate when there was excess work in an existing facility. It appears that the IUE believed that corporate decisions to relocate jobs and build new plants were always predicated on stable or growing markets. Thus, there ought to be no employment losses in the industrial Northeast associated with plant expansions across the low-wage, nonunion south. Yet, the reality was—as Springfield workers painfully learned—that once constructed, a factory would be utilized, expanding markets or not. This shortsighted thinking demonstrated labor's lack at both the national and local levels of a strategic approach to economic restructuring.[30]

Once IUE's organizing efforts were made public, a group calling itself "Citizens" began taking out full-page advertisements in the local newspaper, the *Commercial Dispatch*. Bosch came to Columbus "because our people are not easily influenced to rush into things based on fancy promises, high pressure methods or rosy claims. We are proud that our citizens are stable and that they make their own decisions based on true, complete facts. AB was looking for such a community." "Citizens" argued that workers did not need a union, noting, "Relationships with employees and the community were pleasant, harmonious and satisfactory." "Citizens" reminded readers, "Employees in our industries have not suffered from strikes and job loss. Let's keep this good record." Unions, they concluded, will "interfere with our progress to a happier future."[31] The afternoon before the election "Citizens" reminded everyone that unions cause four negative things, violence, long strikes, lost wages and plants to move. The newspaper ad concluded,

> We are confident the local Bosch plant will continue to expand, provided they are left alone and can deal with any employee on the basis of their ability and initiative without outside help from someone who claims to represent your interests. Could it be your hard earned dollars that really interest them?[32]

Despite the warning and the weight of local history, workers voted for the union 121-74. In the near term, however, wages and benefits stayed far lower in Columbus than in Springfield. Thus, despite successful unionization, work continued to flow south for the rest of the 1950s and into the early 1960s.[33] The urgent question before industrial unions affected by plant closings was: what could they do to slow the exodus of employment from the industrial Northeast? The IUE's national president, James Carey, outlined his program for

[30] *Special Bulletin: The Southern Story* (Fall, 1954), in Local 206 UMALA. The *Special Bulletin* was distributed in Springfield by the Western Massachusetts CIO Council.
[31] CD, "Who Wins If Everybody Loses," 25 July 1954, 5.
[32] CD, "Who Wins If Everybody Loses," 25 July 1954, 5.
[33] CD, "Employees of American Bosch," 21 October 1954, 4; "Bosch Employees Vote for Union," 24 October 1954, 1. The story was barely six lines long.

combating runaway factories. First, federal tax abatements and other financial programs that supported firms on the run needed to be eliminated. This included such measures as provisions in the Taft-Hartley law that allowed firms to pay subminimum wages during start-ups. Local 206 members had already failed to gain the support of the Massachusetts Congressional delegation for this reform. Second, workers affected by a company move should gain preferential hiring status at the newly built facility. In Carey's scheme, laid-off Springfield workers ought to get jobs in Mississippi. Apart from the impracticality of hundreds of laid-off workers selling their homes and moving, Donald Hess ruled this out on March 6, 1954, when he told union negotiators that no Local 206 members "would be taken along in the southward migration."[34] Third, assuming that workers were rehired, all seniority and service should be carried over to the new facility. Fourth, laid-off employees should receive severance payments from their company equal to one week's wages for each year worked. Finally, weekly unemployment compensation should be increased and benefit periods lengthened through the establishment of a federally funded Employment Security Fund.[35]

Carey's plan placed no emphasis on the need for broad-based political strategies or the establishment of labor–community coalitions to deal with the sweeping changes underway in the global economy. This is indicative of organized labor's failure to educate trade unionists about plant closings and capital flight. Subsidies for dislocated workers were no substitute for political action and begged the question of what was to happen as more and more workers lost jobs. Calling for workers to be rehired at new locations with their seniority and benefits intact had no chance of taking place absent a protracted fight by affected workers, because firms moved to *escape* labor agreements. Why would a fleeing company voluntarily bring any part of their labor agreement along in the moving trucks?

For David Brody, in the early 1950s the UAW had two choices when it confronted unstable auto-industry employment: "Either to deal with the causes, or to protect its members from the consequences." Like Carey's call for income security, the UAW focused in the 1950s and 1960s on supplemental employment benefits for laid-off workers, utilizing the consequences-based approach adopted by almost all industrial unions.[36] Unions failed to develop collaborative strategies, testing the limits of capital mobility. By comparison, in 1946 the UE called for the formation of community–labor coalitions to fight plant closings. In the midst of jobs shifting to Mississippi, the Bosch local held two elections for top officers. In 1953 challengers to Parker and Manning campaigned on the innocuous slogan "We will do more for Local 206." One year later Parker and

[34] *SSR,* "Relocation of Bosch Workers Ruled Out," 7 March 1954, 1.
[35] *Special Bulletin.*
[36] David Brody, *Workers in Industrial America: Essays on the Twentieth Century Struggle* (New York: Oxford University Press, 1980), 194.

Manning asked unionists for their votes under the slogan "Get More in 1954." In the available campaign literature from both years, there is no mention of job loss.[37] Looking inward, IUE's agenda never galvanized community support for a fight to preserve jobs.[38]

In 1960 Sumner Slichter wrote that labor's great concern for income security indicated the general conservatism of the union movement. This approach avoided "the necessity of bargaining over such essential management decisions as production schedules, capital improvement plans, and plant location and left management . . . its freedom to make these decisions."[39] This had not been labor's position in the 1940s, when, for example, during the 1945 General Motors strike, an aide to UAW leader Walter Reuther noted that the strike represented

> . . . the first act of a new and significant era in American unionism, an era in which labor might break away from the bonds of business unionism, to wage an economic struggle planned to advance the welfare of the community as a whole, and to lay the foundations for new economic mechanisms designed to win security without sacrificing liberty.[40]

In 1951 Local 206's newspaper echoed this sentiment by arguing that labor needed a voice in the decisions that affected their jobs.

> In Europe unions have been guaranteed the right of co-determination, which implies union participation in corporate financing, pricing, supply, and all other functions of management. This theory has been covered in some of Walter Reuther's writings and we hope in some future issues to bring you a report on this tremendous advance in union responsibility.[41]

Yet, when work left the city, Springfield's unionists never mounted a serious public challenge to management's assumption that work removal was their right. In a 25th-anniversary history of the local, the mid-1950s is recalled as a time when there were steady gains in wages, vacations, and insurance benefits. "Through the years of 1954 and 1955," the history summarized, "it seemed that things were on the move at Bosch and a new era had begun for improved relations with the Local and Management." While unionists predicted that the move to Mississippi would result in higher unemployment and depressed wages, only an occasional call was issued for members to get involved. And while unionists criticized New England's congressional delegation for their failure to

[37] Local 206 UMALA, campaign fliers folders.
[38] For two examples of this, see *UEN*, 14 September 1946, 7 and District Council No. 2, *Unemployment in Massachusetts* (Fall 1949); UE National Office Records, District 2, ff 103, University of Pittsburgh.
[39] Slichter, quoted in D. Brody, *Workers in Industrial America*, 194-195.
[40] Quoted in D. Brody, *Workers in Industrial America*, 176.
[41] *LB*, February, 1951, 2.

prevent "the juicy advantages offered by the South for exploitation of non-union workers by manufacturers"[42] and for their refusal to block defense contracts to runaway companies, there were no political campaigns mounted to elect "true friends" of labor.[43]

SENATOR JOHN F. KENNEDY
WEIGHS IN

Bosch's Mississippi move lengthened the list of closings and work relocations from the Commonwealth and prompted Massachusetts Senator John F. Kennedy to issue a detailed analysis of New England's economic difficulties. On the Senate floor, Kennedy pointed out that "Even after the Korean War boom nearly 40 percent of Massachusetts' textile workers were jobless. . . . Instead of declining during the heavy mobilization year of 1951, unemployment increased 150 percent in Fall River, 103 percent in Lawrence, and more in Nashua, New Hampshire, and Rhode Island's textile mills."[44] Kennedy noted that layoffs and closings were not going to be confined to textiles and apparel. He spoke out against federal laws that permitted corporations to obtain rapid tax amortization certificates for building new factories, arguing that the program amounted to a corporate job relocation subsidy.[45] J. P. Stevens, he observed, received a certificate in 1951, constructed a plant in Stanley, North Carolina, and shuttered its Haverhill, Massachusetts, mill, eliminating 400 jobs. After securing a $20-million certificate, General Electric built a jet-engine plant in Louisville, Kentucky, and when they determined that they needed just a small area of the massive facility for engine production, they filled the remainder of the plant with appliance assembly, moving 19,000 jobs from factories in Trenton, New Jersey; White Plains, New York; South Scranton, Pennsylvania; and Bridgeport, Connecticut. Westinghouse received $30 million in certificates, built factories in Columbus, Ohio, and Raleigh, North Carolina, and shifted jobs from Springfield, Massachusetts, and Newark, New Jersey, to the new facilities.[46]

---

[42] *LB*, April, 1953. Usage of the phrase "This one time" implies that the union rank and file had not been actively engaged in the affairs of the local. There is a sense of urgency here that workers need to, at the very least, come to the defense of their livelihoods.

[43] *LB*, April, October, November, 1954.

[44] Senator John F. Kennedy, "The Economic Problems of New England," *Proceedings of the 83rd Congress, First Session, 99*, May 18, 1953, 5054-5056.

[45] J. Kennedy, "The Economic Problems of New England," *Proceedings of the 83rd Congress, First Session*, 5233.

[46] J. Kennedy, "The Economic Problems of New England," *Proceedings of the 83rd Congress, First Session*, 5235.

In a 1954 *Atlantic Monthly* essay, Kennedy discussed job relocations in the machinery, electrical equipment, paper, and chemical industries already underway. Such moves were subtle at first.

> In only a small number of cases does direct migration take place through closing New England plants and transferring their operations to southern plants. More often, firms start by operating mills in both New England and the South, then tend to abandon their northern plants in periods of decline and later expand their southern operations when prosperity returns.[47]

Kennedy also spoke about the America Bosch situation from the Senate floor, pointing out that, "According to the Springfield Free press, the American Bosch Co., a permanent fixture in Springfield, is leaving its location in that city for a free plant, free taxes for ten years, and low-wage labor in Columbus, Mississippi."[48]

To stop the job drain, Kennedy called on Congress to increase the 75¢-an-hour federal minimum wage. He did not suggest a new figure, but he pointed out that Massachusetts' average manufacturing wage was $1.64. Kennedy worried that development strategies predicated on low wages were sustainable indefinitely, while other parts of the world—particularly Latin America and Asia— industrialized. Kennedy concluded that the South's low-wage strategy would catch up to it, and that it would eventually suffer "the same pangs of aging now suffered by New England."[49] Five years later the minimum wage issue remained unresolved, prompting the *Springfield Daily News* to endorse legislation filed by Kennedy and Senator Wayne Morse of Oregon to raise the federal minimum wage to $1.25. "Many a New England firm has fled to Dixieland to take advantage of low wage rates there. Many a New England factory has found it impossible to compete against goods made in the low-wage industries of the South. Cheap labor pools needed to be eliminated."[50]

---

[47] John F. Kennedy, "New England and the South: The Struggle for Industry," *The Atlantic Monthly* (January 1954), 33.

[48] J. Kennedy, "The Economic Problems of New England," *Proceedings of the 83rd Congress,* May 18, 1953, 5233.

[49] Kennedy, "New England and the South: The Struggle for Industry," 35. In fact, many Southern states are today suffering the same deindustrialization the Northeast and Midwest felt in the late 1970s and early 1980s. Since 2000, the interior South, stretching from Alabama into Mississippi, Arkansas, and Louisiana and up through Tennessee and Kentucky was stuck in the worst downturn in almost two decades. According to economist Mark Zandi, the rural South "is to this recession as Detroit was to the 1980s recession." Zandi is quoted in David Leonhardt, "The Rust Belt With a Drawl," *NYT,* 13 November 2001, D1.

[50] *SDN,* 16 February 1959, 6.

THE WESTINGHOUSE STORY

While the Mississippi saga unfolded there, more disquieting news surfaced when rumors persisted that Westinghouse planned to close its East Springfield plant. The company issued numerous denials, but a letter from the plant's manager James Weaver troubled Springfield's mayor. Weaver wrote,

> If we (Westinghouse) are to get our share of the going business the products we build here must be competitive in price with similar products built by other companies in other cities and states. If we are burdened with higher taxes than our competitors, only because we are located in what others interpret as a listless community, we're in trouble—real trouble, and in order to even stay in business must create off-setting economies in other ways.[51]

Concerned that the city planned to pass its tax burden on to manu-facturers, Weaver asked why his company should have confidence in the city when even the Springfield *Taxpayers Bulletin* called the city "financially sick."[52]

In mid-1958 the local newspapers disclosed a report commissioned by the Westinghouse Board of Directors that called for the factory's closure. Six Westinghouse consumer-products plants were to be consolidated into two facilities. The Westinghouse Board reported, "There is a continuing survey at our various Westinghouse plants across the country to determine what facilities are best fitted or equipped for the various products we manufacture."[53] After several days, unionists learned about the pending transfer of work from East Springfield to Mansfield and Columbus, Ohio. During the recently concluded national strike against Westinghouse, large numbers of workers in its two Ohio factories crossed picket lines, so it appeared that the move rewarded those workers. At the end of 1958, 1,500 workers lost their jobs. Thereafter, the factory stagnated and finally closed in 1970. The land and buildings—sold in 1971 to a real-estate developer for $1 million—stayed empty until the early 1980s, when the Massachusetts Division of Employment and Training situated a dislocated-worker center in one of the buildings.[54]

---

[51] Letter reported on in *DN*, 25 June 1955.

[52] *DN*, 25 June 1955.

[53] *DN*, 29 July 1958, 1.

[54] *SDN*, 30 July 1958, 1; *SDN*, 31 July 1958, 1; *SDN*, 12 August 1958, 1. The union article was quoted extensively in *SDN*, 17 October 1958, 1; *SDN*, 19 February 1971. For a discussion of Westinghouse and General Electric efforts to decentralize production out of the industrial Northeast and away from their unionized workforces, see Ronald Schatz, *The Electrical Workers: A History of Labor at General Electric and Westinghouse 1923-60* (Urbana: University of 1983), esp. ch. 9. For an account of General Electric's move out of Pittsfield, Massachusetts, see Max H. Kirsch, *In the Wake of the Giant: Multinational Restruc-turing and Uneven Development in a New England Community* (Albany: State University of New York Press, 1998). Kirsch states that workers won major concessions from GE during strikes in 1946 and 1969, but that the years after 1969 marked union decline, "fueled by threats by the corporation to relocate production," 38.

While work shifted to Mississippi and Ohio, Bosch and Westinghouse unionists—members of District Two of the International Union of Electrical Workers—failed to engage in serious efforts to build a broad-based response to job loss. There is no doubt that workers across the region were well aware of the layoffs, because several IUE factories were located within a block or two of the Bosch plant. Workers shared lunch breaks at places like Elsie's Café, where over a quick beer and sandwich, oppositional strategies might have been shaped. Knowledge also spread because many workers labored at one time in all three of these factories. These shared experiences could have provided the catalyst for an active cross-plant coalition against deindustrialization.[55]

In 1955 Local 206 officers called for the establishment of a movement to fight runaway shops and safeguard jobs. "The storekeeper, grocer, milkman and all other businesses will suffer from this move by industry out of the area unless something is done and done soon," the *Labor Bulletin* urged. But no such coalition formed.[56]

What happened with defense contracts illustrates how the absence of a coherent strategy plagued labor. On at least two occasions, Local 206 appealed to the state's Congressional delegation for the passage of laws denying Pentagon contracts to firms moving production to break unions. Simultaneously, members of the Westinghouse IUE local secured assurances from Senator John Kennedy and Congressman Edward Boland that they would seek out defense contracts for Westinghouse to keep employment up. Kennedy and Boland had an easier time telling workers they would put contracts in the city than telling Fortune 500 corporations that they were going to lose defense work.[57]

"ANOTHER HOLE IN THE FLOOR"

In the spring of 1955 machines were crated and loaded on flatbed trucks and rail cars for the trip to Columbus, and the windshield wiper, automatic-seat motor, and voltage regulator lines went south. The scene was similar to one described in William Adler's *Mollie's Job*. Adler's narrative describes the postwar migration of factory work from Patterson, New Jersey, to Mississippi in 1963 and Matamoros, Mexico, in the late 1980s. Mollie James describes how "The movers

---

[55] The hiring information is based on my examination of workers' service and seniority information while union business agent at the Bosch. Perhaps 15 percent of Bosch's workforce in 1980 had worked for a time at Van Norman, Moore Drop Forge, or the Armory. This could have provided fertile ground to build a cross-plant coalition of some sort to speak out against deindustrialization.

[56] *LB*, April 1955.

[57] *SDN*, 28 February 1959, 1. See Joan Reilly, "History of Westinghouse Electric Company in Springfield 1915-1970: The Demise of a Giant," unpublished paper, 1986 in the Pioneer Valley Historical Society.

came in at night, like thieves, sometimes just taking one piece at a time. We'd come in in the mornings and there'd be another hole in the floor."[58] During the initial move, five hundred Bosch workers lost their jobs, and where just weeks before they had labored on a variety of automobile components, there were gaping, empty spots along the shop floor. Over the next 30 years the open spaces multiplied, a grim reminder to everyone of how precarious their employment had become. Remarkably, the union leadership believed that very few workers would end up permanently out of a job. But, just after Labor Day 1955, management announced the doubling of the Columbus plant's floor space. And, despite corporate assurances that "specialized precision products" would replace work shipped south, new work did not arrive.[59]

This prompted one unionist to ask, "Where are their so-called new jobs which will tide over the loss of jobs to Mississippi?"[60] Urging management to consider their community obligations, a *Labor Bulletin* editorial called on the corporation "as an employer who has prospered and grown in this community to think of some of the debt it owes to its 44 years in this locality." But the company ignored these appeals.[61] In an early 1956 letter to the *Labor Bulletin*, a worker expressed his concerns: "You buy a house and feel you have some security," he noted. "Before, if you were laid off, you knew that it would be temporary—now it is permanent." To management, he wished "all the best of nothing."[62] In February 1958 the company moved all generator and magneto production to Mississippi "completing the consolidation of electrical manufacturing at the Columbus plant, with the Springfield division concentrating on mechanical and hydraulic products."[63] This time, management made no claims that the plant would remain open or that new work was coming to the city.

Worried about the city's economic vitality, the Springfield Industrial Commission pleaded with Perelle to reconsider this latest move in an open letter in the *Springfield Daily News*.

> As you are undoubtedly aware, the skilled labor and craftsmen available in this area far surpass any other area in the country. Any financial benefit

---

[58] William M. Adler, *Mollie's Job: A Story of Life and Work on the Global Assembly Line* (New York: Scribner, 2000), 16.

[59] *SDN*, "Bosch Arma Announces Huge Expansion of Plant in Mississippi," 9 September 1955.

[60] *SDN*, 25 February 1954, 12. *LB*, February 1954; *SMU*, 7 March 1954; *LB*, April 1954.

[61] *LB*, February 1954; *SMU*, 7 March 1954; *LB*, April 1954.

[62] "Dreams," *LB*, May 1956, 3.

[63] *SDN*, "Generator Dept. Remains At Bosch Div. Plant Here," 11 January 1956, 7. The union learned of the generator line move through an article in the *Springfield Daily News* on 12 February 1958, 6.

that might accrue in another section of the country would be offset by inferior workmanship.[64]

After eleven days, corporate officers responded to the Industrial Commission's letter. Corporation vice president C. A. Sharpe met with Springfield Mayor Thomas O'Connor on February 25 and assured him that work was expected to pick up in Springfield.[65] But, by early 1958 union membership stood at 1,200, less than half of what it had been before work moved to Mississippi. In 1960 there were only 772 members of Local 206.[66]

EUROPE BECKONS

Though the union encouraged management to consider workers "not as units of cost, but as human values," overseas manufacturing opportunities also intrigued ABA's managers.[67] In a June 1959 letter to unionists, Sidney Miller, an ABA vice president, admonished them about foreign competition. "American Bosch's foreign competitors enjoy a greater and too frequently a decisive cost advantage over us. . . . A major cost factor is of course labor costs." The Springfield factory lost several major contracts to foreign firms and, according to Miller, although Bosch's customers "would prefer to do business with us rather than with a foreign manufacturer, and are willing to pay some differential, but that the foreign manufacturing price is so much less they can't do other than buy from them. . . ."

Perelle blamed high wages for the drop-off in commercial sales. What was the wage differential? According to the company, "For every dollar earned by an AB employee, an employee of a foreign competitor is paid an average of only 25 cents. This means that where our average hourly rate is $2.66 the comparable hourly rate in West Germany is 66 cents, in Japan 27 cents and only 80 cents in the United Kingdom."[68] In 1959 and 1960 Perelle searched for precision metal-working suppliers in Germany, Japan, and England in an effort to reduce the Springfield factory to doing only assembly work. With 1960 sales of $125.3 million and assets of $64.5 million, ABA had the financial wherewithal to make location decisions that left the place-bound Springfield workforce vulnerable to product-line relocations and a possible complete shutdown. But production remained in the city for two reasons. First, Perelle failed to locate the lower-wage, highly skilled labor pool required for the precision machining required for diesel components. Second, defense-related orders were on the

[64] *SDN,* 12 February 1958, 1; Industrial Commission letter to Charles Perelle reprinted in *SDN,* 15 February 1958, 6.
[65] *SDN,* February 26, 1958, 1.
[66] Membership records are in UMALA Local 206 files, box 29.
[67] "Frame of Mind," *LB,* November 1959, 1.
[68] Portions of Sidney E. Miller's letter to Bosch employees was reprinted in *SMU,* 4 June 1959. Miller was an ABA vice president. *Progress,* 19 June 1959, 1.

upswing, and Perelle deemed it expedient to do such work domestically. He did, however, complete a licensing agreement with an RCA plant in Argentina for the manufacture of windshield-wiper motor assemblies.[69]

CONCLUSION

During the early 1960s close-tolerance parts machining and the intricate assembly of fuel-injection pumps proved difficult to move. This eventually prompted Perelle and his successor Charles Beck to embark on an automation strategy as a way to cut labor costs. But, for both men, substantial labor savings could accrue only by shifting production to lower-wage plants that had the requisite skills. Just before highly contentious 1967 contract talks started, Beck warned workers that "competitive market conditions," not past history, "will determine the future of any facility in Bosch's corporate structure." He reminded unionists that German-based Robert Bosch—Springfield's chief competitor— had hourly labor costs of $1.52 compared with Springfield's $4.45. In Beck's opinion, because Europe and Japan were closing the technology gap "automation to the nth degree" was essential for the Springfield plant to become cost competitive with its global counterparts.[70]

In the 1960s and again in the early 1970s Beck made numerous investments to lower Springfield's production costs, which will be discussed in a later chapter. Using profits from lucrative Vietnam War defense contracts, he purchased eight companies between 1966 and 1968, and in 1971 he oversaw the construction of two manufacturing facilities in Europe.[71] The acquisitions were symptomatic of accelerated domestic disinvestment and heightened capital reallocation overseas by U.S. corporations. Investment abroad in factories, office buildings, machine tools, and office equipment, which stood at less than $50 billion in 1965, surpassed $213 billion by 1980. Economists Barry Bluestone and Bennet Harrison determined that profits from these investments jumped from $5.2 billion in 1965 to more that $424 billion by 1980. Nationally, plant closings were now endemic. By Harrison and Bluestone's calculations "over the whole decade of the 1970s, a minimum of 32 million jobs were probably eliminated in the United States as a direct result of private disinvestment in plant and equipment." Beck's behavior mirrored that of hundreds of other U.S. corporations.[72] Pressed on the labor-cost issue, management argued that wages had to be lowered for the Springfield plant to be globally competitive. However, "reduce the costs"

---

[69] *Progress,* August 1960.

[70] *SMU,* 13 November 1964, 8; 23 March 1967, 9.

[71] Robert Forrant, "Skill Was Never Enough: American Bosch, Local 206 and the Decline of Metalworking in Springfield, Massachusetts, 1900-1970," University of Massachusetts at Amherst, unpublished Ph.D. dissertation, ch. 8.

[72] B. Harrison and B. Bluestone, *The Deindustrialization of America,* 26, 35.

arguments carried little weight with the rank and file, who dismissed them as a "make the workers pay," approach to the resolution of larger shop-floor problems. At loggerheads, the company's persistent efforts to cut wages provoked a series of bitter, lengthy strikes and other job actions and led to the eventual closing of the Springfield plant.

CHAPTER 5

Skill Was Not Enough:
The Bosch Closes

It's not like they pulled the rug out from under us. It's more like they pulled
the trap door out from under the hangman's noose.
                                                                    — 61-year-old Bosch worker
                                                                    Donald Staples

From the 1950s through the Bosch's 1986 shutdown, unionists sought to engage
in production-related decision making in an effort to save jobs in the city.
Nonetheless, after the Second World War, wild employment gyrations and
increasingly acrimonious labor relations characterized factory life. Bosch
management made investments in new factories outside of Springfield and
also invested in technologies that could replace the skilled workforce. At the
same time, management discouraged workers from applying their production
knowledge to lower manufacturing costs and improve quality. Workers were
treated as a homogenous factor of production, with their skills viewed as
replaceable by high-tech machinery at low-wage production sites.
    When work left Springfield in the mid-1950s, too-high wages were blamed.
Thereafter, unionists protested management's attempts to change the piece-rate
pay system, alter inspection techniques, change long-standing job descriptions,
and introduce new technologies. But relations were not always so poisonous, and
in fact for a few years after the Second World War, management recognized and
praised the skilled workforce. For example, a 1952 company newsletter contained
photographs of an apprenticeship graduation. The accompanying article praised
the graduates as essential to the firm's success. However, by decade's end, only
line supervisors received company-sponsored technical training, and supervisors

spent considerable time learning how to squeeze greater output from machine operators and assemblers.[1]

For several years unionists resisted giving up their shop-floor production roles.[2] In 1951 the union's newsletter reminded members that their stake in American Bosch "is as great or greater than the stockholder. . . . Make suggestions, better the product, give them a dollar's work for a dollar's pay! Don't kid yourself. There are unions more militant than ours that recognize that the increased assumption of responsibility leads to increased benefits." Workers learned that their European counterparts "have been guaranteed the right of co-determination which implies union participation in corporate financing, pricing, supply, and all other functions of management," and that the United Automobile Worker's Walter Reuther, "has been covering this in some of his writings and we hope in some future issue to bring you a report on this *tremendous advance in union responsibility*"(emphasis added).[3]

Shop leaders protected their members' contractual rights while they realized that simple contractualism and an exclusive focus on wage and benefits meant nothing without a job; workers grasped the connections between their skills and job security. For them, job security depended on the company utilizing their hundreds of years of collective production knowledge. A 1951 *Labor Bulletin* account of a Labor–Management Production Committee meeting noted that several high-seniority toolmakers voluntarily worked second shift to resolve nagging production problems with a new fuel-injector part. Rather than deal with the assistant foreman, the general manager "consulted one of the set up men who found the problem and explained how it happened and how to eliminate the problem in the future." The *Labor Bulletin* concluded, "This will illustrate that our people have the know-how and will gladly serve in a supervisor's position if they are asked." But to the union's consternation, in 1955 the company eliminated the Labor–Management Production Committee. In what follows, I tell the story of fouled labor relations, management's concerted efforts to find alternative

---

[1] "New Training Program Looks Good," *Craftsman* (December 1952): 6-7. In 1957 *Progress* reported on a one-day-a-week training program for supervisors studying calibration, timing, maintenance, and repair of diesel pumps, *Progress*, "Back to School for AB Staffers," (August 1957), 4.

[2] For a discussion of postwar labor attitudes and workers' efforts to assert their control on the shop floor, see Steven Tolliday and Jonathan Zeitlin, "Shop-Floor Bargaining, Contract Unionism and Job Control: An Anglo-American Perspective," in Steven Tolliday and Jonathan Zeitlin, eds., *Between Fordism and Flexibility* (Providence, RI: Berg Publishing, 1992): 99-120; Julie Meyer, "Trade Union Plans for Postwar Reconstruction in the United States," *Social Research* 11 (1944): 491-505; David Montgomery, *Workers' Control in America: Studies in the History of Work, Technology, and Labor Struggles* (New York: Cambridge University Press, 1979); Nelson Lichtenstein, "Reutherism on the Shop Floor: Union Strategy and Shop Floor Conflict in the USA, 1946-1970," in Steven Tolliday and Jonathan Zeitlin, eds., *Between Fordism and Flexibility*, 121-143.

[3] *LB*, February, 1951, September, 1951.

production sites for its precision work, and unionists' quixotic efforts to first preserve skill on the factory floor and then save the plant and their jobs. A timeline of Bosch moves is contained in Table 5.1.[4]

Table 5.1. American Bosch Moves 1953-1986

1953	Search for a southern manufacturing site commences
1954	Columbus, Mississippi factory built and work moved there
1957-58	Company searches for European vendors
1960	Joint venture with DeHavilland Holdings, Ltd. to enter British aerospace
1960	Purchase Teledynamics, Inc., Philadelphia-based missile-guidance system
1966	Purchase Bacharach Industrial Instruments, electronic measuring devices
1967	Purchase Hispano Suiza, Netherlands, precision metalworking
1967	Purchase Steelweld, Ltd., England, precision metalworking
1967	Purchase Packard Instruments, Inc., MI, electronics testing equipment
1967	Purchase Wanlass Electronics Co., CA, electronics research and development
1967	Purchase Fluid Power & Accessories, Ill., electronics
1968	Purchase Pace Corporation, Tenn., defense aerospace parts
1968	Purchase Michigan Dynamics, MI, scientific and measuring instruments
1971	Construct new factories in Breda, Netherlands, and Brescia, Italy, for manufacture of diesel fuel-injection parts
1978	Bosch plant purchased by United Technologies Corporation and made part of United Technologies Automotive Division
1982	United Technologies new plant in Columbia, South Carolina, for diesel pumps and fuel-injection work, duplicates Springfield's capabilities
1986	Springfield plant closed

[4]*LB,* May 1951, 4.

THE REORGANIZATION OF CORPORATE LABOR RELATIONS IN THE 1950s

"He Leadeth Many Beside His Still Factory"

Charles Perelle became president of American Bosch-ARMA (ABA) just as the company shifted several production lines to Mississippi. He came to Springfield with a clear record of union hostility, including a stint at Vultee Aircraft during its bitter confrontation with the United Auto Workers in the fall of 1940.[5] To *Fortune,* Perelle was "a doctor of ailing companies." Described as "peppery, ambitious, a master of production," and more disparagingly as a "hot-tempered bantam rooster," Perelle typified executives who sought, in historian Nelson Lichtenstein's words, "the restoration of the managerial prerogatives that wartime conditions had eroded in the areas of product pricing, market allocation, and shop-floor work environment."[6]

Over the spring and summer of 1954 Perelle hired dozens of managers who had previously worked with him, while dismissing several senior Springfield executives, including the plant's vice president for manufacturing, the production manager, and Herbert Riddle, the popular vice president of employee relations. The Springfield *Daily News* reported, "It was learned today that Riddle's only choice was to resign, or be fired and that he left the company with no other job in sight."[7] Employed at Bosch since 1940, Riddle received credit from unionists for establishing nonpareil labor relations during and immediately following the Second World War.

James Mote replaced Riddle, and Charles Tuttle became the director of corporate labor relations. Mote's appointment was an unpopular one with workers, who referred to him as "Mote the Goat." Before becoming vice president of employee relations, Mote set job standards and piece rates in the factory.[8] Tuttle was described to Bosch unionists as "a cold, arrogant man," who turned labor agreements into "technical documents and not co-operative working agreements" in a letter to Local 206 from Frank Fagan, the United Automobile Workers (UAW) Region 1 International Representative. Fagan added that the UAW and Gar Wood enjoyed "the very best of relations and our differences were kept to a minimum," until Tuttle was put in charge. Thereafter the union felt a "severe

---

[5]Workers struck at Vultee and presented a major challenge to the government's desire to avoid work stoppages at plants engaged in war-related production. Nelson Lichtenstein, *Labor's War at Home: The CIO in World War II* (New York: Cambridge University Press, 1982) 54, 57; Wyndham Mortimer, *Organize: My Life as A Union Man* (Boston: Beacon Press, 1971), 170-171.

[6]N. Lichtenstein, *Labor's War at Home,* 228; "Charles Perelle's Spacemanship," *Fortune* 59 (January 1959), 112, 115.

[7]*SMU,* "Riddle Departure at Bosch Seen as Executive Storm Sign," 25 October 1954, 8.

[8]*SMU,* 26 October 1954; *LB,* May 1954.

change in attitude on the part of the Company." Grievances went unsettled and foremen received instruction on ways to limit the scope of the labor agreement.[9] Fagan detailed how Tuttle precipitated a six-month strike at Gar Wood by upholding the discharge of a worker with 28 years seniority for sitting on a stool while performing an operation on his job, a practice the worker had engaged in for over 20 years. Tuttle also fired the union's chief steward when he came to the worker's defense. Fagan warned Bosch unionists about Tuttle's penchant for bypassing collective bargaining for one-on-one deal making with union representatives. For Fagan, Tuttle was

> an outspoken opponent of the Union shop, check-off, seniority agreements, and other basic Union demands. He believes that companies must have freedom to operate without restrictions. He is a cold, arrogant, and highly technical man. He admits having had no experience with working people other than in his present capacity as a Labor Relations man. . . . Since Tuttle left us in 1951, real collective bargaining has been restored and maintained.[10]

During 1954 and 1955 workers repeatedly questioned whether foremen and supervisors knew what they were doing. Foremen received colorful nicknames, indicative of their attitudes toward workers, including Dan "No Answer Today" Sullivan, Art "Hurry Up" Domilla, Ernest "I'll Take Care of it Tomorrow" McLean, Pat "Puddin' Head" Judd, and Charlie "Cut Rate" McCobb.[11] To appease workers, Perelle told them that he needed their help increasing "our business and overall efficiency so that we can maintain our competitive position without drastic changes."[12] Yet, in 1955 he disbanded the plant's Labor–Management Production Committee, established at the insistence of UE Local 206's founding officers in the 1930s. A *Labor Bulletin* editorial argued,

> For nineteen years the American Bosch and the Union have enjoyed good labor relations but now they seem to be on the downgrade. Now it seems we can no longer have an honest and effective means of settling common problems through the Labor-Management Committee. Labor-Management meetings have been held monthly where subjects have been discussed and issues settled before they became a major problem. The meetings were beneficial and should be continued.[13]

Perelle refused unionists demands for the restoration of the problem-solving group. Instead, he dismissed several long-time production supervisors and further consolidated his management team.

[9] *Frank Fagan Letter to International Union of Electrical Workers,* 1 March 1955, UMALA Local 206 collection, Series 2, Box 5.

[10] *Fagan Letter to International Union of Electrical Workers,* 1 March 1955.

[11] *LB,* April and May 1954.

[12] *Craftsman,* August-September, 1954.

[13] *LB,* January, 1955.

Unionists cheered when Perelle established a cost-improvement program (CIP) and purchased several million dollars of new machinery. Under the CIP, workers submitted ideas to "lower costs, improve working conditions or in some way improve the quality of American Bosch products." According to the company newsletter, *Progress,* close to $1.5 million in savings was generated between May 1955 and the end of 1956.[14] But despite such success, in April 1956 Perelle ordered that the union's two CIP representatives could attend just four monthly meetings a year. This was absurd, unionists argued, since from the beginning of the CIP "suggestions authored by members of Local 206 amount to about 95 percent of all submitted."[15] Despite the snub, unionists still suggested ways for the CIP to do a better job. "The average factory worker has good ideas but usually has trouble expressing them in 25 words or less, which is the average on the blanks provided. So it is our belief that a short talk with someone trained in methods or drawing would definitely increase the value of a good suggestion tremendously."[16]

QUALITY AND TECHNOLOGY: CORPORATE STRATEGIES AND LABOR'S RESPONSE

"How Blind Can You Get?"

Despite unionists' displeasure with the Mississippi move and the Labor–Management Production Committee's elimination, a 1954 *Labor Bulletin* editorial "Scrap—What Is It?" discussed the links between scrap, production costs, customer satisfaction, and employment security and urged everyone to do their jobs well.

> It means time wasted, money wasted, material wasted, and it's like water going down the drain. Each person from any level in the American Bosch should take the time to analyze why a certain piece of work was scrapped and that it actually means money out of their pocket, plus maybe eventually the loss of jobs, because we cannot meet the necessary standards and commitments of our customers.[17]

In an open union letter to management, the union asked "How Blind Can You Get?" and offered a critique of the new quality program. Under it, parts were first checked in designated inspection areas off the production floor; when a part failed inspection, a quality analyst prepared a detailed written report cataloging

---

[14] *Progress,* November 1957.

[15] *LB,* April 1956, 2.

[16] For the union's perspective on the production committee and the CIP see, *LB,* April 1954, 3; April 1956, 2; *LB,* May 1957, 1.

[17] *LB,* November, 1954.

why. When the plan took effect, 50 percent of the floor inspectors were eliminated, slashing production costs. In the past, floor inspectors worked in a designated area and four or five times a shift checked parts as they were removed from production machines. Unionists pointed out that the new plan left too few checkers on the floor and could never "correct the reason for the Scrap or Rework at the source when it is being made or before, but is a statement as to the reasons (AFTER THE BULL) [emphasis in original] has been made."[18] Scrap problems were not resolved, and two years later the union noted, "Past experience here at Am. Bosch has taught that Scrap can be repeated after all precautions have been taken unless the source, at the time of machining, is protected."

> Workers have a certain amount of pride, hidden or out in the open as to our accomplishments, our work, etc. . . . Today, thanks to *Operation Speedup*, gone is the pride we had. . . . Through no fault of the workers who can still produce quality unparalleled, the system installed allows for too much leeway, too many reworked parts and a bungling of operations out of sequence. . . .[19]

Unionists argued that these misguided quality efforts, sharp cuts in piecework pay scales, and an aggressive push for higher output caused machine operators to cover up their bad work. To make matters worse, foremen passed scrap out of their departments in an effort to meet increased production quotas. A pointed front page *Labor Bulletin* cartoon entitled "Foremen Solve Scrap Problem" depicted a visibly nervous foreman furtively discarding scrap in a large hole he had chopped through the factory floor.[20] Such "junk cover-ups" continued well into the 1970s. Several foremen lost their jobs in the mid-1970s when a top manager investigating shiny objects in the nearby Connecticut River determined that the objects were Bosch parts. For years, in a widespread scheme to dispose of bad work, supervisors made so-called bombing runs, spiriting rejected parts from the plant and dropping them off a bridge into the river. I witnessed two other long-standing ways to get rid of bad parts. The space under removable metal floor grates routinely became a final resting place for bad work, as did the cavities underneath certain machine tools. My workmates often joked that hollow spots in the floor contained a museum-quality historical record of the Bosch's production.

An observation by labor historian David Brody clarifies what occurred in the plant (Figure 5.1). "What happens on the shop floor is not a secondary affair in the lives of working people. On the contrary it engages their innermost sense of self-worth and honor."[21] Unionists were ignored when they described why defective parts could alienate customers and cost them jobs. Another *Labor*

---

[18] *LB,* October 1954, 1; November 1954, 1.
[19] *LB,* April 1956, 2.
[20] *LB,* April 1957, 2.
[21] David Brody, *In Labor's Cause: Main Themes on the History of the American Worker* (New York: Oxford University Press, 1980), 222.

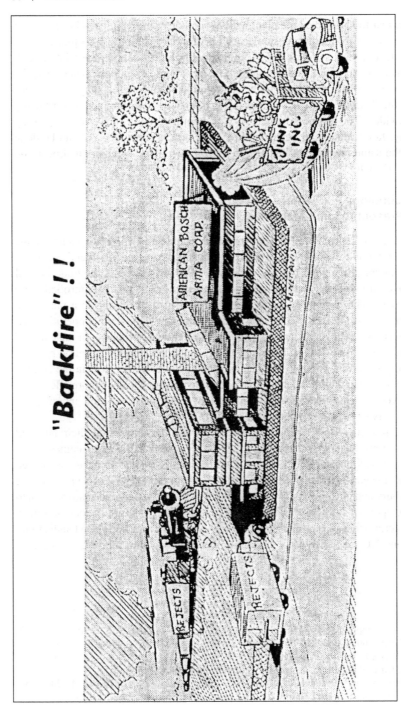

Figure 5.1. Cartoon "Backfire" from *IUE Local 206 Bulletin*, October 1968.

Bulletin cartoon depicted the plant with a locomotive bringing back boxcars with rejected work from angry customers, while a truck brimming with junked parts sped off to a local scrap dealer. Accompanying the cartoon, an open letter read, "With product reliability comes reputation, repeat orders, and jobs. Take away the performance of parts and assemblies and you have customer apathy."[22] In April 1960 the *Bulletin* pointed out that the market for diesel engines was growing worldwide: "The business is there, it won't come to us, we have to secure it by quality, fair pricing, and dependability." The article concluded, "It can be done with the same people that had Bosch on top once—the members of Local 206 IUE, AFL-CIO."[23]

A Technology Fix: Where Workers Are Not Present to Limit Machines

In 1958 Charles Perelle, determined to establish ABA as a leader in the commercial and defense diesel markets, began "risking stockholders' money at the frontiers of machine tool technology."[24] For several years the trade journal *Automation* published testimonials to the virtues of numerically controlled (NC) machines. "The new work performing mechanisms," according to a plant vice president, "must be designed to take advantage of a new freedom of operation that can exist where man is not present to limit the performance of machines." *Automation* editor Roger Bolz reasoned that automation's primary purpose "broadly speaking, is not to displace working people. Rather, it is in the end the means by which the full talents of the operating personnel can be more effectively employed to lower the costs of production and distribution and increase the availability of capital and consumer goods."[25]

But, however Bolz pitched it, machinery builders marketed their NC and multitool products as laborsaving. "One man operates as many machines as the cycle times of jobs permit," read one advertisement. Another ad noted, "You need several general-purpose machines and several operators to keep up with one Kingsbury and one operator." The *American Machinist* cautioned against a rush to reduce operator skill: "At least under the present state of the art, the operator must make certain that all is progressing properly, though he may be able to handle more than one NC machine. Also, since the operator is monitoring rather expensive

---

[22] For a sampling of the union's views on quality, see *LB,* June 1952, 2; August 1957, 3; letter April 1960, 4; February 1968, 1; June 1968, 1.

[23] *LB,* April 1960, 1.

[24] "Charles Perelle's Spacemanship," Fortune (January 1959), 113, 115, 122.

[25] Philip Marvin, "Automatic Machines at Work," *Automation* 1 (August 1954): 34-37, 35; Roger Bolz, "A Successful Partnership," *Automation* 1 (September 1954):13, 13.

equipment, it makes good sense to put a skilled man at the control panel."[26] In an *American Machinist* special issue on numerical control, the editors advised, "Frequently a good machinist can become an excellent programmer," and indicated that maintenance personnel were important and that it was wrong for companies to rely on outside personnel to service their equipment since "no outside maintenance arrangement can match the speed of a properly trained inside staff."[27]

However, Perelle was determined that his $10 million worth of machine tools would lead to greater mastery over the shop floor and production-cost savings. ABA's purchases were part of a nationwide inclination to utilize numerical control equipment, "the one overwhelming metalworking development of the century," according to the *American Machinist* in a 1964 report "Numerical Control: The Second Decade."[28] Perelle believed that the new machines would make it easier for engineers to find the "true time" of machining jobs. So informed, production managers could end machinists' efforts to regulate production.[29]

Automatic milling machines with dual cutting heads and air-clamp fixtures increased output and speeded up parts loading and unloading. Air-operated fixtures permitted the fast and accurate loading of parts, and "because of automatic cycling, the machines are operated back-to-back by one operator." Lathes with powerful drive motors and tungsten-carbide tools cut bar stock to finish dimensions, thus eliminating several secondary cutting operations and the workers who performed them. Burgmaster multispindle drills performed eight or more operations on a part without the need to remove it from a fixture. "Instead of the operator having to move heavy drill jigs underneath the drill spindles, the turret of the new machines automatically indexes six different tools over the part." Such a machine released the operator from standing in front of a single machine manipulating a lever to perform the drilling operation. For once the tool indexed to the proper location, it automatically completed the required drilling operation.

Such a machine allowed a single operator to perform work customarily done by several other workers. "No attention is needed," *Progress* reported, "except to load, press the start button, and unload. This permits the operator to operate a second machine. . . . It's obvious that outdated machine tools are a handicap which AB cannot afford." According to management, "Working back-to-back,"

---

[26] *Progress,* March 1959, 1. *American Machinist,* 26 October 26, 1954, NC16. Management said that the new machine tools allowed workers to move up from "the Model T to a Lincoln." *Progress,* May 1959, 1; June 1959, 1; September 1959, 1. For a typical Kingsbury ad, see *American Machinist,* June 1950, 26. *American Machinist,* November 1954, 8-9, 32, 39; December 1954, 52-53.

[27] *American Machinist,* October 25, 1964, NC16.

[28] *American Machinist,* 26 October 1954, NC2.

[29] Donald Roy, "Quota Restriction and Goldbricking in a Machine Shop," *American Journal of Sociology* 57 (1952): 427-442; Donald Roy, "Efficiency and "The Fix": Informal Intergroup Relations in a Piecework Machine Shop," *American Journal of Sociology* 60 (1954): 255-266.

on newly acquired Kingsbury horizontal drilling and tapping machines "two units are capable of drilling, counter-sinking, and tapping up to 26 holes simultaneously. Internal to the drilling time on the first machine, the holes are being threaded by tapping in the second machine. Versatile quick-changing fixtures and tools provide a means of rapid changeover for various parts."[30]

One hundred drill-press and miller operators lost their jobs. Unionists labeled the machinery purchases the "consolidate effort—eliminate personnel" campaign. "Battery of new Operator-Eliminator machines being set up rear of Department 160," read a *Bulletin* headline. "There will be so much new machinery by July of next year that there will undoubtedly be fewer people working here. *Automation means—Meet the market competition by fewer Union Members*. Without a doubt this definition should be in Webster's dictionary."[31] But, because a great deal of the work that remained in Springfield was nonrepetitive, a core of skilled workers remained essential. Perelle hoped to persuade these workers to be willing partners in the technology program, yet management made all of the technology decisions and Perelle turned a deaf ear to union calls for a joint committee to study the impact of technology and automation on workflow, quality, training, and employment. Instead, in January 1958, he established a management-only technology "thinking group." For workers, the insinuation was clear, and a rancorous debate over technology followed.[32]

SHOP-FLOOR TENSIONS ESCALATE

A dysfunctional grievance system added to disquiet on the shop floor. A *Labor Bulletin* cartoon depicted Director of Industrial Relations Mote at a table across from a sweating and gagged foreman. Mote rubbed a magic "answers" lantern while "NO" floated in a cloud above his head. Off to the side, a file cabinet had grievance forms spilling from every drawer, while a wastebasket contained a torn copy of the labor agreement. The accompanying article described the old days when an open-minded labor-relations office reached settlements rather than issued ultimatums. "We cannot help but recall," the article concluded, "the many pleasant hours spent with men of high principles who treated us as human beings and received the proper respect reserved for those who lead us." Just as the UAW's Frank Fagan predicted, foremen no longer resolved grievances on the shop floor, and justice delayed heightened tensions between grievants and supervisors.[33]

[30] For discussions of technology acquisitions, see *Progress*, November 1956; January, March 1957; March, April, May, September 1959 (PVHM American Bosch collection).
[31] *LB*, October 1959.
[32] "Technical Advisory Group Organized by Bosch ARMA to Study Needs of the Future," *SMU*, 13 January 1958, D7.
[33] *LB*, April 1956, 1.

Stephen Meyer found that there were two important categories of grievances at Allis-Chalmers between 1937 and1940. One group "a significant challenge to the shop floor authority of straw bosses, foremen, and supervisors"; the other "touched on the complicated question of new production technologies."[34] Meyer made the point that much of this grievance activity sprang from workers' sense of equity and fairness; it "constituted a means for resisting new technologies and new production methods." When management introduced automatic machinery, rate grievances afforded workers a protest vehicle, a way to defend themselves "against the inexorable penetration of new industrial and managerial methods" on the shop floor.[35]

How do Bosch grievances compare? Table 5.2 summarizes a random sample of 200 grievances filed from the early 1950s through 1970.[36] On one rate grievance, a worker wrote, "I find the rate given to me to be extremely low. I want a new rate taken that will be fair and equitable." On another, a worker argued, "Time study eliminated my fatigue allowance." A third stated, "I cannot possibly do the work assigned, I am already overloaded; I claim speed-up." When the company reorganized work in the factory's drill-press area in the late 1950s, well over 50 percent of grievances filed concerned piecework rates. Union leaders warned workers to not walk off the job over unresolved rate grievances: "Employees, if walking out in a body, are subject to disciplinary action."[37]

An undated union report analyzed rate problems in Department 110 from 1942 to 1966.[38] In the department, skilled set-up men, mechanics, and machine operators kept Warner and Swasey chucking machines and Acme Gridley bar-fed automatic screw machines running. Workers operated two or three machines and everyone was paid on total department output. "During the war years and for a period afterwards the many problems were kept in the department and resolved by an aggressive group of old timers, so written grievances were at a

[34] Stephen Meyer, *Stalin Over Wisconsin: The Making and Unmaking of Militant Unionism, 1900-1950* (New Brunswick: Rutgers University Press, 1992), esp. 111-117.
[35] S. Meyer, *Stalin Over Wisconsin*, 113; Stephen Meyer, "Technology and the Workplace: Skilled and Production Workers at Allis-Chalmers, 1900-1941," *Technology and History* (1988): 839-864, 855.
[36] The local maintained excellent grievance files by worker and department. Hundreds of grievance files are cataloged in the UMass Local 206 archives, providing a rich source for a more exhaustive study of grievance activity. In many instances the grievance committee's notes are attached to the original grievance and in almost all cases the company's formal written response is included.
[37] UMALA Local 206 files, Series III, grievance files. Letter to Officers and Stewards in Series 3. The job-classification issue is analyzed in chapter 7 when the job rating and seniority systems are described.
[38] *Local 206 1941 Labor Agreement,* 36. The 1941 contact read, "The policy regarding the speed of operations is that time studies shall be made on the basis of fairness consistent with quality workmanship, efficiency of operations, and the reasonable working capacity of normal operators."

Table 5.2. Sample of 200 Local 206
Grievances 1953-1970

Rates of payment on piece work	30%
Job classifications	26%
Foremen performing union work	11%
Miscellaneous	11%
Seniority in layoffs and recalls	8%
Working out of classification	3%
All others	11%

minimum," the report summarized.[39] When Perelle's modernization campaign started, Department 110 was his first target. He wanted machines with simplified set ups, automatic parts loading and unloading attachments, and increased tool capacity in order to break the group power exhibited by workers, who routinely slowed or stopped production to protest changes in their work.

The new machines had automatic cycle controls, so Perelle insisted that operators perform their own set-ups and inspections. This prompted a series of grievances when set-up personnel and floor inspectors were terminated. Workers filed grievances over the number of machines they were assigned and the ways in which the company proposed to calculate their compensation when machines broke down.[40] Grievances also attacked management's authority to alter customary staffing patterns. In reply, the company insisted that the new machines made work easier and suggested pay cuts were in order; this prompted more complaints.[41] In Department 110, workers utilized a highly effective form of protest: the group grievance. During a departmentwide group hearing, all affected workers left the shop floor and production stopped. In one carefully orchestrated scene, workers left their machines, cleaned up, and strolled through the factory to the hearing room to the cheers of other workers.[42]

The second-most-common grievance involved job classifications, usually in opposition to a foreman ordering someone to do work outside their formal job description. Workers argued that this was an attempt to reduce the workforce. Should workers be induced to perform the functions of laid-off workmates these

[39] *Department 110 Grievance History Memo,* author unknown, UMALA Local 206 grievance files.
[40] *Ibid.* It is instructive to compare the collaboration Derber described in Westinghouse with the continuous battle in Bosch's most important production department.
[41] UMALA, *Department 110 Grievance History Memo.* Grievances for a job upgrade were seldom successful. In a review of 15 arbitration cases, the union won one upgrade.
[42] UMALA Local 206 files, Series III, Box 12 grievance files.

cuts could become permanent. Management reasoned that since they "purchased" a worker's time for eight hours, if a machine broke down or an operator was waiting for work, they had the right to reassign the worker. "Not so fast," said the union. "We have specific job classifications and job descriptions and this is what we are hired to do, nothing more." For unionists, "anyone working out of classification on day work jobs must be halted. Let's hire the needed help for efficiency and productivity's sake."[43] Unionists had cause for concern, for under Perelle's shop-floor reorganization, close to 100 stock handlers, packers, and inspectors lost their jobs in the late 1950s.[44]

Managers also ordered workers running machines with long operating cycles to work at other equipment outside their contractual job classification. A personal example clarifies this point. For several years I operated a multitool cutting machine that completed a single part every four minutes. Once the machine was loaded and running there was little for me to do. I considered the time my own but management thought otherwise. Periodically they announced their plans to have me operate additional machines during the "four minutes," including a drill press and a hole-tapping machine. These machines had job descriptions and classifications and workers assigned to them or already on lay-off status. In my estimation, by running the machines, I cost others their jobs. Such conflicts were a day-to-day occurrence, and it is not hard to see how such activities, which impinged upon Perelle's and his successors' shop-floor control, provided the company with an incentive to find alternative manufacturing facilities.

1958 WILDCAT STRIKE

In the fall of 1958 Local 206 members supported members of the Bosch's striking engineer's union. The previous autumn, Local 206 accepted a small wage settlement after management had agreed to hold new wage talks in mid-1958. In April 1958, Bosch received a sizable government order for B-52 bomber test equipment, and unionists believed this enhanced their bargaining position.[45] Union negotiators pointed out that hourly pay rates fell 9¢ below the local average; management countered that Bosch's $2.66 hourly average exceeded 10 similar, nearby firms by 19¢. Not wanting to jeopardize the on-time completion of the bomber work, the company stated that they did not want a strike. "However," their public statement concluded, "we don't want to go through negotiations similar to

[43] UMALA Local 206 files, Series III, Box 12, ff 125, grievance files. Two workers in the department, Vincent Motyl and Donald Staples, filed several grievances. Each man became a union steward and got elected to more responsible positions in the union during the 1960s and 1970s. Both men earned reputations as strong unionists during these skirmishes.
[44] LB, October 1959, 3.
[45] SMU, 31 August 1957, 14; 6 September 1957, 1.

these each year, and we're not going to."[46] The rank and file authorized a strike, and management moved finished and nearly finished products from the plant as strike momentum built. But, for some unfathomable reason, union president Ernest Depathy told local newspaper reporters that divisions existed among the rank and file over the strike. The union accepted a 7¢-an-hour increase, but failed to obtain the automatic cost-of-living language they sought.[47]

Two months later, perhaps still angry over the failure to get the cost-of-living language, unionists honored picket lines set up by striking members of Bosch Engineering and Architectural Local 112. Local 206 business agent Jim Manning stated, "We cannot promote or assist a strike without being in violation of our contract with the company." But, "We cannot control the actions of individuals in our local." On the first day of Local 112's walkout, Local 206 members refused to enter the plant for their paychecks. Workers received their pay when the company agreed to distribute checks in the cafeteria across the street from the main production facility. The October 10 *Daily News* carried a front-page photograph of massed striking Local 112 workers and their Local 206 allies blocking the plant's front gates. Hundreds of unionists could be seen perched on a hill across from the plant.[48]

On day two of the Local 206 stay-away, the company charged that the union was in violation of their contract's no-strike clause, and personnel manager Mote sent letters to Local 206 members informing them that they were participating in an illegal work stoppage. Manning responded, "I have told my people the plant is open and they can go to work but they say they don't want to be called scabs."[49] Compounding the company's difficulties, the Columbus, Mississippi, IUE local went on strike October 9, when their contract expired. ARMA's head of labor relations, W. Gerard Tuttle, raced to Columbus hoping to end the strike there. With Tuttle in Mississippi, no contract talks were scheduled in Springfield.[50]

Local 206 members ignored a second company return-to-work letter and remained on the hill for nine days; not one unionist crossed the picket line. There is no evidence that management filed unfair-labor-practice charges against the union or sought injunctive relief from the courts. Nor is there any evidence that they pressured the city to provide a large enough police presence to escort willing workers into the plant.

When Tuttle returned from Mississippi, he refused Local 112's offer to return to work and submit outstanding issues to binding arbitration. Local 206 members received still another letter urging them to end their walkout: "Next Friday you will receive no pay—is it worth it for the small amount that divides

[46] *SMU*, 14 August 1958, 1.
[47] *SDN*, 14 August 1958, 19.
[48] *SMU*, 10 October 1958, 1.
[49] *SDN*, 11 October 1958.
[50] *SMU*, 11 October 1958; SDN, 11 October 1958, 1; *SDN*, 13 October 1958, 24.

Local 112 and us? If it is not money, what is it then? There must be a great principle involved." Referring to the local's August wage settlement, the letter concluded, "After lengthy negotiations your union gained for you increases averaging approximately seven cents an hour, which is $2.80 a week. Do you realize that you have already lost 43 weeks of your recent increase by your six days absence from work? You will never make up the pay you are losing." Close to 400 Local 206 members filed unemployment claims during the second week of the walkout, and many received one check despite the company's threat to fight every claim.[51]

Local 112 members finally ratified a new contract on October 20, and Local 206 members returned to work on October 21. On the first day of the walkout, a reporter described what he believed Local 206's protest was about. "A vivid contrast in business conditions was provided by today's walkout," he wrote. "In 1955, a strike idled 3,500. Today, just three years later, no more than 1,300 were involved."[52] The walkout set the tone for labor–management relations for several years. Perelle and his successors, determined to never again be mocked by hundreds of workers perched on a hill, sought to hold down wages in Springfield while they launched an aggressive effort to acquire alternative manufacturing sites.

"Morale—And No Bread"

Nine months after the wildcat walkout, Local 206 members returned to the picket line seeking cost-of-living protection. However, with unemployment high, and the nation gripped by recession, some workers wondered whether a strike made sense.[53] The company presented the union with its wage proposal just two hours before the contract expired. Company spokesperson Lesile Neville informed the media that "The Company is in good shape for a long strike and has a warehouse stocked with products." Management wanted a three-year agreement and informed the union that money issues would not be discussed until the local acquiesced to this demand. A week into the strike management sent letters to workers' homes describing how global competition made only a small wage increase possible. After 13 days, the union agreed to a three-year agreement, and yet again failed to obtain cost-of-living protection.[54]

[51] *SDN*, 18 October 1958, 1.
[52] *SMU*, 10 October 1958, 1.
[53] *SMU*, 17 August 1959, 3. The U.S. Department of Labor determined that Massachusetts had 7 of the 33 labor markets in the country with unemployment rates exceeding six percent. Springfield was one of them. A Federal Reserve Bank study released in August noted that in all three post-war recessions employment declined more on a percentage basis in New England than in the rest of the country, *SMU*, 18 August 1959, 1.
[54] Strike stories appeared in the *SMU*, August, 14, 15, 17, 21, 26, 29, 1959.

In the early 1960s the company intensified its argument that wage gains need to be tempered due to foreign competition. A 1966 *Bulletin* editorial, "Morale—And No Bread," summarized the enmity in the plant.

> Let us go back five years before the Hot Shots took over the Bosch via New York City. Machines not so fast; parts good. Local 206 members were in the main contented to give a good week's work for a good week's pay and good parts to boot. Morale was high, the Bosch wasn't the worst place to work. Today, morale is what you can get a cup of coffee for if you also have a dime. . . . The human has a strange knack for adapting himself to any situation. If you have 2,000 people with problems and no attempt is made to correct these same problems you will have 2,000 people adapting themselves, if you follow.[55]

COMPETITION INTENSIFIES AND SALES, PROFITS, AND JOBS FLUCTUATE

In the midst of the plant's technology-investment program, Perelle announced that Springfield's sales would double between 1958 and 1961 on the strength of increased business with the automobile industry. Springfield-designed fuel-injection systems were options on new Ford, Lincoln, and Packard models, and Mercedes Benz installed Bosch fuel-injection systems on many of its most expensive vehicles. Perelle planned to add 600 workers and a third shift by the summer of 1959, bringing total employment to 2,300. However, the various auto deals fell through as the national economy slumped, and a push-button transmission designed for Ford's new Edsel models never went into production either because the car was an abysmal failure. From glowing forecasts, by late spring 1960 Perelle told anyone who would listen that management needed to defeat the foreign competition.[56] Following a two-week summer shutdown, the plant went on a four-day week and when workers resumed a five-day week after Labor Day, 400 production workers were laid off. Corporate sales fell under $71 million by 1964, down from $133.6 million in 1960.[57]

Perelle, still bound to the local skill base and desperate to lower his production costs, now installed a $3.5 million state-of-the-art International Business Machines (IBM) data-retrieval system. The company needed "a data processing system sensitive enough and fast enough to run our modern factory. . . ." The system's 25 data-entry stations spread across the factory calculated payroll,

[55] "Morale and No Bread," *LB*, June 1966, 1.
[56] "Foreign Competition Basis for Bosch Reorganization," *SMU*, 3 June 1960, 36.
[57] "Bosch Plans Cutback," *SMU*, 25 June 1960, 10; "Bosch Returning to Five-day Week Here," *SMU*, 18 August 1960, 7.

tracked parts production, and monitored all inventory. The company also implemented a value-analysis engineering program that required a cost evaluation and redesign of over 100,000 machining and assembly operations. The paper system in use was cumbersome and contributed to scheduling problems and expensive overtime to meet delivery dates. With the new system, components could be allocated from inventory or scheduled for production within three minutes, regularizing set-ups. The system enabled supervisors to check the output of individual workers. Unionists feared that the information could be used to speed up workers when their output was low and cut incentive rates when compensation rose.[58]

Production needed to be reorganized by products, as opposed to machine functions. Under the functional system, parts went to specific areas of the factory for grinding, milling, and drilling. The sequential layout by product family could cut the costs associated with inventory control and material handling. Engineers developed new layouts for major product lines, but the effort stalled and inefficiencies remained. The company never discussed the values-engineering program and the shop-floor redesign with workers, even though stock-handlers and parts expediters understood the problems associated with workflow. In the end, the values-engineering program provided minimal cost relief.[59] Thus, despite investments dating back to the mid-1950s, production problems persisted.

The Vietnam war's defense build-up breathed life into Springfield and the corporation's Diesel Systems Division. In 1961 Bosch received a $2.5 million order for weapons control systems for B-52 bombers and a $3 million order for fuel-injection systems for 800 tanks. In 1962 Studebaker-Packard Corporation of South Bend, Indiana, ordered 4,000 multi-fuel-injection systems for military trucks, and in 1963 the Army began purchasing fuel-injection systems for its 5-ton trucks from Bosch. The Studebaker and Army orders totaled almost $30 million, and the increased work required an expansion in assembly capacity. In 1969 diesel-division sales rebounded to $47.9 million, up from $33.9 million in 1965. However, defense orders masked a vexing problem: commercial automotive products still faced stepped-up global competition. German competitors captured 70 percent of Springfield's commercial diesel fuel-injection business. Near the end of the Vietnam War, Massachusetts received over 10 percent of the nation's prime defense contracts; by the mid-1970s the state achieved the

---

[58] "New System Cuts Production Costs," *SMU,* 24 May 1960, 12.

[59] *Progress,* September-October 1964, 2; *Progress,* April-May 1966, 2; *SMU,* 10 December 1963, 17; 14 February 1964, 1; For an insightful discussion of the evolution of sequential layout, see Michael Best, *The New Competition* (Cambridge: Harvard University Press, 1990), esp. 52-55. The reorganization was never completed at Bosch.

dubious distinction of having the nation's highest unemployment rate as these military sales ended. Hundreds of Bosch workers lost their jobs.[60]

Perelle retired in 1964, replaced by Charles Beck, the former president of the Philco Corporation. As defense orders increased, Beck announced the construction of a $6-million research center and assembly building. The assembly building contained an automated monorail system to move machined parts between the production and assembly buildings and a temperature-controlled room for the final machining and hand fitting of extremely close-tolerance special products. Beck planned to hire 700 workers, bringing total union and nonunion employment to 3,000.[61] The new building and hiring projections seemingly solidified Springfield's future as the largest facility in one of ABA's most profitable manufacturing divisions. But this changed because Beck achieved important bargaining leverage over the union with the construction of factories in Brescia, Italy, and Breda, Holland, to produce newly designed fuel-injection systems for the automotive and agricultural equipment markets.[62] Unable to beat the foreign competition, Beck joined it. The European plants were a major blow to Springfield's future for two reasons. First, Local 206 members had completed the prototype work for the new systems and believed it would lead to employment growth. Second, work could now be moved to plants with lower wages and highly skilled machinists and engineers.

Adding to workers' problems, the corporation began to shift its market orientation from diesel and defense work to scientific and medical equipment. The company even changed it name to AMBAC Industries, excising "Bosch" from the title. Diesel and aerospace sales fell to $30 million from $48.1 million between 1968 and 1971; the only division registering strong sales gains was scientific and medical instruments, which jumped to $36.6 million from $22.6 million (Table 5.3). AMBAC's 1971 Annual Report celebrated the fact that "27 percent of total sales and 40 percent of total profits came from scientific, medical, environmental, and industrial instruments, products all acquired or developed in the last five years." Workers' production expertise was far less as most fuel-injection work went to the Netherlands and Italy.[63]

---

[60] For the impact of defense spending in Massachusetts during the 1960s and 1970s, see Jack Tager, "The Massachusetts Miracle," *Historical Journal of Massachusetts* 19 (Summer 1991): 111-132. The Springfield unemployment rate was 11.2 percent in 1975, significantly higher than the 8.5 percent rate nationwide.

[61] *SMU*, 28 January 1965, 16; 2 March, 1965, 15; 23 March, 1965, 12; 14 May 1965, 12; *Progress*, March 1965, 1; *Progress*, February-March 1966, 2; *SMU*, 1, 2 March 1966, 1.

[62] Brescia is in Northern Italy, approximately 60 miles west of Milan, and Breda is about 60 miles from the North Sea coast. For wage comparisons, see Jules Backman, *The Economics of the Electrical Manufacturing Industry* (New York: New York University Press, 1962), 291, 361.

[63] AMBAC, *Annual Report,* 1971; AMBAC, *Securities and Exchange Commission Prospectus,* 1971.

Table 5.3. Corporate Net Sales in Millions by
Division 1964-1971

	1964	1965	1966	1967	1968	1969	1970	1971
Diesel systems	27.7	33.9	40.6	43.6	48.1	47.9	34.0	30.0
Electrical products	13.4	14.9	17.4	16.4	19.9	21.6	21.7	26.0
Scien/Med. Inst.	11.6	13.7	18.1	22.5	22.6	26.4	32.3	36.6
Aerospace	31.2	25.4	32.0	28.5	25.6	20.7	20.5	14.8
Industrial products	3.6	3.8	4.7	8.2	12.3	12.2	16.9	10.6
Ordnance					22.5	31.2	30.4	16.8

BOSCH JOBS IN GLOBAL PLAY

Demand for the plant's commercial products for the automotive, agricultural, and truck industries remained weak, and foreign competitors were gaining market share in these sectors at the expense of Springfield. At the end of the 1950s Bosch employed a core of high-seniority workers supplemented by large numbers of workers with little seniority and no historical attachment to the contract and the union. In 1956, 30 percent of the workforce had over 25 years seniority; five men with a combined 180 years of service worked in one department; and in 1959, 40 workers celebrated 45 years of service. This sizable group of high-seniority workers remained vocal and unified at contract time, with interests that could not be ignored.[64] After striking only once since 1936, and then for just 2 days, workers struck three times between 1959 and 1971, while their ranks thinned the factory floor was reorganized and production lines were sent around the world (Figure 5.2—Local 206 membership).

Unionists regularly heard from the company that their wages were excessive when compared with their counterparts in Europe, South America, and the nonunion southern United States. In the General Electric plant 30 miles west in Pittsfield, Massachusetts, the company's "coordination of a huge network of integrated production facilities significantly reduced the control which craft workers had customarily exerted over their labor, even as they retained the skills

[64] In 1956 there were 378 members of the 25-year Club out of 1,200 working (*LB*, April 1956, 3). The quote is from *LB*, April 1957, 1. See also *Progress*, 23 January and 13 March 1959. The company newsletter continually ran articles about long-service workers and their importance to the success of the plant even as they disdained their input on the shop floor.

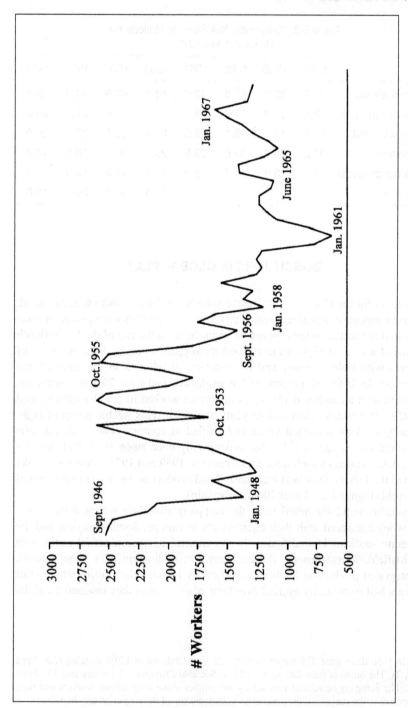

Figure 5.2. Local 206 membership September 1946–January 1968.

which have been depicted as the cornerstone of their power in the workplace and of their status in life."[65]

Though Van Norman, Bosch, and GE workers were in the same New England-wide district of the International Union of Electrical Workers, there is no evidence that they coordinated a campaign against runaway jobs. Historian Nelson Lichtenstein contends that a "system of interclass accommodation" developed in the late 1940s between unions and managers, serving, over time, to blunt worker power on the shop floor. Skilled machinists and others intent on maintaining control over the pace and content of their work used this power on the shop floor during the 1930s and early 1940s. Quickie work stoppages and departmental slowdowns escalated among workers. Lichtenstein estimates that by 1944 one of every two workers in the auto industry took part in some sort of work stoppage. In 1944 a GM vice president reported that most GM strikes were "caused by the refusal of workers to meet production standards."[66] Bosch unionists pressed for a measure of control, with management's answer the move to Mississippi, various joint production ventures, and the construction of plants in Italy and Holland. Defense-related decline and the corporation's national and international expansion provided the backdrop for four contract negotiations between 1962 and 1971. The decade started uneventfully. Bolstered by a rank-and-file strike vote and plentiful military work, the local achieved significant wage and benefit improvements in 1962. But for the rest of the decade, two lengthy work stoppages punctuated the company's efforts to get wage relief through modifications of the incentive system.[67]

Several months before 1965 contract talks, managers expressed their unhappiness with the *Labor Bulletin*'s incessant attacks. Undeterred, the union blasted the company's efforts to re-rate all piecework jobs. "All there is in the shop is tension, and it is getting worse," read a *Bulletin* article. "Today most any employee you ask will tell you that he or she hates to come to work. Some of us get so

---

[65] Donald Hess letter quoted in Forrant, 1994, 72. *SMU*, 15 April 1953, 1; Senator John F. Kennedy, "The Economic Problems of New England," *Proceedings of the 83rd Congress, First Session*, 99, 18 May 1953, 5054-5056. Philip Leahey, "Skilled Labor and the Rise of the Modern Corporation: The Case of the Electrical Industry," *Labor History*, 27 (Winter 1985-1986): 31-53, 53.

[66] Quoted in Nelson Lichtenstein, "Conflict Over Workers' Control: The Automobile Industry in World War II," in Michael Frisch and Daniel Walkowitz, eds., *Working Class America* (Urbana: University of Illinois Press, 1983): 284-311, 295. The workforce Lichtenstein describes as being actively involved in shop-floor job actions is similar in make-up to the one found in the Bosch plant. During the 1940s and early 1950s close to 50 percent of the workforce set up and operated manual machines and could significantly control output by controlling their own pace. Information gathered from Local 206 seniority and occupations lists, UMALA American Bosch files.

[67] *LB*, June 1962, 1.

irritable that we take the job home with us—this is not good."[68] Because of pressures to increase output, "We have had more stomach disorders and heart conditions amongst pieceworkers than ever before in the history of AB."[69]

Union president Al LeBeau blamed layoffs on the company's decision to subcontract work and charged that the elimination of floor inspectors caused an increased scrap rate. LeBeau also compared management's staffing with overseas firms and urged that "the level of Top Management be brought down to what most foreign companies have, not a heavy overloaded drain on the profits of the company with high salaries, but competitive in the same sense as the average worker is informed he must be."[70] LeBeau warned unionists, "This is only the beginning of a long hard struggle in which everyone must do his or her part to survive the viciousness of management in protecting our jobs and security."[71] The rank and file voted 670-310 against the negotiating committee's strike recommendation, accepting a three-year contract that was short on wage gains but did contain an upward wage adjustment for the skilled trades, early-retirement language, and a fifth week of vacation for workers with 30 years of service or more.[72]

Filming Set-Ups:
"He Clobbers Our Rates with New Methods"

A year later the union withstood management's attempt to film workers performing machine tool set-ups. Lichtenstein discusses the role of set-up personnel in the automobile plants in the 1930s and 1940s and notes that set-up specialists were "somewhat free of the harsh, mechanical discipline imposed by the moving mechanical assembly line."[73] With a degree of autonomy, they occupied a critical role, ensuring that machines ran quality parts and were instrumental in maintaining production schedules. Their "black box artistry" frustrated production managers: in the middle of a set-up—with gears, tooling, and fixtures spread about the work area—parts were not being made and supervisors, who knew little about the set-up process, were powerless to speed up the process. Bringing tools to their proper settings required fine adjustments, making the work difficult to time with a stopwatch, so the company sought a cinematic record of several set-ups. Because the labor agreement called for set-up personnel to be paid on an hourly basis, the union charged that the attempt to establish piecework rates on set-ups was a contract violation. When, on May 27, the company tried to film a machine set-up, the union steward called the worker off the job for a meeting with business agent

---

[68] *LB*, March 1964, 1.
[69] *LB*, June 1964, 1.
[70] *LB*, June 1964, 1.
[71] *LB*, June 1964, 1; September 1964, 1.
[72] *SMU*, 21 August 1965, 1; *LB*, September 1965.
[73] N. Lichtenstein, "Conflict Over Workers' Control," 286.

Steve Jaross. The company agreed not to film set-ups, giving the union a short-lived victory; management accelerated its search for other production facilities and laid off nearly 200 workers. A *Labor Bulletin* poem captured the mood among many unionists.

My Boss
He's my boss, tho' he looks down
As if I crawled out of the ground
When I make a little mistake
He jumps on me, there is no break.
Why can't he learn I'm not a machine.
I have faults, if you know what I mean
Even an automatic breaks down,
I'm not the one wearing a frown.
We are people, human beings,
Do you know just what that means.
Children, problems, bills and such
Things that get us into dutch
We are working hard and true
Why do they just make us blue?[74]

No Pay Concessions

In 1968 the company once more sought wage relief. Cognizant of the corporation's global acquisitions, workers argued that there was obviously money available for wage and benefit improvements and pushed for automatic wage increases tied to inflation, an extra increase for the skilled trades, and more vacation time for high-seniority workers. After a three-week strike workers ratified a three-year contract with a wage package worth 56¢ an hour, 12¢ above the company's original offer, but they did not get the cost-of-living protection they wanted.[75]

In the months before and after the strike, unionists tried working with management to resolve production problems. In February 1968 business agent Jaross made the company's plans to relocate the toolroom a primer on worker involvement. The tool room had been moved to the first floor of the main plant from the third floor, but the new location proved disastrous. "Now does it make any sense," Jaross asked,

> to take a department such as the toolroom, where all the tools, fixtures, and gages to be used throughout the plant are to be manufactured at close tolerances . . . and place it in an area just recently vacated by a cast iron manufacturing department with the added inconveniences of poor lighting, uneven flooring for machines which must hold close tolerances, and dust

[74] *LB*, June 1966, 3.
[75] *SMU*, 15 April 1968, 1; *SDN*, 15 May 1968, 1.

from the nearby manufacturing departments which settles on plates and size blocks used in the daily performance of these tool room employees and makes their work of CLOSE tolerance almost guess work? There are some tool room grinders, whose skill in determining the precise amount to be ground from a tool, fixture, or gage is judged by the sound of their grinding wheel and this can no longer be done.

Implicit was the notion that problems like these were avoidable when unionists were consulted.[76]

The union also provided the company with a description of five pressing problems: the consistent failure to repair defective equipment, resulting in excessive lost production time and scheduling problems; a lack of proper tooling when needed to complete set-ups and keep production jobs running; incomplete data on job processing sheets and work orders leading to inventory and planning problems; the generally dirty conditions in the plant; and poor workflow and production bottlenecks, resulting in a lack of work for some departments and excessive overtime for others.

Unionists poked fun at the company in a *Labor Bulletin* cartoon entitled "The Chain of Command" (Figure 5.3). Depicted were a cigar-smoking stockholder, one hand full of money with the other out searching for more; the plant manager, with formulas swirling around in his head, eyes crossed, and a vacant stare on his face; four foremen, identified as "the pinheads"; and a worker chained to a drill press. Free the operator, the cartoon implied, and you gain all the problem-solving expertise required to make the plant run smoothly. Management rejected LeBeau's request for meetings, and the plant lurched into the 1970s with declining commercial sales, lay-offs, heightened international competition, and deteriorating labor–management relations.[77]

For corporate officers, the millions of dollars invested in Springfield should have generated a financial return, not resistance to cameras and strikes. The Springfield–Europe wage differential represented the stumbling block in 1971 contract talks. In an April 16 "Dear Worker" letter, vice president Ralph Hershfelt reminded everyone that 1000 Bosch workers had lost their jobs since the start of 1970. To halt the employment skid, the company needed improved controls over the organization of work, a streamlined grievance procedure, and an updated incentive plan, "one which will make possible increased productivity and reduce unit costs." Unionists must admit "the necessity for changes in the Agreement to enable the Company to maintain its competitive position and thus continue to provide and expand employment in Springfield."[78]

[76] *LB*, February 1968, 1.
[77] *LB*, October 1968, 1.
[78] Hershfelt letter to workers 16 April 1971, UMALA Local 206 Archives Series III, Box 8, ff 86.

Figure 5.3. Caratoon "Chain of Command" from *IUE Local 206 Bulletin*, October 1968.

These "reduce-the-costs" arguments carried no weight after what the union considered repeated failures by management to involve them in their production-improvement efforts. In an April 13 leaflet, the negotiating committee condemned the company's proposal to re-rate incentive jobs using predetermined engineering times as tantamount to "rolling us back to the 1930s working condition era" when workers had no say over rates or rights to argue how they were set.[79] Workers walked off the job when the contract expired, with the company charging that the union failed to respond to their piece-rate proposal. Throughout the strike the union never mentioned what it believed to be a retrograde plan, while management pressed that the existing system was inaccurate, unfair, and impractical. The company tried playing workers off against each other. "Some employees with less than a reasonable effort," vice president of operations Hershfelt charged, "can attain higher than average earnings, and many employees have a limited earning opportunity in spite of their very best effort." Only a new incentive system would improve costs so "we could earmark a reasonable amount for wage and pension increases in the years to come."[80]

During the stoppage, the company assured unionists there were no plans to shift production to Europe, but workers must have recognized their precarious position. Military work was already scheduled to shrink by close to 80 percent with the wind down of Vietnam War defense spending and the factories in Italy and Holland about to open. After six weeks Hershfelt told unionists,

> It is our responsibility to plan a course of action for American Bosch that can ensure the survival of the Division. At this time the improved technology and capabilities of European manufacturers, their advanced engineering, low import duties and the low cost of transportation bring new competition and new pressure to bear with our efforts to maintain a volume of business in the heavy-duty truck manufacturing industry of this country.[81]

For added emphasis, he reminded everyone that several Springfield-area factories were closed: "Some of these are substantial firms, national in scope, and not really affected by a temporary set-back or recession. They left Springfield because of a limited future considering manufacturing costs in this area." After 15 weeks workers ratified a contract with a 75¢-an-hour raise over 3 years, an improvement from the company's early June proposal of 41¢, an amount they had

[79] Local 206 1971 contract flier in UMALA Local 206 Archives Series III, Box 8, ff 86.

[80] Hershfelt letter to employees, 8 June 1971, UMALA Local 206 Archives, Series III, box 8, ff86.

[81] Hershfelt letter to employees, 8 June 1971.

made contingent on the local's acceptance of the new predetermined time system. In a defeat, management did not secure its new incentive program.[82]

CLOSURE

Whatever sense of satisfaction strikers felt dissipated when AMBAC put the entire diesel division up for sale. Seven years later, Hartford, Connecticut-based aerospace giant United Technologies Corporation (UTC) purchased the division in what *Business Week* called a friendly takeover for cash and preferred stock valued at $210 million.[83] UTC already owned Pratt & Whitney Aircraft, Sikorsky Aircraft, Hamilton Standard Technologies, Carrier Air Conditioner, and Otis Elevator. Since becoming UTC's chief executive officer in 1971, Harry Gray had built the corporation from a $2 billion aerospace company into a $15 billion conglomerate, one of the country's biggest industrial firms. Gray's reputation—his nickname was the "gray shark"—as an antiunion, hostile-takeover artist preceded him to Springfield, and Local 206 members noticed Gray's penchant for downsizing or closing older plants. One notable casualty was Otis Elevator Company's flagship factory in Yonkers, New York, which once employed 1,300 workers represented by the International Union of Electrical Workers Local 484. UTC acquired the plant in 1976, started layoffs in 1979, and closed it in 1983.[84]

The Springfield factory became part of the United Technologies Automotive Group, along with the Breda, Holland, and Brescia, Italy, manufacturing facilities. The three plants concentrated on the manufacture of diesel fuel-injection systems for medium- and heavy-duty vehicles, including trucks, construction equipment, and agricultural equipment. The Springfield plant also manufactured electric governors, hydrotors, and accumulators. The Columbus, Mississippi, plant became headquarters for United Technologies Electro Systems. Its product lines included automobile ignition systems and small DC motors for automobile power windows, door locks, and windshield wipers.[85]

[82] Company to workers, 16 April 1971, UMALA Local 206 Archives, Series III, Box 8, ff 86; "Hershfelt to Employees," 8 June 1971, Local 206 Archives, Series III, Box 8, ff 86; *SDN*, 25 July 1971, 1.
[83] "UTC Acquires AMBAC," *Business Week*, 20 March 1978, 46.
[84] *SMU*, 10 October 1980, 52; James Feron, "Otis Elevator to Leave Birthplace," *New York Times*, 1 December 1982, B2; Franklin Whitehouse, "Yonkers' War Over Otis Gathers Force," *New York Times*, 12 December 1982, Section 11, 1; Charles Stein, "What Would Harry Gray Think Now: UTC Cuts, And More May Be On The Way," *Boston Globe*, 14 December 1986, A1.
[85] United Technologies Corporation press releases, 29 June 1982 and 21 March 1983, PR Newswire Association, Inc.

New Standards Plan: The Screws Tightened

Between 1978 and 1981 Springfield production lines went to Italy and Holland, and 40 percent of the workforce was terminated. UTC also forced the union to grievance arbitration several times in an effort to weaken or eliminate long-standing seniority, job bidding, and job classification contract language. In May 1981, 10 years after the former owners failed to change the incentive system, UTC presented Local 206 with its own ultimatum. A memo sent to each worker's home pointed out that to "preserve job security" in Springfield, the piecework incentive system had to be scrapped and a new one installed. If the change was made, a $20 million–$30 million modernization program could begin; absent a new payment system, there would be no further investments in Springfield. Six months before the memo, on November 6, 1980, UTC announced plans for the construction of a $120 million manufacturing facility in Columbia, South Carolina. Incentives to build there included reduced property and utilities taxes and state-supported workforce training. UTC planned to produce the same fuel-injection components made in Springfield there.

At the membership's direction, the negotiating committee discussed a new incentive system with management in the middle of an existing three-year labor agreement.[86] When negotiations on the so-called New Standards Plan (NSP) began, workers received a letter from company vice president Henry Fuller, reminding them

> The competitive position of the Springfield facility has deteriorated in recent years. Productivity has declined while our operating costs have skyrocketed. Some of our machines and processes have become outdated. Our options are clear. We must modernize our Springfield facilities, introduce advanced machining concepts and develop new processes and systems. Or, we must develop another modern manufacturing facility in addition to the South Carolina plant. Either option will require a major investment on the part of the Company. The main obstacle we face in modernizing Springfield is the deteriorated piecework system. . . . In order to be competitive, we must restructure our incentive system in addition to modernizing the facility.[87]

Fuller pointed out that investments would be made elsewhere "unless we can secure an agreement by the union to cooperate by modifying the wage incentive system."[88] Negotiations dragged through the summer while UTC completed the construction of its nonunion, 322,000 square-foot state-of-the-art South Carolina plant. While the company assured the union that the South Carolina plant "is only

[86] Henry Fuller memo, 8 May 1981, Local 206 Archives, Series III, Box 8. For a discussion of South Carolina's recruitment program: George Matusky, "South Carolina Means Business," *Forbes,* 148, no. 21, 1991, 69-77.
[87] H. Fuller memo, 8 May 1981.
[88] H. Fuller letter, 15 May 1981, Local 206 Archives, Series III, Box 8.

an expansion of Bosch's activities and is not intended to replace it," many workers believed otherwise.[89]

A broad-based coalition of stewards and local officers—myself included—opposed the NSP, pointing out that this was an attempt to study and reengineer jobs before moving all of them south and abroad. Company proposals, it was argued, should be considered in 1983 during the next normally scheduled round of contract negotiations, when the local could demand stronger plant-closing language, better pension protection, and limitations on subcontracting. The divided negotiating committee made no recommendation to the membership before a secret ballot vote on October 22, 1981 ratified the NSP 531-453. The *Springfield Morning Union* called the yes vote proof-positive that American Bosch was in Springfield for good, and that the company stated, "Investments will now be made."[90]

One month after the vote, I was elected the local's business agent and less than one year later protests erupted against a two-week plant shutdown, blamed on a lack of work. A union press release I helped to write stated,

> No more crawling—no more concessions. We are opposed to this company shipping out work to other plants in this country and overseas. And we are opposed to the politicians who come to the plant gates looking for votes, but are nowhere to be found when their help is needed to pass plant closing legislation.[91]

Between 1980 and 1986 UTC relocated production from Springfield to Italy and Holland and started joint manufacturing ventures with companies in Japan, France, England, and Italy. UTC president Robert Daniell commented, "Our markets are increasingly global. And over the next five years international sales are likely to grow faster than domestic sales." According to *Business Week,* the key motivation was that "UTC earns a higher profit on foreign sales than on domestic sales."[92] The promised plant modernization and product diversification did not take place, and job losses mounted; between 1982 and 1985, 600 Springfield workers were fired as part of what UTC called its "redirection program."[93]

---

[89] United Technologies Corporation press release, March, 1980, Local 206 Archives, Series III, Box 8.

[90] Leaflets and campaign fliers in Local 206 holdings, UMass Amherst Archives; *SMU,* 23 October 1981.

[91] *SDN,* 4 September 1982, 3.

[92] United Technologies Corporation Annual Report, April, 1985; "UTC Adds Westland to Its Growing Foreign Arsenal," *Business Week,* 24 February 1985, 88-89.

[93] Judith Leff, "United Technologies and the Closing of American Bosch," *Harvard Business School Case Study 386-174* (May 1986), 3.

In-Plant Conflicts Escalate and Quality Suffers

As layoffs mounted, labor relations deteriorated and grievances escalated.[94] During the summer and fall of 1985, the two sides engaged in a group grievance that rivaled the 1970s fight over the timing of set-ups. The grievance was precipitated by the company's lay-off of 33 inspectors, followed by their replacement with the same number of inspectors and lower pay grades. The union unsuccessfully sought injunctive relief through the federal courts, arguing that well over 100 workers could be adversely affected due to the labor agreement's complex layoff system. The moves, we pointed out, could cause financial hardships for wrongly laid-off workers and create a chaotic scene should the company lose the arbitration case and be compelled to return everyone to their former positions and reimburse lost wages.

During the arbitration case, the union contended that layoffs were possible only when there was a demonstrated lack of work. Since the company posted job opportunities for an identical number of inspectors, albeit at lower wages, no lack of work existed nor had the work appreciably changed. For unionists, the company move was a ham-fisted attempt to not only slash wages but to also weaken the contract's seniority provisions. Company lawyers countered that the newly posted inspectors' classifications were in the contract and that management had the exclusive right to assign work for the good of their business. The arbitrator dismissed the company's maneuvers as an ill-disguised ploy to circumvent unambiguous contract language and ordered them to pay lost wages of close to $150,000 and reinstate all affected workers to their former positions.[95]

Charles Perelle denied unionists the opportunity to play a constructive role when he eliminated the Labor–Management Committee, and the corporation's antiunion animus prohibited their acknowledgment that worker suggestions had merit. This approach to quality continued well into the 1970s and 1980s as this personal example attests. A novice to the world of complex machine tools before I went to work at the Bosch, I built up a stock of knowledge over my years in the plant. I first held an entry-level position, and then I availed myself of the labor agreement's job-bidding system and landed a job on the exotically named

[94] *Local 206 Grievance files,* UMass Amherst Labor Archives, Series II. For a discussion of the escalation of grievances at General Motors after 1960, see Nelson Lichtenstein, "Reutherism on the Shop Floor: Union Strategy and Shop-Floor Conflict in the USA 1946-1970." For Lichtenstein, the rise in grievances was in part a consequence of workers' concerns for such in-plant issues as speed-up, automation, health and safety, and production standards. Wildcat strikes increased at Chrysler and GM in the late 1960s in response to what GM Department Director Leonard Woodcock called the industry's gold-plated sweatshops. Nationally publicized strikes at GM's Lordstown and Norwood assembly plants in the early 1970s centered on similar issues related to how production was done on the shop floor.

[95] *SDN,* 22 August 1985, 8. NLRB charges were filed and the Board essentially mimicked the court and told the local to arbitrate the case.

New Britain CAM-O-MATIC chucking machine. Under the tutelage of a 40-year machinist named Stanley, I learned how to keep the machine set-up and running. Once I mastered the job, Stanley was going to retire; I stood between him, his fishing boat, and an end to punching a clock at 6:30 a.m.

Department 206, where I worked, performed machining functions on fuel-injection housings destined for cars and trucks. Housings were quite complex, with numerous internal holes and various shapes and angles milled and ground on what began at one end of the plant as a steel bar. Before reaching me, the housing passed through several other departments and its estimated dollar value, including invested labor time, approached $500 when I got my hands on it. Paid on a piecework incentive basis, with normal effort, I completed eight housings an hour and received my base rate of pay; any housings I completed above 64 earned me an incentive bonus. To generate what I believed was an acceptable pay rate, I usually completed 75 to 80 housings in an eight-hour shift, earning an approximately 25 percent bonus above my hourly base-pay rate of $10.50. While training, Stanley warned me not to exceed 75 to 80 housings, because to do so, would likely trigger a time-study engineer's rate review.

In a week's time I could finish eight or nine parts an hour, then my serious education began. The complex aspect of the job entailed performing change-overs (set-ups) on the machine for different size housings. Set-ups occurred, on average, three times a month and required the replacement of sundry parts including gears, cams, complex tooling, and fixtures. It was an exacting process, as the machine had to hold finished dimension within two ten-thousandths of an inch; a human hair split several times. The complexity of the task, the precision required by the machine, and the costs involved should parts be scrapped, meant that set-ups often took two eight-hour shifts. In other words, absent any company-recognized standard time for executing the set-ups, I finished when I finished. While I performed a set-up I received 125 percent per hour of my previous week's hourly average. Thus, doing set-ups furnished me with an extraordinary degree of discretionary control over my work time and the size of my paycheck.

After a month and a half, I performed the set-ups reasonably well, and on the afternoon of Stanley's last departure, he handed me three oil-stained notebooks, which contained the richly detailed personal notes, diagrams, and descriptive short-cuts he compiled over years operating the CAM-O-MATIC. Ingenious shortcuts decreased the time required for set-ups. There were also ingenious tips for how to alter the machine's operating speeds to generate greater output. Armed with this historical knowledge, I completed set-ups in a few hours and produced 70 to 80 finished parts in six hours. I asked Stanley why he had not used the notebooks during training and he replied, "I had to make sure you were smart enough to use the books the right way and smart enough to make sure that management would never get their hands on them. I needed to make sure you were on the right side!"

This exchange symbolized what had become an adversarial relationship when it came to improving shop-floor quality, a labor–management conversation dating back to the union's criticisms of Charles Perelle's quality moves in the 1950s. During my time at the Bosch, management often launched a campaign to lower the plant's scrap rate and urged workers to make suggestions for how to reduce defective work. Workers held these antiscrap campaigns in contempt, even though they understood that their employment was linked to customer satisfaction.

In the 1970s and 1980s, when workers did offer suggestions, they were ignored, and by the time the plant closed, we believed that top management wanted us to produce bad work so that they would have an excuse to shutter the factory. For example, to finish a set-up, I was required to produce a so-called "first piece," which had to be approved by one of the plant's head inspectors. The first piece remained at my machine while the job was run. Customarily a perfectly good piece from somewhere up the line from my machine was used during this procedure, and quite often several good housings were used before one passed muster; until then, the housings I used were scrap. Rejects cost the company $1,500 to $2,000 for each set-up I did; all around me workers completed similarly wasteful set-ups. We devised a simple process to eliminate this waste, or so we thought. Housings scrapped elsewhere in the factory could be identified through the application of a spot of bright red paint and become a stock of trial-and-error set-up housings. Our supervisor labeled the scheme too difficult to implement, citing the work necessary to track the scrap pieces. It was easier, he said, to toss bad parts into the numerous scrap bins located about the shop. Shaking our heads, we returned to work. While I ran the CAM-O-MATIC, the notebooks helped me preserve a good deal of discretionary control over the workday. My tricks, multiplied many times by other workers' shortcuts, ran counter to the long-term viability of the plant. Yet this behavior amounted to a perverse form of job security so long as the plant remained open.

February 1986:
The Closing Officially Announced

The union's arbitration triumph in the "inspectors case" represented a hollow victory, for on February 4, 1986, at the start of scheduled contract talks, the company informed union negotiators in a 20-line memo that they were closing the Springfield plant. Vice president of Operations Jon Adamson told negotiators,

> We are unable to continue operating four facilities with this continuing over-capacity situation. I, therefore, regret to inform you that a very difficult business decision has been made to close the Springfield manufacturing operation by the end of August of this year. The military products will be

moved to Columbia, South Carolina; injectors to Brescia, Italy; and industrial products to Fluid Power of the Components Division.[96]

Three weeks later UTC spokesperson Alan Muncaster stated, "We have to do something or we're not a viable company anymore. We're stuck with manufacturing space and nothing to fill it and no hope of filling it." The $140-million Columbia, South Carolina, plant represented a significant investment by UTC, while Springfield's 650 Local 206 jobs made up less than 0.5 percent of its worldwide payroll.

Local 206 was no match for UTC, nor were the region's local, state, and national political leaders ever up to the challenge. They acted wounded when the closing was announced.[97] Springfield Mayor Richard Neal stated,

> I feel betrayed, because the city of Springfield, in good faith, held a series of meetings, that began eight to ten months ago, in which we offered all kinds of assistance. And I never knew until today what was going to happen. Each step of the way we were told not to worry, that they were not going to close. . . . To tell me at 2:00 p.m. that the eventual phase out was imminent does not, to my mind, demonstrate high regard by that corporation for this community.

Massachusetts Secretary of Labor Paul Eustace labeled UTC's previous assurances that they would remain in the city "bold-faced lies." While in an ironic twist, Massachusetts Governor Dukakis spoke in South Carolina about the Massachusetts employment and training system's programs for laid-off workers only four days after the closing announcement. Sixty-one-year-old Donald Staples, a 36-year veteran in the Bosch, summed it up for workers: "It's not like they pulled the rug out from under us. It's more like they pulled the trap door out from under the hangman's noose."[98]

The announcement confirmed predictions union leaders had made for years. After watching 300 workers lose their jobs in the spring of 1985, I prepared a memorandum to city, state, and federal officials that read in part,

> If all that was involved here was the loss of 300 or more well-paid jobs, there would be enough cause for very serious concern. But, these job losses are only the beginning. A clear pattern of mismanagement and disinvestment on the part of United Technologies, the parent corporation of American Bosch, point toward a phase-out of all operations at American Bosch's Springfield plant. Repeated management assurances that American Bosch and UTC have a

---

[96] Jon Adamson to all employees, *Plant Closing Memorandum,* 4 February 1986, UMALA Local 206 files.

[97] *HTT,* 1 March 1986, 1.

[98] *SMU,* 5 February 1986, 1; 7 February 1986, 1; Andrew Dabilis, "South Carolina Gives Dukakis the Rub on Springfield Plant Closing," *BG,* 8 February 1986, 9.

strong commitment to continuing operations are contradicted by management actions. . . . All of this occurs while the markets for AB's traditional product lines are booming. Other firms are becoming more cost competitive and investing heavily. Meanwhile we see UTC milking this plant for whatever remains here to be taken in profit and moving all its jobs, all its commercial product lines and much of its machinery elsewhere.

It concluded, "The union has cooperated fully in trying to stem absenteeism, in trying to increase production. We've shown results. Such cooperation has been repaid with layoffs and the promise of more layoffs. We see clearly the impending closing of this plant."[99]

A carefully worded company response noted,

> We want to maintain all four of our plants, including the two in Europe, but we have to redirect a number of product lines to better utilize our manufacturing capacity. Nothing has changed since we announced those 80 layoffs. We've done exactly what we said we'd do. There are no plans to shut the plant down.[100]

Within seven months, 1,200 people lost their jobs, while in South Carolina UTC paid approximately $20,000 a year in property taxes on the new plant compared with roughly $140,000 a year in Springfield.[101]

Seven weeks after the closing announcement, during a meeting at the Massachusetts State House, UTC officials and federal and state politicians announced a $600,000 UTC contribution to a workers' retraining and assistance program to be matched by a state contribution. Not one Local 206 representative was asked to attend the meeting despite the fact that the subject of help for fired workers remained a contentious bargaining issue. For Springfield Congressman Edward P. Boland, the contribution indicated that

> The company recognizes that it has a responsibility to do what it can to mitigate the effect of the closing on workers and their communities. I am pleased that the company has responded favorably to our suggestions in this area.

The *Boston Globe* called the $600,000 a UTC gift! But for Local 206 it was blood money "so they can look good in the eyes of Springfield" and get the union off their back. "The $600,000 donation—roughly $600 per fired worker—pales

[99] Local 206, UTC Disinvestment Points Toward American Bosch Closing, Summer, 1985, UMALA Local 206 files.

[100] *HTT*, 27 June 1985, 10.

[101] Jean Mooney, "For United Tech Closing Plant Made Good Business Sense," *HTT*, 1 March 1986, 1.

when juxtaposed to UTC's $9 Billion in assets at the time of the shutdown" [102] (Figure 5.4).

Figure 5.4. To UTC shareholders, I.U.E. local 206 open letter to UTC shareholders, appeared in *The Hartford Courant*, April 28, 1986.

[102] Randi Eldredge, "$1.2 Million Offered to Help Workers," *SMU*, 27 March 1986, 29; "UT Gives State Jobless Cash," *BG,* 27 March 1986, 73. A week earlier, Boland's office had informed unionists that "a decision by a private company to close a manufacturing facility is not grounds upon which to debar that company from defense contracts," dashing hopes that a work denial threat would force UTC to possibly keep the plant open ("Congressmen to UTC Workers: No Grounds to Deny Contracts," *SMU*, 22 March 1986, 18).

CONCLUSION

At the start of the 21st century the repercussions from the Bosch and other closings in the region are still felt. For workers and the regional economy, the Bosch closing's costs were staggering. Between 1986 and 1988 $31.1 million in income disappeared; there was an additional expenditure of $9.1 million in unemployment insurance, welfare, and other benefits; and an $8.6 million drop in federal and state tax revenues. Fired workers' average hourly wage was $11.38, supplemented with medical insurance and pension plans and a generous vacation allowance. According to figures compiled by the dislocated-work center that handled Bosch claims, the average replacement wage for workers fortunate enough to find a job was $9.22, and most jobs lacked basic medical insurance.

Since the late 1980s much of Massachusetts' economic growth bypassed the western part of the state. Between 1989 and 1999 real median income in Massachusetts climbed 6 percent to $54,077, but in Hampden County it declined by 12 percent, and in Springfield it fell 9 percent, to $30,417, the largest decline in the Commonwealth. Adding to the region's employment woes, no expansion of high tech manufacturing occurred in Springfield, Holyoke, Greenfield, and other river-valley factory cities.[103] In Springfield's North End, once home to 20 metalworking and machinery plants, block after block of triple-decker wood-frame apartment buildings, first homes for the thousands of German, Scottish, Italian, and Irish immigrant workers who made their way to the city, were burned down or torn down. In 2007 Springfield, still in severe economic distress, was being run by a state-appointed finance-control board, which had final authority over all city spending decisions. The city's plight nearly 20 years after the Bosch shutdown is examined in chapter 8.

[103] Figures on income from Andrew M. Sum, Paul Harrington, et al., *The State of the American Dream in Massachusetts, 2002* (Boston: MassINC, 2002). Anthony Flint and Bill Dedman, "Urban Renaissance Eludes State's Mid-sized Cities," *BG*, 23 June 2002, 1; Marcella Bombardieri, "Richer, Poorer," *BG*, 5 May 2002, B1; Janny Scott, "In Some Pockets, 90's Boom Was a Bust," *NYT*, 17 June 2002, A16; Robert Forrant and Shawn Barry, "Winners and Losers: High-Tech Employment Deals an Uneven Hand," *Massachusetts Benchmarks* 4, no. 3 (2001):12-16.

CHAPTER 6

Too Many Bends in the River—
The Larger Valley's Demise

After outpacing the world in the 1950s and early 1960s, the U.S. machine-tool industry entered a "death spiral" precipitated by managerial deficiencies, corporate reorganizations, and heightened international competition. Japanese and German machine-tool builders presented a concerted challenge for global market share and greater access to the extremely large U.S. market. This had very adverse consequences for the Connecticut River Valley. In an astonishing role reversal, the country became the world's largest importer of machine tools, while goods producers lost their early access to top-notch conventional and state-of-the-art machine tools and the notable competitive advantages they conveyed. The story of valleywide degeneration reveals the role played by a series of forces that have come to typify globalization. These include outsourcing, capital flight, and consolidation of ownership by takeover. Attention focuses on the impact of these forces on the valley's viability through a series of firm-specific case studies and an analysis of what happened to the computer numerical-control sector of the machine-tool industry.

TAKE A LITTLE TRIP

In 1981, stung by their rapid loss of global market share, the presidents of several U.S. machine-tool companies undertook a two-week fact-finding tour of Japan in hopes of gaining fresh insight into the industry's future. Arranged by the National Machine Tool Builders Association (NMTBA), participants learned how their Japanese counterparts increased their global market share. No "magic bullet" explained Japan's precipitate advance to machine-tool prominence.

> Nowhere in the thirteen factories toured by our study group did we see any unique manufacturing technology. In general Japanese machine tool builders use the same types of machinery to build their products as in America. However, the equipment and technology are very intelligently applied and many builders are investing heavily in the latest technology to improve productivity further.

117

The U.S. delegation learned that Japanese tool builders emphasized collaborative research in developing new products, spent a considerable amount of profits upgrading equipment, and promoted continual shop-floor improvement and skills training. By comparison, industry analyst Anthony DiFilippo found that capital investments by U.S. tool builders had dropped noticeably after 1970, when Vietnam War orders dissipated. By 1980 these expenditures were lower, in inflation-adjusted dollars, than in 1965. Shortly after the NMTBA's Japan trip, a National Research Council (NRC) survey of 43 U.S. machine tool firms found that 40 percent of the equipment on factory floors was at least 20 years old, compared with 18 percent in Japan. The NRC also learned that many firms had abandoned their apprenticeship programs. In other words, critical aspects of what U.S. builders had determined were reasons for success among their Japanese rivals were neglected at home.[1] Such systemic failure had grave consequences for the valley economy.

POST-SECOND WORLD WAR WEAKNESSES
IN THE REGIONAL ECONOMY

Starting in the late 1960s the Connecticut River Valley metalworkers suffered a series of devastating layoffs and plant closings as the machine-tool industry's global fortunes sank. Across Massachusetts, 12 percent of manufacturing jobs disappeared each year between 1969 and 1976. Half of Greater Springfield, Massachusetts' manufacturing facilities closed between 1950 and 1987. Machinery building and precision metalworking, as we saw, prospered in the river valley from the 1930s through the mid-1950s, long after textile and apparel cities like Holyoke, Fall River, Lawrence, and Lowell ceased their population and economic growth.[2] Now, the valley's metalworkers endured a similar fate.

Metalworking and machinery firms with 500 or more workers, plentiful in the valley after the Second World War, were hit hard. Among the firms that survived,

[1]National Machine Tool Builders Association (NMTBA), *Meeting the Japanese Challenge* (McLean, VA, 1981), 5. On the study trip were the top managers of several leading U.S. machine-tool builders, including Cross & Trecker, Giddings & Lewis, and Bridgeport Machines. Firms visited included Toyoda Machine Works, Mori Seiki, and Fujitsu Fanuc. Anthony DiFilippo, *Military Spending and Industrial Decline: A Study of the American Machine Tool Industry* (New York, 1986). National Research Council (NRC), *The US Machine Tool Industry and the Defense Industrial Base* (Washington, DC, 1983), 2.

[2]Robert Forrant, Plant Closings; U.S. Department of Commerce, *Manufacturing Censuses*. For the Holyoke story on mill ownership changes and disinvestment, see William Hartford, *Working People of Holyoke* (New Brunswick: Rutgers University Press, 1990), esp. ch. 8; employment figures in Frederick Weaver, *Economic Literacy: Basic Economics With an Attitude* (New York: Rowan & Littlefield, 2002), 7.

average employment fell from 79 to 35 workers between 1947 and 1977[3] and by 1990, 90 percent of establishments employed fewer than 20 workers.[4] The closings crippled the valley's trade-union movement, dominated since the 1930s by industrial unions of skilled and semiskilled machinists and metalworkers in large plants.[5]

To the dispassionate observer, the warning signs were apparent. Signals included the shutdowns of several Springfield manufacturers, large-scale layoffs at Westinghouse, Bosch's Mississippi move, and ownership changes among leading companies, including the American Bosch and its next-door neighbor, Van Norman Industries. The Springfield Thread Works, a 52-year-old family business, closed in July 1954. Among its 70 employees were 10 with over 40 years service. In 1958 the 75-year-old H. L. Handy provisions company fired 500 workers and exited the valley. Swift and Company had purchased it, and the closing was part of Swift's "program to close uneconomical units, improve others, consolidate operations where possible into the most modern facilities." The Fleming Foundry, a three-generation family-owned business, ceased operations in 1959, leaving 50 workers unemployed.[6]

In 1956 Future Springfield, Inc., a local business and industry trade association, published an economic blueprint for the city. They identified 12 city manufacturers employing over 1,000 people; 20 years later five remained. The original 12, all union shops, were American Bosch, Chapman Valve, Gilbert and Barker, Package Machinery, F. W. Sickles, Springfield Armory, J. Stevens Arms, U.S. Rubber, Van Norman Machine, Westinghouse, Monsanto Chemical, and Spaulding. Only Monsanto Chemical and Spaulding were open in 2003.[7] The cumulative impact of closings and layoffs created a breach in the historical continuity of the Connecticut River Valley as a world leader in precision metalworking and devastated the regional economy.[8]

---

[3] Robert Forrant, Plant Closings; U.S. Department of Commerce, *Manufacturing Censuses.* For the Holyoke story on mill ownership changes and disinvestment, see W. Hartford, *Working People of Holyoke.*

[4] United States Department of Commerce, *Manufacturing Censuses.* In Worcester, by comparison, average firm size there fell from 90 to 30 workers.

[5] Data on firm size and workforce is taken from United States Department of Commerce *Census of Manufacturers and Population Censuses* for the years under review.

[6] *SMU,* 24 July 1954, 10; *SDN,* 21 August 1958, 1; *SMU,* 5 March 1959, 13.

[7] Future Springfield, Inc., *Report* (1956) located in PVHM Business Collection series.

[8] Robert Forrant, Elyse Cann, Kathleen McGraw, *Industrial District or Industrial Decline? A Survey of Western Massachusetts Metalworking* (Springfield: Machine Action Project, 1991).

DECLINE OF A CRITICAL SUBSECTOR: "THE WORLD NO LONGER NEEDS THE U.S. MACHINE-TOOL INDUSTRY"

The machine-tool industry, a small but nonetheless essential sector of manufacturing, accounts for approximately 2 percent of manufacturing employment in developed countries. Machine tools cut or form metal, and are utilized in the manufacture of products or to make machines upon which goods are produced. Long-term collaborative relationships between final-goods producers and machinery builders generate productivity-enhancing innovations. In William Corcoran's view, "technological change within the machine tool industry translates into technological change in manufacturing processes themselves, yielding lower costs, higher quality, and new products."[9]

There are several market segments, including low-cost basic machines like the drill press, computer-controlled machines, and expensive and complex computer-controlled multiaxis machining centers.[10] Heavily capitalized firms produce customized multimillion dollar transfer lines for automobile manufacturers and machining centers for the aerospace industry. Small, typically family-owned enterprises build general-purpose machines that cost as little as $10,000-$20,000.[11]

Distinctions exist in how machines are controlled. Conventional machines are operated by a worker who places the part to be machined in a fixture and manipulates a handle to bring a cutting tool in contact with the part. In the case of a numerically controlled (NC) drill press, the machine is guided by a computer program, most often written by an engineer. The cutting tool travels into the part as instructed by the program, making it possible for the operator to run several machines. More elaborate computer numerical control (CNC) automation permits operators, parts designers, and engineers to enter the dimensions and details for

[9]William Corcoran, "The Machine Tool Industry Under Fire," in Donald Losman and Shu-Jan Liang, eds., *The Promise of American Industry: An Alternative Assessment of Problems and Prospects* (New York: Quorum 1990): 227-247, 227. For useful general histories of the industry, see Joseph Wickham Roe, *English and American Tool Builders* (New York: McGraw-Hill Publishing Co., 1926); John Glover and William Cornell, *The Development of American Industries* (New York: Prentice-Hall, Inc., 1941), esp. ch. 26, "The Machine Tool Industry," 557-76; L. T. Rolt, *A Short History of Machine Tools* (Cambridge: MIT Press, 1965); David Hounshell, *From the American System to Mass Production, 1830-1932* (Baltimore: The Johns Hopkins University Press, 1984); Max Holland, *When the Machine Stopped: A Cautionary Tale from Industrial America* (Boston: Harvard University Business School Press, 1989).

[10]See Robert Forrant, "The Global Machine Tool Industry," in Malcolm Warner, ed., *International Encyclopedia of Business and Management* (London: International Thompson Publishing, 2002): 2309-2316.

[11]Glynnis A. Trainer, "The Metalworking Machinery Industry in New England: An Analysis of Investment Behavior" (master's thesis, Massachusetts Institute of Technology, 1979), 73.

numerous highly intricate parts into a computer linked with several machines. With numerous programs stored in its memory, a CNC machine can perform highly complex work on parts of varying shapes and sizes throughout the workday with little lost manufacturing time caused by setting and resetting equipment for the various parts, diminishing the need for several skilled workers. Individual machines can also be programmed to work together to perform a series of machining operations on complex parts with very little, if any, worker handling involved.[12] Due to their productivity-enhancing capabilities and versatility, NC and CNC machines have replaced many conventional machines on factory floors. For example, in 1976, the share of CNC grinding machines sold among all grinding machines was 1 percent in the major tool-producing countries. By 1984 sales of such machines amounted to 11 percent of market share and climbed to over 60 percent of market share by 2000. The U.S. machine-tool industry failed to capture a healthy share of the burgeoning market for computer-controlled machines, and this contributed to the collapse of several venerable Connecticut River Valley tool builders. Why this took place is discussed later on in this chapter.

Adding to the industry's difficulties, merger waves in the late 1960s, the mid-1980s, and the late 1990s "resulted in the acquisition of machine tool firms by large, diversified companies that had not previously been in the machine tool business." For example, Bendix acquired the Warner & Swasey Company in 1983 and transferred most of Warner & Swasey's production to the Japanese company Murata. When machine-tool sales soared, the new owners invested the profits in other businesses, but during downturns, the assets of their machine-tool divisions were sold off to generate cash, thus weakening the tool builder when business returned.[13] A detailed analysis of employment and establishment change by ownership for the periods 1969 to 1972, 1972 to 1974, and 1974 to 1976 concluded, "In every period under consideration, non-independent firms experienced greater mortality (closings) than did the independent firms."[14] This pattern of acquisition and consolidation in the Connecticut River Valley resulted in many long-established firms losing their financial independence. As the U.S. industry restructured, thousands of highly skilled workers lost their jobs in the Northeast and Midwest. Between 1975 and 1995 total industry employment declined from 88,000 to 57,000, while the number of production workers fell to 35,700 from 57,400 (Table 6.1).

[12] R. Forrant, "The Global Machine Tool Industry"; U.S. Congress, House Subcommittee on Special Investigations of Small Business Problems, *Problems of the Tool and Die Industry and Associated Problems of Manufacturers and Distributors of Machine Tools,* 89th Cong., 2nd session, July 26 and 27, 1966.

[13] M. Holland, *When the Machine Stopped,* p. 84. NRC, *The U.S. Machine Tool Industry,* 44.

[14] NRC, *The U.S. Machine Tool Industry,* 44; G. Trainer, "The Metalworking Machinery Industry in New England," 163.

Table 6.1. U.S. Machine-Tool Employment
in Thousands, 1979-1995[15]

Year	Total employment	Production workers
1975	88.0	57.4
1977	88.5	57.4
1979	104.3	68.9
1981	104.4	67.3
1983	69.1	39.8
1985	73.0	45.7
1987	63.4	39.9
1989	67.3	43.6
1991	59.5	36.9
1993	51.4	31.4
1995	57.0	35.7

In 1998, of the world's top 200 machine-tool firms by sales, 56 operated in Italy, 49 in Germany, and 25 in the United States., while for most of the 1990s the 4 largest builders were Japanese owned. For 1999 Japan ($7.7 billion) and Germany ($7.5 billion) were the world's top producers, accounting for close to half the world's output (Tables 6.2 and 6.3). Its machine-tool trade surplus in 1999 was $4.9 billion, compared with Germany's $1.6 billion. By comparison, in 1999 the United States incurred the world's largest machine-tool trade deficit, $2.8 billion. Contributing to Japan's strength, Fujitsu Automatic Numerical Controls (FANUC) was the world's largest producer of computer control systems, the brains of advanced machine tools.[16]

[15] Data from Association for Manufacturing Technology, *Economic Handbook of the Machine Tool Industry* (McLean, VA, 1996). For comparison purposes, between 1980 and 1995 Germany lost 31 percent of total employment (99,000 to 68,000); Japan lost 16 percent of total employment (33,767 to 28,354); the U.S. lost 35 percent of jobs. Figures in Robert Forrant, "The Global Machine Tool Industry."

[16] Association for Manufacturing Technology, *The Economic Handbook of the Machine Tool Industry* (McLean, VA, 1995, 1999); M. Tsuji, M. Ishikawa, and M. Ishikawa, *Technology Transfer and Management in East Asian Machine Tool Industries* (Osaka, 1996, esp. 31-35).

Table 6.2. Ten Largest Machine-Tool Builders in
1997 by Sales in Millions $U.S.[17]

Company	Country	Sales
Yamazaki Mazak	Japan	1253.0
Amada	Japan	1214.3
FANUC	Japan	1007.4
Thyssen Maschinenbau	Germany	922.3
Okuma Machinery Works	Japan	873.5
Fuji Machine	Japan	815.4
UNOVA, Inc.	United States	789.8
Trumpf Group	Germany	778.2
Mori Seki	Japan	740.7
Toyoda Machine Works	Japan	650.9

Table 6.3. Global Market Share by Percent among
the Top Three Producers[18]

	1964	1970	1975	1980	1985	1990	1996	1999
United States	25.1	18.5	17.3	18.1	12.6	6.7	12.6	12.8
Japan	6.4	14.2	7.8	14.4	24.8	23.2	23.6	23.0
Germany	15.9	18.9	17.6	17.8	14.8	18.9	20.1	21.0

The next section describes the post-war downward trajectory of three firms,
Van Norman Company, Jones & Lamson, and Bryant Grinding. Their stories
typify what happened among river-valley tool builders and by implication their
various metalworking partners.

STUDIES IN REGIONAL DECLINE

Van Norman

Hamilton, Ontario, brothers Charles E. and Fred D. Van Norman founded
the Waltham Watch Tool Company in Watertown, Massachusetts, in 1888.

[17] Data from Association For Manufacturing Technology, *1997 Machine Tool Scorecard,*
(McLean, VA, 1998).
[18] Data from Association For Manufacturing Technology, *Economic Handbook of the
Machine Tool Industry* (McLean, VA, 1996, 1999).

Springfield's Board of Trade recruited the company as part of its larger effort to attract more skill-based firms to the region. It was incorporated as the Van Norman Machine Tool Company in 1890, and at start-up, 25 workers produced bench lathes, molding dies, and engravers' equipment. By 1910 its engineers had designed the first milling machines with adjustable cutter heads and the first cutter grinders. Customers purchased these machines in Greater Springfield and in the Midwest's growing auto industry.

Van Norman earned its national reputation during the First World War, when it designed and built machines that produced industrial ball bearings. Until then, ball bearings had been largely imported from Germany, thus U.S. war production would have been crippled without this engineering feat. The company grew in the interwar years, building specialized equipment for the automotive industry and labor-saving, multipurpose machines for the global market. Van Norman advertised its machines in the *American Machinist*, noting that the machines performed "the work of many single-purpose machines," and cut operator idle time as much as 50 percent "because there is no waiting for specific machines," and no "continual changing of the workpiece."[19]

Turning a handsome profit, in the early 1950s Van Norman purchased several other Massachusetts machine-tool firms to gain complementary product lines. Enlarged in this way, the company caught the attention of New York industrialist Herbert Segal, and in 1956 he acquired a 35 percent controlling interest in company stock from the original owners' descendants. Springfield-area directors were replaced, and the company's headquarters was moved to New York City, where the offices of Segal's other holdings were located. Van Norman Machine Tools was now one of eight divisions in Van Norman Industries (VNI), a conglomerate with factories in California, Michigan, New Hampshire, Ohio, and Pennsylvania, and $50 million in annual sales.[20]

When he purchased Van Norman, Segal envisioned it becoming the centerpiece of what he referred to as the "General Motors of the machine tool industry." Plans for the construction of a Springfield factory to house VNI's entire machine-tool division were announced March 1957. But by late spring 1957 the national economy slumped and machine-tool orders fell as manufacturers curtailed their equipment purchases. Construction halted, 100 Van Norman workers lost their jobs, and the remainder of the workforce was employed only 32 hours a week. At year's end sales were $47 million, down from $49.8 million the previous year. With corporatewide profits a meager $722,611, the machine-tool division stagnated, and the new plant was abandoned.

[19] *American Machinist*, 90, 31 January 1946, 12.
[20] Larry Gormally, "Van Norman: A Jewel of a Company," *Springfield Journal*, 15, no. 14 (1990): 4-5; Amy Glasmeier, *Manufacturing Time: Global Competition in the Watch Industry, 1795-2000* (New York: Guilford, 2000), esp. ch. 3; *SMU*, 1 March 1957, 1, 28; *SMU*, 30 March 1957, 1.

At the start of 1958, a group of Chicago investors provided VNI with a much-needed cash infusion by purchasing 100,000 company shares. The Chicago group assumed three seats on the 15-person Board of Directors and led cost-cutting efforts: Segal's compensation was reduced 10 percent; corporate officers and supervisors were forced to absorb 5 percent pay cuts; and annual fees paid to corporate directors were cut in half to $2,000.[21] More layoffs and workweek reductions followed, and rumors circulated that VNI was going to discontinue production in the city. Demise seemed imminent when in November 1958 the 64-year-old Segal announced his retirement. When he left, only 350 workers labored in the machine-tool division, an astonishing drop from the 1,500 workers in place in 1956 when he took over.

Despite mounting losses, hope was kindled when Charles Meyers, the president of the Morse Twist Drill and Machine Company, a cutting tool division of VNI, replaced Segal. When the economy accelerated at the end of 1960, Meyers invested in the development of several new machines, including an NC grinder; an NC machine for miniature ball bearing manufacture for the missile, aircraft, and medical instruments industries; and a multiaxis drilling machine.[22] These machines were a part of Meyers' Integrated Design Program, whereby VNI customers were surveyed regarding their future manufacturing requirements. However, after a member of the Chicago group became vice president for finance, an internal struggle for the corporation's still meager profits resulted in the termination of the Integrated Design Program before its long-term potential for providing the firm with an expanded customer base was analyzed. Without the promise of new work, by the end of 1963 half of the factory's 500 workers were on a 35-hour week, and every worker feared for his future.[23]

VNI merged with the Universal American Corporation in 1962, and five years later it was acquired by the Gulf & Western Corporation. Under Gulf & Western, employment skidded under 300, the lowest level in over 30 years. The factory limped into the 1970s, when in the fourth ownership change in 20 years, it became an appendage of Minnesota-based Winona Tool Manufacturing. It soon became apparent that Winona had purchased the plant simply for its globally-recognized reputation, not for its skills and production capacity, and the factory remained open only four more years. A skeleton crew of workers expended their last days performing a task that must have rankled; they affixed

---

[21] *SMU*, 4 December 1957, 6; 2 February 1958, 1.

[22] *SMU*, 26 April 1958, 13; 22 July 1958, 1; 18 August 1958, 1; 13 November 1958, 1.

[23] *SMU*, 7 April 1960, 1; 5 May 1960, 16; 18 June 1960, 11; 10 December 1960, 33; 3 August 1961, 2; 14 November 1961, 7. The machine cut the groove in the ballbearing's inner ring to tolerances of 50 millionths of an inch and could be either manually or power fed.

the Van Norman nameplate on Italian machine tools being imported by Winona for North American distribution.[24]

Jones & Lamson

Springfield, Vermont, and surrounding communities "thrived through the 19th century by supplying machines to most major industries," from guns and bicycles to steelworks, railroads, and automobiles. The area, formed by the joining of the Black River and the Connecticut River, gained the nickname "Precision Valley" for the exacting tolerances of the machines it produced and the work that customers generated using them.[25] In 1920, fifty firms and 4,000 workers in central Vermont crafted machine tools, fixtures, and specialized parts for final-goods producers around the world. At the conclusion of the Second World War, 8,000 machinists plied their craft in central Vermont.

The "big three" machine tool firms—Jones & Lamson, Fellows Gear Shaper, and Bryant Grinder—employed 817, 530, and 229 workers respectively in 1939; in 1941 an intense wartime production schedule hiked employment to 2,220 at J&L, 1,584 at Fellows, and 861 at Bryant. From 1941 to 1945, they shipped over 12,000 machines. Without an increase in worker housing, many machinists spent the harsh Vermont winters living in canvas tents pitched on relatively flat land near the railroad lines that hauled new machine tools to aircraft and tank factories across the United States.[26]

Started in Windsor in 1824 as the Connecticut River Company, and after several permutations, the custom gun shop Robbins and Lawrence was formed in 1849. Open under that name until 1856, the company benefited from lucrative federal contracts for rifles before and during the Civil War. To complete these contracts on time, the company's skilled mechanics devised their own production machinery, and over time machine-making became the company's core business. Reincorporated in 1879 as the Jones & Lamson Machine Company, the firm relocated to Springfield, Vermont, in 1888. There the company produced the country's first flat-turret lathes. Other innovative products followed, including an optical comparator in 1919 and a thread-grinding machine in 1920. J&L's

---

[24] Van Norman's demise is similar to that of New Hampshire-based Burgmaster. According to Max Holland, because profits were high and the hold on the domestic market seemed secure, in the 1960s tool builders were enticing to conglomerates like Gulf & Western and Textron. He estimates that two-thirds of the industry was negatively affected by "A distant managerial capitalism. . . ." M. Holland, *When the Machine Stopped,* 266.

[25] Norman Boucher, "A Natural History of the Connecticut Valley Metal Trade," *Regional Review* (Winter 1994): 6-12, 11. For a history through the 1950s of the Springfield Vermont machine tool industry, Wayne Broehl, *Precision Valley: The Machine Tool Companies of Springfield Vermont* (Englewood Cliff, NJ: Prentice-Hall, 1959).

[26] Information on J&L gathered during a May 2001 interview in Springfield, Vermont, with Faye Kingsbury, who retired from the company in the 1970s after working there for over 40 years, first as an apprentice machinist. J. Roe, *English and American Tool Builders,* ch. XV.

workforce peaked at slightly over 3,000 in late 1944, with workers on grueling 12-hour shifts for six days a week.

Soon after the Second World War, J&L's founding families relinquished day-to-day control of the company, and it was acquired outright by Textron in the late 1960s. At the time Textron also purchased Connecticut-based Bridgeport Machine and Bryant Grinding, J&L's near neighbor. From the late 1960s to the early 1980s, conglomerates like Textron purchased several machine-tool companies. In paroxysms of hubris, the managers of these conglomerates felt that their central engineering staffs and corporate level R&D could overcome what they felt were the industry's weaknesses.

Textron sold J & L in 1984 to a financial holding group. Prior to the sale, production mangers with well over 100 years of collective machine-building experience were dismissed, replaced by Textron's management team. While the new team may have known how to manufacture something, then J&L quality manager Faye Kingsbury recalled that it was not machine tools.[27] Workers "laughed at their new managers and wondered what the hell they were trying to do," he recalled. Textron's top management located their office in a nonmachine-tool plant over 125 miles away in Connecticut. For Jim Halvorsen, a long-time manager at nearby Bryant, "having no strong local operations manager contributed mightily to product line decline at J&L in the 1970s." Unable to boost sales, in 1986 J&L filed for bankruptcy protection. The Goldman Industrial Group purchased it in 1988 and filed for its own bankruptcy protection in 2002. In describing Textron's takeover strategies, industry historian Arthur Alexander concluded that profits from its machine-tool division were regularly diverted to other business activities rather than to enhance the machine-tool business. "Over a decade-long continuation of this policy, these two Textron divisions lacked new lines of competitive products, especially in numerical control."[28]

Ironically, J&L brought out a basic low-cost computer-controlled lathe in the late 1960s, and its order book quickly filled up. However, scant investments were made in figuring out how this burgeoning demand could be satisfied. Assuming that they controlled the U.S. domestic market, J&L informed far too many potential buyers to expect a one-year wait for machines. Kingsbury felt

---

[27] Michael Gabriele, "Goldman, building a machine tool empire," *Metalworking News,* 15 August 1988, 1; Arthur J. Alexander, "Adaptation to Change in the U.S. Machine Tool Industry," in Hong W. Tan and Haruo Shimada Kingsbury, eds., *Troubled Industries in the United States and Japan* (New York: Palgrave, 1994): 321-367, 333; interview with Faye Kingsbury; interview with Jim Halvorsen in June 2001 at the American Precision Museum in Windsor, Vermont. Halvorsen was a manager at the Bryant Grinding Company for much of the 1970s and early 1980s. Little research has been done on the decline of Vermont firms. The American Precision Museum in Windsor, Vermont, has many records from these companies. In mid-2001 production at J&L, Bryant, and Fellows Gear Shaper—all now owned by the Goldman Group— was consolidated in one wing of the Bryant factory.

[28] A. Alexander, "Adaptation to Change in the U.S. Machine Tool Industry," 333.

that this cavalier attitude toward customers was understandable in the 1950s and early 1960s, when even conventional lathes built in Japan suffered numerous design and mechanical flaws. However, at a 1971 international tool show in Los Angeles, Kingsbury viewed Japanese lathes that were "foolproof for accuracy," were cheaper than J&L's lathes, and most importantly, could be delivered on time.[29]

Max Holland uncovered a similar situation at New Hampshire-based Burgmaster. When the company introduced its first series of NC lathes in 1964, orders doubled to $16.4 million for the machines in one year, yet shipments increased only 18 percent. By January 1966 Burgmaster had a $30 million backlog for its lathes, yet it was shipping $900,000 worth of machines monthly.[30] Japanese firms, eager to fill the vacuum created by the failures of companies like J&L and Burgmaster, produced basic lathes and NC lathes in sufficient quantity to meet U.S. customer demand by the early 1970s.

During a 2001 interview, a still incredulous Halvorsen described one firm that proudly proclaimed that it built its various lathes on a "different size a month" schedule. A customer placing an order in February for the type of machine produced during January politely was informed that a one-year wait was likely for the desired machine to be built again. Burgmaster and J&L were abandoned by hundreds of disgruntled customers because of the even more profound abandonment of both companies by their corporate owners' refusal to invest in the expanded manufacturing capacity and shop-floor improvements needed to grow market share and, at the very least, preserve existing jobs.[31]

Bryant Grinding

Bryant Grinding opened its doors in the early 1900s after William Bryant, who had studied engineering at the University of Vermont, received a patent for a revolutionary grinding machine that became the company's core business. The machine ground the internal and outer surfaces of a part without it having to be repositioned or placed in a second machine. This saved precious set-up time, and equally important, because the part was located just once in the machine, the finished part's quality improved a great deal. Like J&L, Bryant prospered during the Second World War.

For a time, Bryant dodged the problems attendant with buy-outs already vexing its Vermont neighbor. For example, when in 1958 it became a subsidiary of the diversified machine-tool manufacturer Ex-Cell-O, local management remained. However, Textron's purchase disrupted Bryant's management

---

[29] Faye Kingsbury interview, June 2001.

[30] M. Holland, *When the Machine Stopped;* Artemis March, *The U.S. Machine Tool Industry and its Foreign Competitors* (Cambridge, MA: MIT Press, 1990).

[31] James Halvorsen interview, June 2001; W. Broehl, *Precision Valley*, 184-189.

structure, and the company began to drift. Orders dropped in the early 1980s as European countries protected their domestic markets. Furthermore, buoyed by their success in several basic machine-tool markets, Japanese firms now produced computer-controlled grinding machines in a direct challenge for Bryant's lucrative U.S. car-builders market. According to Halvorsen, "when auto production went global we lost important engineering relationships with our customers and now foreign proximity built some business for European competitors." Bryant's executives, including Halvorsen, felt that it would take at least 10 years for Japanese companies to build computer-controlled machines equal to Bryant's. However, just as Faye Kingsbury's assumptions were proven false, Halvorsen was chastened when he viewed an exhibit of extremely well-built Japanese NC grinding machines at a 1983 international tool show in Hanover, Germany. He recalled thinking "the world no longer needs the U.S. machine tool industry."[32]

Bryant preserved a semblance of its markets by providing excellent customer service. Technicians accompanied all new machines to set them up and guarantee performance on their customers' shop floors. But "when the financial world fully took control of the manufacturing world in the mid-1980s this customer-builder link was deemed too costly by Textron's accountants," according to Halvorsen. Across the country, Bryant's field technicians and engineers were fired and after-sales customer service scaled back. After alienating its once-secure customer base, Bryant's market for high-end grinders dwindled. A series of debilitating mergers, acquisitions, and flirtations with bankruptcy culminated in the company's 1990 purchase by The Goldman Industrial Group, a financial holding company.[33]

For most of the 1990s, the United Electrical, Radio & Machine Workers union, which represented workers in the Vermont plants purchased by Goldman, charged that the holding company was not reinvesting in the companies. In 1990 and again in 2000, workers protested that no new machinery had been bought since Goldman took over. During a bitter round of contract negotiations in 2000, Goldman's negotiators admitted that this was true. Goldman's continued ownership, unionists charged, would result in the slow destruction of the Vermont machine-tool industry. At the start of 2001, fewer than 400 workers were

---

[32] Kingsbury interview, June 2001. During other research efforts I interviewed the owners of close to 100 tool and die and precision metalworking firms in western Massachusetts, most of which employ fewer than 50 workers. There was a common response when I discussed with them the fact that a goodly number of their machine tools were foreign made, mostly from Japan: "We needed the equipment right away and we needed decent service. U.S firms could promise neither of these things."

[33] J. Halvorsen and F. Kingsbury interviews, May 2001. Gerry Khermouch, "Vermont USA shifts focus, turns profit," *Metalworking News,* 3 September 1990, 6; "Bridgeport, Conn., Machines Firm, Parent Seek Bankruptcy Protection," *The Connecticut Post,* 16 February 2002, 9.

employed in the three Vermont firms. In February 2002 Goldman filed for bankruptcy in U.S. Bankruptcy Court, and machinery production ceased in central Vermont after 170 years. Goldman owed its employee pension fund nearly $8 million and had failed to make its required payments into the plan, thus prompting the federal Pension Benefit Guarantee Board to place liens on the Goldman-owned factories. Bankruptcy filing and production cessation followed.[34]

"FROM THE ROOF, INSTEAD OF THE FOUNDATION": NUMERICAL CONTROL IN THE UNITED STATES AND JAPAN

Significant differences existed in the development of NC technologies in Japan and the United States, and these differences help to clarify why the U.S. industry lost so much market share in the 1970s and 1980s. With their government's technical and financial support, Japanese firms collaborated in the development of the low-cost basic NC machinery. A single company, FANUC, focused on the development of machinery controls and software to establish an industrywide standard. These machines provided Japanese builders with a solid entry point into the U.S. market.[35] On the other hand, a dozen U.S. builders constructed expensive, highly specialized machines, mainly for defense contractors, usually with their own proprietary controls. No effort to establish an industrywide standard for controls gained favor in the United States, and very quickly FANUC's "controls became the de facto world standard, with an estimated 70 percent of the global market, providing Japanese machine-tool makers with a substantial first-mover advantage."[36]

U.S. industry leaders were cognizant of ongoing efforts in Japan to develop NC equipment. In 1959 the trade publication *American Machinist* dutifully reported that firms there were "moving into the international arena big time." However, it pejoratively concluded that Japanese machinery was nondescript and appealed simply to "Southeast Asian and other industrially backward nations." *American Machinist* also noted that Japan's Ministry of International Trade and Industry championed research on a numerically controlled jig

[34] *UE News*, "Local 218 Keeps Jobs in Springfield, Vermont," *UE News archives*, www.ranknfile~ue.org/uen; Greg Gatlin, "Machine tool firms file for Chapter 11," *Boston Herald*, 20 February 2002, 31.

[35] A. Wagoner, *The U.S. Machine Tool Industry*, 327; Kenkichiro Koizumi, "In Search of Wakon: The Cultural Dynamics of the Rise of Manufacturing Technology in Postwar Japan," *Technology and Culture*, 43 (2002): 29-49.

[36] CTI, *The Decline of the U.S. Machine Tool Industry*, 22; Anderson Ashburn, "The Machine Tool Industry: The Crumbling Foundation," in D. Hicks, ed., *Is New Technology Enough? Making and Remaking U.S. Basic Industries* (Washington, DC: American Enterprise Institute for Public Policy Research, 1990): 19-85. 80-81. In 1978, 40 percent of machine tools in use in the United States were over 20 years old, in Japan the figure was 18 percent.

borer suitable for use in small shops. However, there is no evidence that the industry's leaders ever fully grasped the long-term market threat posed by these activities.[37]

In the United States, NC machine-tool research and development became convoluted, because too many firms were involved in a thoroughly uncoordinated way, the all-important controls were developed without uniform standards, and the machine tools and the controls were too often built to engage in exotic and difficult tasks with minimal application to the broader customer base. This was a far cry from the Connecticut River Valley's 19th-century collaborative culture. According to Anderson Ashburn, "A common expression among people involved in the early years of NC was that it had developed from the roof instead of the foundation." The machines built in the United States were, according to Max Holland, "far more sophisticated than anything a civilian manufacturer might need or be willing to pay for."[38]

In sharp relief to the helter-skelter approach in the United States, controls were built in Japan by FANUC in an "Armory-like" collaborative endeavor with tool builders, and the controls became the globally recognized standard. While FANUC developed machine controls and software, tool builders worked on machinery designs and improved manufacturing techniques to meet antici-pated customer demand. In other words, work commenced at the foundation, and when organizational learning increased, more complex designs were considered.

Japan's Ministry of International Trade and Industry (MITI) and the Japan Machine Tool Builders' Association (JMTBA) formulated a comprehensive strategy to rebuild the country's manufacturing base. The JMTBA was formed in 1952 by 40 of the country's largest builders. It acted as their members' voice with the government and facilitated the exchange of technical information between firms.[39] Two national laws, the *Gaishi-ho* (Foreign Capital Law, 1950), and the *Kikaikogyo Rinji Sochio-ho* (Temporary Measures for the Development of the Machinery Industry Law, 1956) helped machine-tool builders gain access to capital and foreign technology. MITI brokered 29 licensing agreements with foreign machine makers between 1961 and 1964, while it discouraged direct foreign investment in Japanese machine-tool firms. Licensing helped U.S. firms gain limited and only temporary entry into Japan.[40] Machinery exports to Japan fell 50 percent in 1963 and another 50 percent in 1965; by comparison,

[37] *American Machinist,* 1 June 1959, 38.

[38] A. Ashburn, "The Machine Tool Industry," 48; M. Holland, *When the Machine Stopped,* 34-35.

[39] M. Tsuji, M. Ishikawa, and M. Ishikawa, *Technology Transfer and Management in East Asian Machine Tool Industries.*

[40] Toshiaki Chokki, "A History of the Machine Tool Industry in Japan," in M. Fransman, ed., *Machinery and Economic Development* (New York, St. Martin's, 1986): 124-152.

Japan's exports to the United States skyrocketed from $2.4 million in 1964 to $26.2 million in 1967, and they climbed steadily thereafter. In the early 1970s MITI advocated that 50 percent of Japan's machine-tool output should be NC equipment, and builders were encouraged to design NC machine tools that would be useful to the typical small Japanese manufacturer becoming increasingly interested in automation.

These efforts were on display at the 1970 International Machine Tool Convention in Osaka, Japan. There, a system of 28 linked machine tools was guided by FANUC controls. Four years later in *World Manufacturing*, Tokyo Bureau chief Michael Mealey reported that the entire production process at FANUC's Hino factory was under computer control. "Computers keep track of orders, parts inventory, parts purchase, production schedules, and parts testing," he wrote.[41] In 1975 FANUC opened a service center in the United States and the rout of U.S. builders was on. By the mid-1980s FANUC dominated the control market worldwide, and Siemens, General Electric, and General Motors were forced to enter joint ventures with FANUC to maintain even a small presence in the controls market.[42]

THE VALLEY GRINDS DOWN

A plentiful pool of skilled machinists and engineers, a well-practiced reciprocal relationship among machine-tool builders and their customers, and the presence of hundreds of tool-and-die shops enhanced the valley's innovative capabilities and its competitiveness for nearly 200 years. For 20 years after the Second World War, the country's preeminence in machine-tool design and manufacture, coupled with the productivity advantages that accrued to goods producers that utilized the machines, enabled tool builders and goods producers to prosper. Global prominence was aided by the fact that there was only minimal foreign competition for domestic machine-tool sales to the automobile, aircraft, and other durable-goods sectors. In such a virtuous circle of profitability, U.S. builders employed thousands of well-paid machinists, many of them belonging to trade unions. But the good times did not last.

Tool builders and final-goods producers went through a tortuous decline in the 1970s and 1980s, punctuated with plant closings and the loss of thousands of jobs. The valley's long-standing reputation as a center for innovation now badly tarnished, the ACCURACY sign atop the Pratt & Whitney Machine Tool building became a distant memory. This 1945 description of the Pratt workforce, "It is not uncommon at Pratt & Whitney for succeeding generations of families to

---

[41] Michael Mealey, "NC and Computers Build NC," *World Manufacturing*, November 1974, 31-34.
[42] Robert S. Eckley, *Global Competition in Capital Goods: An American Perspective* (New York: Quorum Books, 1991), 123.

work here—grandfather, father, son—each passing his skill and knowledge to the next in true New England fashion," was no longer applicable.[43] How far was the fall? In 1954 Connecticut had 119,000 workers in skilled metalworking occupations; by the early 1970s there were 102,000 people so employed; and in 1982 approximately 95,000. Massachusetts factories employed 241,816 such workers in 1954 and 150,000 in 1982. The greatest collapse occurred in central Vermont, where about 1,000 machinists were employed in the early 1980s, down from over 10,000 in 1947.

Up and down the river valley, research and development was constricted in the small firms, and when conglomerates subsumed larger tool builders, out-of-touch top management halted investments in their machine-tool divisions.[44] In his 1966 history of the machine-tool industry, Harless Wagoner offered a prescient critique of the industry's lack of ongoing investments, explaining how this hurt national productivity.

> The machine tool industry or, at least, particular firms in the industry deserve full credit for having greatly improved machine tool capacity and performance on a wide range of machining problems. This is true even though it is believed that greater technical progress could have been made had the industry devoted greater effort to research and development and had been given greater support in these efforts by machine tool users, and the federal government. It also appears, however, that as machine tool builders became more preoccupied with business problems, cost accounting, statistics, controlling price competition, profit ratios, reserves, etc., they devoted less attention to purely technical problems.[45]

Echoing Wagoner, Ashburn concluded that since about 1970 the management of most machine-tool companies shifted into the hands of people with financial rather than technical backgrounds.[46] Overall, the industry failed to invest enough in itself, relying instead on Department of Defense prime contracts and the manufacturers of computers and controllers to spur innovation. Even when innovations took place, such as Van Norman's customer-builder design program

[43] Pratt & Whitney Tool Catalog, 1945, located in the catalog collection at the American Precision Museum, Windsor, Vermont.
[44] For a discussion of another machine-tool region, with strong parallels to events in the Connecticut River Valley, see Charles Craypo, "The Deindustrialization of a Factory Town: Plant Closings and Phasedowns in South Bend, Indiana, 1954-1983," in Donald Kennedy, ed., *Labor and Reindustrialization: Workers and Corporate Change* (University Park, PA: The Pennsylvania State University, 1984): 27-67. All data from the U.S. Department of Commerce, *Manufacturing Census.* The census is published by the U.S. Government Printing Office and is carried out at five-year intervals. There are separate national and state reports. Contained in the state reports, is county-level and in some cases city-level data on manufacturing activity.
[45] H. Wagoner, *The US Machine Tool Industry,* 327.
[46] A. Ashburn, "The Machine Tool Industry," 80; NRC, *The US Machine Tool Industry and the Defense Industrial Base,* 14-15.

or J&L's NC lathe, efforts were short-circuited by the financial constraints of conglomerate ownership. Ashburn, citing a 1985 study by the Technical Change Centre of London, summarizes this failure:

> . . . both European and U.S. firms seemed to view investment in improving productivity as an exercise in short-run cost reduction for new products. In contrast, the Japanese firms viewed manufacturing engineering in a much more fundamental way, considering such investment as an important element in product design and development and a major long-run source of international competitiveness.[47]

According to Kingsbury and Halvorsen, even with the domestic market shrinking, U.S. builders eschewed exports. The failure to market globally during these years was a major problem because the primary locus of consumption had moved from the United States to Europe and the Pacific Rim.[48] Into the 1980s U.S. builders did not sell large numbers of computer-controlled machines in the domestic or foreign market.[49] The National Research Council determined that

> The traditional practice of order backlog management, which served U.S. machine tool builders well for several decades, was based on an implicit assumption that potential foreign competitors did not have the resources to take advantage of wide swings in the U.S. tool market. Whether this assumption was ever valid, it certainly was not so by the late 1970s. By that time many foreign firms had the resources to offer fast delivery of quality machines to U.S. customers who did not wish to wait for backlogs to be worked down by their domestic suppliers.[50]

Japan's NC design-and-build path established a domestic market, which became the springboard for global success. Between 1970 and 1974, small-to-medium-size firms made up from one-third to one-half the market for NC machine tools in Japan.[51] Computer-controlled machine tools composed 9 percent of unit output in Japan and less than 2 percent in the United States in 1979; output figures were 42 percent and 7 percent respectively in 1991. The adjusted market values of all NC machines shipped by U.S. builders in 1991 sank below

[47] NRC, *The US Machine Tool Industry,* 53.
[48] CTI, *The Decline of the U.S. Machine-Tool Industry,* 65; Artemis March, *The US Machine Tool Industry,* 12, 106-107. Such disregard for exports dated back to the early 20th century.
[49] Wagoner, *The United States Machine Tool Industry,* 227; Department of Commerce, *Federal Manufacturing Census 1987* (Washington, DC: GPO, 1990).
[50] NRC, *The U.S. Machine Tool Industry and the Defense Industrial Base.*
[51] William Corcoran, "The Machine Tool Industry Under Fire," 239.

1982 levels, even as over the years domestic demand soared to $2.2 billion in 1991 from $1.25 billion in 1983.[52]

Leading U.S. builders focused their postwar research and development efforts on Pentagon-size problems, lured by large payoffs and lucrative cost-plus contracts. In one classic case, the government ordered the manufacture of 11 four-spindle, five-axis machines at a cost of $1 million each, when an existing four-axis machine costing $150,000 was already available. This insistence on customized machines raised design-and-build costs without affecting performance, and it deterred firms from designing with applications for their nondefense customers.[53]

Japan's market developments were augmented with training that promoted maximum shop-floor participation from machinists, something Charles Perelle and his successors at the Bosch discouraged. While in Japan, U.S. builders learned that machinists' training in shop-floor participation bolstered their rival's competitiveness. Investments in state-of-the-art technology and the integration of shop-floor workers into the process of NC technology development provided the foundation for Japan's success. The travelers noted,

> Keeping their workplaces and machines in good order is a responsibility assigned to the operators themselves, along with maintaining output, helping fellow-workers and assuring that every part produced meets or exceeds quality standards . . . each worker is trained to correct the minor problems that often arise in the course of the day, to conduct regular preventive maintenance to monitor and adjust equipment, and to search continually for ways to eliminate potential disruptions and improve efficiency.[54]

By comparison, the Bosch, Van Norman, J&L, Bryant, and Burgmaster stories demonstrate how conglomerate ownership eroded shop-floor skills and managerial talent. J & L lost its on-site operations manager after its purchase by Textron. Houdaille's acquisition of Burgmaster transformed it from a plant predicated on knowledge and ability to one that rested on the corporate way of doing things. Burgmaster's machinists and engineers were uninvolved in reorganization efforts and numerous failed shop-floor reorganization campaigns followed.

A critical component of Japan's success—one seen by the touring U.S. machine-tool builders—was the integration of skills throughout the firm, from

---

[52] Using Manufacturing Census data and reports from the NMTBA, Ashburn determined that in the mid-1980s all types of NC were accounting for almost half the U.S. consumption of machine tools and more than 60 percent of the NC machines were being imported. Ashburn, "The Machine Tool Industry," 1990.

[53] According to the National Research Council, custom-design requests diverted scarce engineering and management time to the construction of machine tools that "will not be useful to other machine tool customers" (NRC, *The U.S. Machine Tool Industry,* 67).

[54] NMTBA, *Meeting the Japanese Challenge.*

managers to shop-floor production workers. In contrast, "U.S. companies tended to use their managerial organizations to develop and utilize technologies that would enable them to dispense with shop-floor skills so that 'hourly' production workers could not exercise control over the conditions of work and pay."[55] The Rand Corporation concluded that U.S. competitors utilized their factories "as test beds for the latest tools, relying on workers to come up with new incremental improvements in products or the process of making them. This includes not only engineers, but production workers as well."[56] Meanwhile, U.S. firms terminated apprenticeship programs, partially in response to the cyclical nature of the business; if managers were going to survive the industry's vagaries through massive layoffs, why invest in the workforce?

Skill and historical production knowledge became expendable, shearing innovation's underpinnings. Between 1982 and 1987, under the weight of heightened global competition, a lack of consistent machinery purchases from the U.S. Big Three automobile producers (themselves in sharp decline), a drop in defense procurement, and the general malaise in the manufacturing economy, 600 of 900 U.S. tool builders with fewer than 20 employees closed. Of the approximately 650 builders left, only 30 employed more than 250 people; 450 employed fewer than 50 people.[57] In the end, Springfield, Massachusetts, contained a number of aging, empty, multistory factories, which were no match for the new, one-story facilities being constructed across the South and by global competitors.

Ironically, Japan's progression to world leadership was strikingly reminiscent of early developments in the Connecticut River Valley. In Japan, government agencies played the facilitating role of the Springfield Armory in the development and diffusion of new technology to cooperative networks of developers, producers, and users of machine tools. This was supported by high levels of investments in worker training and work systems, which reflected a high regard for workers' technical expertise and knowledge and maximized shop-floor participation in product and process innovation and improvement. The "fools gold" of defense spending during the Korean War rearmament boom and the Vietnam War allowed firms and workers to ignore their internal and external problems; but this was hardly enough to stimulate sustainable growth or fend off the series of crushing plant closings in the 1970s and 1980s. The full

[55] NMTBA, *Meeting the Japanese Challenge,* 13; William Lazonick and Mary O'Sullivan, "Maximizing Shareholder Value: A New Ideology for Corporate Governance," in W. Lazonick and M. O'Sullivan, eds., *Corporate Governance and Sustainable Prosperity,* (New York, Palgrave, 2002): 11-36, 13.

[56] Critical Technologies Institute, *The Decline of the U.S. Machine Tool Industry* (Rand Corporation, 1994), 49.

[57] Robert Forrant, "Good Jobs and the Cutting Edge," in W. Lazonick and M. O'Sullivan, eds., *Corporate Governance and Sustainable Prosperity* (New York, Palgrave, 2002): 78-103.

implications of the collapse were realized in 2004 when Springfield, poised on the brink of insolvency, came under a state-appointed finance control board. Unable to pay its bills, the city's spending decisions shifted into the hands of individuals whose only interest was to balance the city's books. Municipal workers lost their jobs, the city's unions were forced into lengthy and acrimonious contract talks, and essential services were eliminated. But, before we examine Springfield's plight, one more trip is necessary to look at how the ups and downs in the machine-tool and metalworking industries affected Pratt & Whitney aircraft workers in Greater Hartford, Connecticut.

CHAPTER 7

The International Association of Machinists, Pratt & Whitney, and the Struggle for Connecticut's Blue-Collar Future

> And here, now, this little loop in the box before Paul, here was Rudy as Rudy had been to his machine that afternoon—Rudy, the turner-on of power, the setter of speeds, the controller of the cutting tool. This was the essence of Rudy as far as his machine was concerned, as far as the economy was concerned. . . . The tape was the essence distilled from the small, polite man with the big hands and black fingernails; . . . . Now, by switching on lathes from a master panel and feeding then signals from the tape, Paul could make the essence of Rudy Hertz produce one, ten, a hundred, or a thousand of the shafts.
>
> —Kurt Vonnegut, *Player Piano*

Riding down Main Street in East Hartford, Connecticut, toward the six smokestacks dominating the front of Pratt & Whitney's mammoth aircraft-engine factory, one cannot help noticing numerous artifacts of industrial decline: empty and trash-strewn lots, boarded-up storefronts, and vacated triple-deckers, once homes for Pratt & Whitney workers. A short drive away on the other side of the Connecticut River, one can observe the dichotomies between East Hartford and downtown Hartford, with its glittering insurance companies, banks, and the headquarters—known around Hartford as the "Gold Building"—of Pratt's parent, the United Technologies Corporation (UTC). Our minitour makes apparent the economic uncertainty and painful "pulling apart" of the social fabric in Hartford and the rest of the once-industrial northeast United States' older cities caused by the disappearance of well-paying manufacturing jobs.

With over 1 million industrial jobs lost during the early 2000's U.S. recession, including hundreds of machining jobs at Pratt & Whitney, Pratt workers fear for their futures. The union hall for East Hartford's IAM Local 1746 sits across the street from the Plant. Inside, local president Mike Stone observed, "Well-paying, secure jobs, which both provided a career for thousands of hard-working people and their families, and supported hundreds of retail and service establishments across the state—jobs workers in the past were able to pass along to their children—continue to disappear." This is why "with 4,500 members in the four Pratt & Whitney locals, job security needs to be the focus of everything we do."[1] Members of Local 1746 and three other Connecticut Pratt & Whitney locals were not supposed to be worrying about their jobs.

Highly contentious 1993 contract negotiations resulted in tax concessions from the Connecticut legislature and agreements on wage cuts and weakened seniority language from the IAM in return for Pratt's commitment to employment growth. But, thereafter, Pratt workers clashed numerous times with UTC over its failure to live up to the bargain. Events culminated in the first strike in nearly 40 years.[2] After watching thousands of unionists lose their jobs in the 1980s and 1990s—Local 1746 had over 9,000 members in 1983 and barely 2,500 in 2001—and despite the threatening economic climate, at 12:01 a.m. on December 3, 2001, unionists struck, mainly in opposition to further job erosion.[3] The IAM's fight for job security in the face of deindustrialization and capital flight is an important part of the larger story about the Connecticut River Valley's decline.

[1] Interview with Mike Stone by author, March 2001, *Hartford Courant,* 20 June (1993), B4.
[2] For discussions of plant closings and community dislocation, see Robert Forrant, "'Neither a sleepy village nor a coarse factory town': Skill in the Greater Springfield, Massachusetts Industrial Economy 1800-1990," *Journal of Industrial History,* 4 (2001): 24-47; JoAnn Wypijewski, "GE Brings Bad Things to Life," *The Nation,* 12 February (2001): 8-23; Jefferson Cowie, *Capital Moves: RCA's 70-Year Quest For Cheap Labor* (Ithaca, NY, 2000); William A. Adler, *Mollie's Job: A Story of Life and Work on the Global Assembly Line* (New York, 2000); Kathryn M. Dudley, *The End of the Line: Lost Jobs, New Lives in Postindustrial America* (Chicago, University of Chicago Press, 1994). For community studies of deindustrialization, Gordon Clark, *Unions and Communities Under Siege: American Communities and the Crisis of Organized Labor* (New York, 1989); June C. Nash, *From Tank Town to High Tech: The Clash of Community and Industrial Cycles* (Albany, NY, 1989); Roger Keil, *Los Angeles: Globalization, Urbanization and Social Struggles* (New York, 1998). Doreen Massey and Richard Meegan, *The Anatomy of Job Loss: The How, Why and Where of Employment Decline* (London, 1982).
[3] Daniel Altman, "Nation's Unemployment Rate Rises to 5.8%," *New York Times,* 5 January (2002), B1; Reed Abelson, "AT&T Plans to Lay Off 5,000 Workers," *New York Times,* 5 January (2002), B1; Sue Kirchhoff, "U.S. jobless rate reaches 5.8%," *Boston Globe,* 5 January (2002), C1; David Leonhardt, "The Rust Belt With a Drawl," *New York Times,* 13 November (2001), C1.

THE CONNECTICUT AND NATIONAL ECONOMIES RESTRUCTURE: ANY ROOM FOR BLUE-COLLAR WORKERS?

Less than 50 years ago, the United States accounted for close to half of global manufacturing output. After 1945, war-induced prosperity and increasing productivity, coupled with the benefits of Keynesian fiscal and monetary policies, contributed to rising living standards. Gross national product expanded from $213 billion in 1945 to more than $500 billion in 1960 and $1 trillion in 1970. Connecticut's capital city of Hartford sat within the 200-hundred-mile-long Connecticut River Valley industrial corridor that ran between Bridgeport, Connecticut, and Springfield, Vermont. As we have already seen, for much of the 19th and 20th centuries the valley's firms and its machinists and metalworkers related to the rest of the country and the world as an innovative and powerful manufacturing center. This premier position was eroded during the 1970s and the 1980s as Japan, continental Europe, and several Asian nations emerged to challenge U.S. preeminence in autos, steel, major household appliances, and consumer electronics.

Job loss intensified during the 1973-1975 recession and spiked between 1979 and 1983, when over 2 million jobs (almost 16 percent of the national total) in several highly unionized durable-goods sectors were lost, mainly due to the use of labor-saving technologies and the movement of large segments of manufacturing overseas. Among the Fortune 500's largest manufacturers, employment fell to 12.4 million from 15.9 million between 1980 and 1990. General Motors, Ford, Boeing, GE, and UTC collectively eliminated 230,000 jobs from 1990 to 1995. Firms like UTC and Bosch expanded their direct foreign investments in factories, office buildings, office equipment, and machine tools. Whereas in 1965 this investment amounted to less than $50 billion, it reached $124 billion in 1975, surpassed $213 billion in 1980, and climbed to $610.1 billion in 1994. Even in industries like jet engines, where U.S.-based producers had successfully maintained their global market share, success did not insulate workers from the effects of global restructuring.[4]

---

[4]By 1996 about three-quarters of all employed Americans worked in service industries, up from two-thirds in 1979. For a discussion of these trends, see S. Herzenberg, J. Alic, J. and H. Wial, *New Rules for a New Economy: Employment and Opportunity in Postindustrial America* (Ithaca, 1998); Kim Moody, *Workers in a Lean World: Unions in the International Economy* (New York, 1997); Barry Bluestone and Bennet Harrison, *Lean and Mean: The Changing Landscape of Corporate Power in the Age of Flexibility* (New York, 1994); Robert Forrant, "Between a Rock and a Hard Place: U.S. Industrial Unions and the Lean, Mean Global Economy: Unions on the Shop Floor as the Next Century Approaches," *Cambridge Journal of Economics*, 24 (2000), 751-69.

Declining Unions—Declining Standards of Living

Unionized workers felt the full force of these changes. One in three American workers belonged to a union in the mid-1950s compared with one in seven in 1999. As manufacturing declined, companies routinely threatened work removal to quash organizing campaigns. And, during most rounds of collective bargaining, corporations received wage-and-benefits concessions from workers.[5] This resulted in wage depression, declining household wealth, and increased income inequality. Yet, productivity rose 7 percent through the 1990s, due to enormous gains in certain sectors, and corporate profits in 1997 were 11.8 percent of revenues, their highest level since 1959, when the Commerce Department started to track the numbers.[6] Between 1987 and 1996 average employee compensation in the United States grew just 1.1 percent, compared with 4 percent between 1977 and 1986, and for most workers, real wages fell under 1973 levels as labor's share of the national income dropped from 66.2 percent in 1970 to 59 percent at the start of 1996. In 1998 the International Labour Organization summarized these trends:

> Recently, while many trade unions have been pressing for reduced work time, guarantees of employment security and measures to combat unemployment, some employers have been seeking to modify many of the hard-won social protection measures in an effort to make labour markets less rigid.[7]

General Electric's "Model Behavior" and Employment Security

In the postwar period, Pratt & Whitney and General Electric were the global market leaders in supplying engines to power aircraft of all types. But in the 1990s

---

[5]For union membership, see L. Belsey, "Labor's Place in the New Economy," Christian Science Monitor, 27 March (2000), 1. For a discussion of the global aspects of capital flight, see William Greider, One World Ready or Not: The Manic Logic of Global Capitalism (New York, 1997), esp. chs. 5 and 7; International Labour Organization, The Impact of Flexible Labour Market Arrangements in the Machinery, Electrical and Electronic Industries (Geneva, 1997); William Lazonick and Mary O'Sullivan (eds.), Corporate Governance and Sustainable Prosperity (New York, 2002); J. Tagliabue, "Buona note, guten tag: Europe's New Workdays," New York Times, 20 October (1997), D1; L. Uchitelle, "Global Good Times Meet the Global Glut," New York Times, 16 November (1997), D1; Teresa Hayter and David Harvey (eds.), The Factory & The City: The Story of the Cowley Automobile Works in Oxford (London, 1993); Andre Lipietz, Mirages and Miracles: The Crisis of Global Fordism (London, 1987).

[6]United States Department of Commerce, Bureau of Labor Statistics (2000); Mary O'Sullivan, "Shareholder Value, Financial Theory and Economic Performance," paper presented at the 52nd Annual Meeting of the Industrial Relations Research Association, Boston: 2000b.

[7]International Labour Organization, The Impact, p. 1; Frank Hansen, "Compensation in the New Economy," Compensation and Benefits Review, 30 (1998): 7-15.

the employment picture was gloomy; the blue-collar and the white-collar workforces had shrunk by 35 percent since 1988. Much of the employment downsizing was due to a decline in defense orders, and when the aircraft market recovered in the mid-1990s employment levels in the jet-engine sector did not. Jobs remained one-third below 1990 employment levels and average hourly earnings were flat.[8]

GE's aggressive search for cheaper production facilities put intense pressure on Pratt to follow suit. In the late 1950s GE moved to parallel production by building several production facilities capable of handling the identical work. Alternative production sites made it possible for GE to extract concessions from its unionized workers and reduce the threat of strikes under the threat of work removal. In the late 1980s GE implemented a continuous improvement strategy called the "GE Workout" in most of its aircraft engine plants, designed to accomplish four things: establish trust on the factory floor between workers and managers; empower employees to make production-improvement suggestions; eliminate unnecessary work; and establish a new shopfloor paradigm of boundaryless work. GE also sought to change its labor agreements to eliminate job classifications and broaden the tasks workers were expected to perform. Workers were urged to welcome the freedom that boundaryless work offered and "to take advantage of it by using their minds creatively to figure out how to improve the company's operations." Unionists at GE's Evendale, Ohio, aircraft engine facility refused to embrace the freedom, and in retaliation, 40 percent of the parts made at Evendale were removed and 3,900 workers were fired.[9] Lynn, Massachusetts, blue-collar workers at first rebuffed GE, but the Lynn local eventually agreed to the contract modifications and the introduction of the multi-skilling program.[10] Parallel production and continuous improvement proved rewarding for GE shareholders: in 1998 the company registered $1.7 billion in operating profits on $10 billion in sales, an operating margin of 17 percent.

[8] This analysis borrows heavily from the work of Beth Almeida. See, in particular, "Good Jobs Flying Away: The U.S. Jet Engine Industry," in Lazonick and O'Sullivan (eds.), *Corporate Governance and Sustainable Prosperity* (New York, 2002): 104-140.

[9] Robert Slater, *The GE Way Handbook* (New York, 2000), 50; Konzelmann and Forrant, "Creative Work Systems." Employment at Evendale was close to 20,000 in 1988; at the end of 1994 only 8,000 workers remained.

[10] Former GE engineer Oswald Jones cites GE manager Charles Pieper, who supervised several plant reorganizations in Europe, and describes how workers relate to participation programs. According to Piper, "I have never seen a group of people who are not interested. Never. Never. Never. Whether you are Chinese, Hungarian, Japanese, Swedish, people love to go and make their workplace better. . . ." While Pieper was president of GE Lighting Europe, passionately committed workers saw factories drop from 24 to 12 and employment from 24,000 to 13,000. Jones concluded "It is hardly surprising that workers regard GE managerial initiatives to make the workplace better with considerable skepticism." Oswald Jones, "Changing the Balance? Taylorism, TQM, and Work Organisation," *New Technology, Work and Employment,* 12 (1997): 13-24, 20-22.

In 1999 GE flexed its global muscles with the launch of its "Globalization and Supplier Migration" strategy. Components suppliers needed to achieve 10 percent to 14 percent annual cost reductions to keep their GE work. By and large such savings could only be realized by shifting work to countries with lower cost structures. In presentations across the country, GE told its suppliers, "Migrate or be out of business; not a matter of if, just when. We expect you to move and move quickly." There was a carrot: "We sincerely want you to participate and will help, but if you don't we will move on without you." The benefits of a move to Mexico included average daily wage rates of $6.00, friendly unions, and the promise of long-term low labor costs. According to IAM economist Beth Almeida, what occurred "should serve as a warning to those who would maintain that the U.S. will always win out in the high-tech manufacturing race. The idea that only poor quality jobs in low-tech industries are being lost to competitor nations is refuted by the experience of aerospace workers. . . ."[11] In the context of GE's restructuring, Pratt contemplated moves of its own. Economic analysts, elected officials, labor-union leaders, and blue-collar workers across Connecticut confronted the possibility that Pratt might close its Connecticut factories.

DEINDUSTRIALIZATION AND ECONOMIC RESTRUCTURING IN CONNECTICUT

In Connecticut, four of ten manufacturing jobs disappeared between 1980 and 2000. At the start of 2000 there were 18,700 fewer jobs in primary metals (–66.6 percent), 37,300 fewer jobs in industrial machinery (–54.2 percent), and 48,500 fewer jobs in transportation equipment (–53 percent) than in 1967.[12] Connecticut gained 113,000 new jobs from 1985 to 2000. But, by and large, these were jobs in the low-paying service and retail sectors, including health care, copy centers, temporary-help agencies, restaurants, and entertainment. Finance, insurance, and real estate (FIRE) added 10,000 jobs over the 15-year period. With the exception of FIRE's average weekly wage of $1,359, wages in the growth sectors trailed manufacturing wages. The 2000 average weekly manufacturing wage was $1,117 compared with $717 for services and $427 for retail trade. Across Connecticut the fastest growing occupations included eating and drinking establishments, cleaning and lawn-care services, catalog and mail-order houses, and household audio and visual equipment sales. None of these occupations made

[11] Aaron Bernstein, "Welch's march to the South," *Business Week,* 6 December (1999), 74. J. Millman, "GE boosts Mexican output as labor talks in U.S. near," *The Wall Street Journal,* 5 January (2000), 8; J. Millman, 1998. "Mexico is becoming auto-making hot spot," *Wall Street Journal,* 23 June (1998), 17; B. Almeida, "Good Jobs Flying Away," 106.

[12] Wage data comes from the Connecticut Department of Labor Web site; 1999 is the last year reported. www.ct.dol.ct/us/lmi/20299ct.htm

use of the precision manufacturing skills held by Pratt & Whitney workers, and none of these occupations pay a remotely similar wage (see Tables 7.1 and 7.2).[13]

In their research on deindustrialization, Doreen Massey and Richard Meegan pointed out that the parties to the process—labor and capital—do not share the same outcomes. Corporate profits had returned to peak post-World War II levels by the mid-1990s, yet in Connecticut, home to the corporate headquarters of several leading global corporations, median real family income fell 14 percent between 1990 and 2000.[14] Adjusted for inflation, U.S. workers' median income was 5 percent lower in the mid-1990s than in the late 1970s. The top 5 percent of households (those making $133,000 or more) controlled 21.4 percent of all income, while the bottom 60 percent controlled 27.6 percent. This represents a reversal of the 20 years after the Second World War, when the country's industrial base expanded and there was a steady decline in family income inequality. Accompanying the wage effects, large-scale community/social effects following the rapid disappearance of well-paying work led to demoralization, impoverishment, and out-migration, things that "might lead to the potential for recovery in de-industrialized regions being compromised. . . ."[15]

There was a 1.5 percent drop in population and no net employment gains in Connecticut's capital city, Hartford, over the 10-year period. This stagnation was "reflected to a lesser degree in all of Connecticut's large cities with the exception of Stamford in Fairfield County," resulting in a "widening economic and racial segregation in Connecticut, which is the richest state in the country."[16] The think tank MassInc found that for seven of the nine northeast states, "median real incomes were below those of 1989, with Connecticut, Massachusetts, New Hampshire and New York faring the worst in the region." Connecticut's median household income in constant 1999 dollars fell to $49,267, from $56,916 in 1989, the largest drop among the 10 northeast states.[17]

[13] *Connecticut Economic Digest,* April (2001), 7; August (2001), 5; September (2001), 2.

[14] D. Massey and R. Meegan, *The Anatomy of Job Loss,* vii; Andrew Sum, *The Story of Household Incomes in the 1990s* (Boston, 2001). The report can be located at www.massinc.org/publications/reports

[15] Chuck Collins, B. Leondar-Wright and Holly Sklar, *Shifting Fortunes: The Perils of the Growing American Wealth Gap* (Boston, 1999); Hansen, "Compensation in the New Economy"; David Weinberg, "A Brief Look at Postwar U.S. Income Inequality," *Current Population Reports* (Washington, DC, 1996), 60-91; Bert Altena and Marcel van der Linden, "Preface," *International Review of Social History,* 47 (2002), 2.

[16] David M. Herszenhorn, "Behind Census Numbers in a Declining Hartford," *New York Times,* 22 March, 2001, A22; Jenny Scott, "Connecticut Population Shifts Toward New York," *New York Times,* 20 March, 2001, 1; United States Department of Housing and Urban Development, *The State of the Cities 2000* (Washington, DC, 2000).

[17] www.massinc.org

Table 7.1. Structure of Connecticut Economy by Employment Categories

	1985	1999	Job change	% Change
Total employment	1,558,100	1,671,500	113,400	7
Manufacturing	408,000	269,200	−138,800	−34
Transportation and public utilities	68,300	78,200	9,900	15
Services	349,600	526,600	177,000	50
Finance, insurance, real estate	130,400	140,700	10,300	8
Trade (wholesale/retail)	346,000	359,500	13,500	4
Construction	65,400	60,900	−4,500	−7
Government	188,800	235,600	46,800	25
Mining	1,600	800	−800	−50

Source: Connecticut Department of Labor, www.ctdol.state.ct.us/lmi

Table 7.2. Connecticut Employment by
Percentages 1985 and 1999

	1985	1999
Manufacturing	26.2	16.1
Transportation and public utilities	4.3	4.6
Services	22.4	31.5
Finance, insurance, real estate	8.3	8.4
Wholesale and retail trade	22.2	21.5
Construction	4.1	3.6
Government	12.1	14.0
Mining	< 1.0	< 1.0

Source: Connecticut Department of Labor,
www.ctdol.state.ct.us/lmi

David Harvey and Erik Swyngedouw documented a similar phenomenon in their discussion of massive layoffs at a Rover assembly plant in Coley, an industrial suburb of Oxford. There, restructuring

> meant not only the loss of many of those secure jobs which secured community affluence for many, but a transition in the qualities of the jobs that remained (through speed-up, deskilling, and the like) so that the difference between the marginalized and the employed became less rather than more marked.[18]

Turret-lathe operator and IAM Executive Board member Ted Durkin noted that while there were some jobs available with decent wages for fired Pratt workers, they required considerable training. "I'm 45, and lots of other workers are older. Not too many folks will want to start all over again and go back to school." The jobs that are available absent education are at gambling casinos, Home Depot, and at small machine shops, but for a lot less money and few, if any, benefits. Machinist and union-shop committee member John Cloutier added that years ago "you could get your foot in the door here [Pratt], project into the future, and see yourself with a steady job for 30 or more years; but no more. How do you sign for a mortgage, buy a car, save for your kid's college when your employment future is so insecure?"[19]

UTC, PRATT & WHITNEY, AND THE CONNECTICUT ECONOMY

Pratt & Whitney, a major business segment of United Technologies Corporation, employed roughly 12,000 people in Connecticut, and 30,000 worldwide in 2000. In 2001, with 2,000 locations in 220 countries, UTC ranked 57th among U.S. corporations and 125th in the world. UTC's global workforce totaled 150,000 in 2000, down 25 percent from 1990. As a result of the transfer of capital commitments abroad, 54 percent of UTC's employment was outside the United States. UTC's other major business segments were Flight Systems, which includes Hamilton Sundstrand and Sikorsky, producer of such things as engine controls, environmental control systems, aircraft propellers, and helicopters; Carrier Air Conditioner, the world's largest manufacturer of heating, ventilating and air-conditioning systems; and Otis Elevator, the world's leader in the manufacture of elevators, escalators, and automated people movers. It operated in Arkansas, California, Connecticut, Georgia, Maine, Michigan, Minnesota, Oklahoma, and

---

[18] David Harvey and Erik Swyngedouw, "Industrial Restructuring, Community Disempowerment and Grass-Roots Resistance," in Hayter and Harvey, *The Factory and the City*, (New York, Mansell Publishing, 1993): 11-25, 16.

[19] Author interviews at the Pratt & Whitney Local 1746 Union Hall in December 2000 and January and March 2001.

Texas. European and Asian joint ventures were in Dublin, Ireland; Tapei, Taiwan; Kiev, Ukraine; and Singapore. Hamilton Sundstrand, also in Connecticut, employed 17,000 people worldwide, with about 4,000 in Connecticut. Jet-engine manufacturing, overhaul, and repair operations were located in eight states and Puerto Rico, and there were international overhaul and repair operations in Canada, China, England, France, Germany, Ireland, Italy, Malaysia, the Netherlands, Russia, and Singapore.[20]

Pratt & Whitney and General Electric were world leaders in the manufacture of jet engines. A truly indigenous New England industry, 128 New England firms and 34,000 people built complex parts, components, subassemblies, and control systems for engines during 1999; the majority of these firms were subcontractors to the Lynn, Massachusetts-based General Electric plant and/or Pratt & Whitney. This represented 28 percent of total U.S. aircraft-engine manufacturing employment.[21]

Originally a machine-tool builder, Pratt & Whitney Company was incorporated in Hartford in 1855. In 1925 businessman Frederick Rentschler and engineer George Mead approached Pratt about the manufacture of a new air-cooled airplane engine. The two men came to Connecticut for the same reason Rolls Royce had settled in Springfield around the same time: an available network of precision metalworking firms and a deep pool of skilled machinists. Pratt provided the two men with start-up funds and some manufacturing space. Four years later, Pratt joined with Sikorsky Aviations Corporation, Chance Vought, and the Hamilton Standard propeller corporation to form Hartford-based United Aircraft, which was renamed United Technologies Corporation in 1975. Dynamic growth during and right after the Second World War made Pratt Connecticut's most important industrial employer and fueled the growth of hundreds of small- and medium-sized metalworking and precision manufacturing firms across Connecticut and western Massachusetts.[22]

Pratt's manufacturing and engineering projects soon took place in nine states and several European and Asian countries. This made it possible for Pratt to whipsaw unions, communities, and entire nations to exact concessions for jobs.[23] As though playing a giant board game, Pratt shifted work between Connecticut, Florida, and Maine, while participating in multiple overseas ventures. For the

---

[20] UTC 2000 *Annual Report.* Germany.

[21] For the impact of General Electric's abandonment of Pittsfield, Massachusetts, see Max. H. Kirsch, *In the Wake of the Giant: Multinational Restructuring and Uneven Development in a New England Community* (Albany, New York, 1998). Kirsch notes that GE expanded during the 1970s, adding 30,000 jobs abroad while decreasing domestic employment by 25,000, 13.

[22] The company's early history is from "Soaring Through Time" and "Key Elements in the History of United Technologies" at www.utc.com; Anne Markusen et al., *The Rise of the Gunbelt* (New York, 1991).

[23] Robert Forrant, "Too Many Bends in the River: The Decline of the Connecticut River Valley Machine Tool Industry," *Journal of Industrial History,* 5 (2), 2002: 71-91.

IAM in Connecticut, these maneuvers weakened contractual seniority and job-classification language and significantly reduced the strike threat.[24]

UTC's investors and top managers were handsomely rewarded. In 2001 UTC was on *Forbes* prestigious Platinum List of 400 U.S. corporations. *Forbes* pointed out that when compared with its aerospace and defense industry peers, "UTC had the second-best five-year average for return on capital (21 percent) and virtually tied for first place in the five-year average for earnings per share growth (21.9 percent)."[25] Its revenues of $26.6 billion in 2000 were well above 1996's $19.9 billion, and earnings per common share of $3.55 in 2000, compared favorably with $1.74 in 1996. Pratt's 2000 operating profit of $1.2 billion accounted for 35 percent of UTC's $3.4 billion total. The corporation's 2000 *Year in Review* proclaimed, "Investors do prize consistency, and UTC is committed to this above all. UTC's total shareowner return has compounded at an average thirty percent annually since 1994, well above market indices." Added the *Review,* "Our $1.8 billion in available cash flow also provides the engine of growth for acquisitions." Thirty-five acquisitions costing $7.6 billion were completed in 1999-2000. However, profit increases did not translate into employment growth. During 1999 UTC terminated 15,000 employees from its global workforce—41 firings a day for the calendar year. Pratt & Whitney worldwide accounted for 5,200 terminations.[26]

1993 CONCESSIONARY BARGAINING

Faced with sharp defense-spending cuts at the end of the Vietnam War, UTC purchased several companies, including Sikorsky Helicopter, Carrier Air Conditioning, Otis Elevators, and American Bosch. When coupled with the late-1980s boom in the commercial airline industry, these moves produced several profitable years for Pratt. However, in 1991 Pratt's first-quarter earnings dropped 75 percent, and new UTC chief executive, Robert Daniell began to slash $1 billion in manufacturing costs.[27] To achieve this, 6,700 hourly and salaried jobs at Pratt's U.S. facilities were scheduled for elimination, but as losses continued across the corporation, a more radical two-year restructuring program was proposed. UTC-wide, 14,000 jobs were to be eliminated—7 percent of the global

---

[24] Kapstein, "Workers and the World Economy"; Almeida, "Good Jobs Flying Away"; Jones, "Changing the Balance?"; Bryn Jones, *Forging the Factory of the Future: Cybernation and Societal Institutions* (Cambridge, England, 1997).

[25] Howard Banks, "No More Yo-Yo," *Forbes,* 11 January (1999): 130-131; Claudia H. Deutsch, "Private Sector: Even His Soufflés Can't Relax," *New York Times,* 19 November (2000), Section 3, 2; Brian Zajac, The 400 Best Big Companies in America," *Forbes,* 8 January (2001).

[26] UTC Year in Review, 1, 8.

[27] In the first quarter of 1991 earnings at Pratt dropped 75 percent—less than half the predicted earnings. But with UTC relying on Pratt for two-thirds of its operating income, this was a hard hit. Jonathan P. Hicks, "United Technologies Bumpy Ride," *New York Times,* 1 May (1991), D1.

workforce—and 100 facilities were to be closed. Even before the proposed cuts, the membership of Pratt's East Hartford union local was 6,000, a decrease of one-third since 1983.[28] In 1993 George David, formerly head of Otis Elevator, became UTC Chief Operating Officer under Daniell, and Karl Krapek was named president of Pratt & Whitney. The trio called for the termination of 10,000 Pratt employees worldwide.[29]

In early spring 1993 UTC gave the IAM and the Connecticut legislature an ultimatum: generate $30 million each in cost concessions right away or Pratt, "crown jewel of UTC and a pillar of Connecticut's economy for 70 years," will cease its manufacturing in the state. Elected officials and union leaders were warned that absent the concessions, 2,300 jobs would be cut before the end of 1993 with the rest of the jobs phased out over several years.[30] Bill Cibes, the state's budget director commented, "If you let 2,300 jobs leave Connecticut, that means the state is not competitive to retain the rest."[31] "Pratt &Whitney is part of the business heritage of Connecticut," Governor Lowell Weicker stated. "It's done well by Connecticut and its people. It belongs here. You've got to give up something in the tough times. We all do."[32]

David and Krapek presided over marathon bargaining sessions with the union and the state legislature while deftly courting legislative delegations from Georgia and Maine—the sites of smaller Pratt & Whitney plants—which offered Pratt lucrative incentives to move work to their states. Connecticut's hourly manufacturing costs, Krapek intoned, averaged $6 to $8 higher per worker than in other states. These costs needed to come into line for Pratt to continue to make aircraft engines in its birthplace, he warned.[33] While state leaders complained that Pratt's cost figures were exaggerated, they nonetheless struggled to meet them because they believed that Krapek's threat was all to real. Unionists approached the talks with dim hopes, convinced that the East Hartford plant's fate was already sealed.

Ultimately, the legislature granted a series of incentives that included a research-and-development tax credit, loan guarantees for job training, grants to train Pratt workers in Japanese-style lean-production, and electricity-rate reductions. The legislature also enacted policies that granted all Connecticut employers savings on their workers' compensation insurance. For its part, the IAM agreed

[28] George Judson, "Pratt & Whitney Threatening to Shut 2 Connecticut Plants," *NYT,* 15 April (1993), A1.
[29] Robert Weisman, "Real struggle for Pratt's future played out in private," *Hartford Courant,* 26 December (1993), A1.
[30] R. Weisman, "How Pratt flexed its muscle, and state, union relented," *Hartford Courant,* 27 December (1993), A1.
[31] R. Weisman, "Real struggle," A1.
[32] R. Weisman, "How Pratt Flexed," A1.
[33] Kirk Johnson, "By Pratt & Whitney's Math, Connecticut Costs Too Much," *NYT,* 23 April (1993), A1; G. Judson, "Pratt & Whitney Threatening."

to a wage freeze, new productivity targets, and numerous work-rule changes and received a vague company commitment to keep jobs in the state, limit subcontracting, and halt the move of jobs to Maine and Georgia. The concessions were approved in a close vote, but even the workers who voted for the givebacks remained suspicious of Pratt's true intentions. But, in the words of one member, it was "better to preserve jobs and live to fight another day." In the first year after the concessions, UTC achieved a 20 percent earnings increase on just a 1 percent increase in sales; workers were not so fortunate.[34]

THE AFTERMATH: THANKS—BUT NOT REALLY

After the concessions were made, Pratt boss Karl Krapek sent a letter to Pratt & Whitney workers telling them, "By agreeing to the plan, the workers had expressed faith in the future of our company." The company will undertake "significant redesign of our manufacturing, engineering and administrative processes" and will keep work in the state. Pratt placed a full-page advertisement in the *Hartford Courant* on Sunday, June 27, 1993, that contained a public thank-you to the state's taxpayers and the union for the cost relief. Pratt credited the legislature for measures that "make business more competitive" in Connecticut, praised the IAM for "convincing us to keep jobs in Connecticut" and applauded workers for their trust. "The spotlight now shines on Pratt & Whitney to deliver on our promises," the ad trumpeted. It concluded with this proclamation: "SOME DAY OUR BUSINESS WILL PICK UP AGAIN. THANKS TO YOU, IT WILL PICK UP IN CONNECTICUT."[35] Yet, the movement of work intensified and the membership of IAM District 91—which included all of Connecticut's union locals representing UTC production and maintenance workers—fell from 13,000 in 1993 to fewer than 10,000 by 1999. In 2000 UTC announced its intention to trim an additional 14,500 jobs corporationwide over three years, with more cuts in Connecticut.[36]

In March 2001 I discussed 1993's events with Warren Occhialini, Ted Durkin, John Cloutier, and Mike Stone, Pratt workers and active union members. They concurred that despite the corporation's insistence that they wanted an open style of industrial relations and an atmosphere of trust, events after 1993 made this impossible. In particular, despite expansion promises, thousands more workers lost their jobs. "In the end the Pratt workforce is always smaller, despite assurances that this will not take place," noted Cloutier. Occhialini observed that the local lost jobs because UTC believed that it could do whatever it wanted. Cloutier also noted that in 1998, even after a signed agreement was reached between

[34] Author interviews, 2001.
[35] *Hartford Courant,* 20 June (1993) B4; Thomas Lueck, "Jet-Engine Workers Accept Harsh Reality," *New York Times,* 25 June (1993), B6.
[36] T. Lueck, "Jet-Engine Workers"; Tim Smart, "Global Mission."

the union and the company to send 80,000 hours of work from East Hartford to North Berwick, Maine, with 100,000 hours of the Maine plant's work shifting to East Hartford, work went to Maine, but the reverse trek never occurred. The work shifting agreement in the 1998 collective-bargaining agreement between District Lodge 91 and Pratt & Whitney reads in part, ". . . approximately 21 part numbers associated with LPT Blades will be moving from Maine to Connecticut. This work represents approximately 100,000 hours of work annually."[37]

In describing blue-collar attrition, Cloutier concluded, "Two generations of workers are not on the shop floor." At the time of my interviews, 75 percent of Connecticut's Pratt & Whitney workers were over 45 and the average seniority in the plants was 22.1 years. With layoffs and restructuring, there were almost no machinists and machine operators in their 20s and 30s; no additional hiring was taking place, just the occasional recall of laid-off workers to fill vacancies caused by retirements. Cloutier noted that, "Serious, long-term education and training to upgrade the skills of shop-floor workers does not take place. This would indicate there is no future here." Durkin commented that Pratt has done such a poor job training people that they often rehired retirees at inflated salaries to train workers in the various skills lost through early retirement and layoffs. Shaking his head, Durkin remarked "We don't use logic with them when we discuss this kind of thing."

For Cloutier and Durkin, management's restructuring had little to do with workers being unable to perform the job. Unionists had participated in several efforts to redesign jobs in order to lower production costs and save jobs. Yet, according to Cloutier, when most job-redesign projects were completed, the work "gets pulled out of the factory and shipped to an overseas business partner or a local job shop." The workforce is so lean that there is almost no way for new work to come into the shop because the existing workforce can't handle it. People are already working tremendous amounts of overtime because the plant is run so much on the margin in terms of needed workers.[38]

Reacting to proposed cuts at Pratt & Whitney's North Haven, Middletown, and East Hartford factories, IAM District 91 directing-business representative James Parent expressed unionists' frustrations:

They don't realize that when they talk about a worker, it's not just one worker. They are talking about a whole family, whose future is up in the air. They are talking about the tax base of North Haven and all the surrounding communities where workers live.

[37] According to Cloutier, a 1994 management survey of employee morale at Pratt was reported on in *Business Week* in 1995. While 78 percent of employees reported pride in their work, fewer than half the workers felt any loyalty to the company. Author interviews, 2001.

[38] Author interviews. On industry restructuring, see Randy Barber and Robert Scott, *Jobs on the Wing: Trading Away the Future of the U.S. Aerospace Industry* (Washington, DC, 1995); Tim Smart, "Global Mission," *Business Week,* 1 May (1995): 132-135.

In a January 2001 interview, Parent reiterated his concern for keeping jobs in Connecticut and wondered where work would come from that could generate a stable tax base. "Why not grow jobs in Connecticut," Parent asked, "instead of walking away from a workforce that averages 22-plus years seniority?"[39]

In their description of Rover's investment diversions, capital flight, and work relocation, Harvey and Swyngedouw point out that

> Innumerable companies have cashed in on local productive capacity for decades only to determine that this capacity is no longer useful to them, leaving behind thousands of lost jobs, a desolated local economy, and citizens, local governments as well as other community-based institutions (varying from trade unions to the churches) in confusion and disarray.

To Parent, it appeared likely that Pratt & Whitney and UTC were ready to cash-out in Connecticut. For example, in 1998 Pratt took a majority interest in Singapore Airlines' engine shop and Hamilton acquired Ratier-Figeac in France, and Carrier commenced a joint venture with the Japanese manufacturer Toshiba. In 1999 Otis formed LG Otis Elevator Company in Korea with LG Electronics, Inc. UTC held an 80 percent equity interest in the new company.[40]

THE TEN THOUSAND JOBS QUESTION: OR, WHAT—FLIP BURGERS?

In the midst of job loss, in December 1998 IAM District 91 reached agreement on a three-year contract with Pratt. At the time of the negotiations, the company indicated that 1,000 additional jobs might be eliminated over the next three years due to what it referred to as "production scheduling problems." But unionists were assured that no drastic cuts like in 1993 were anticipated. Company officials emphasized that Pratt & Whitney was in fact committed to Connecticut. Increased orders for lucrative engine repairs were expected to boost jobs. But eight months later, without talking to the union, Krapek announced plans to shutter the North Haven, Connecticut, factory and relocate Pratt's engine repair and service work to Oklahoma and Texas. The announcement prompted a 4.7 percent increase ($3.19) in the price of United Technologies stock, while the business press

---

[39] Author interviews.

[40] Harvey and Swyngedouw, "Industrial Restructuring, Community Disempowerment and Grass-Roots Resistance," 20. Beth Almeida, "Linking Institutions of Governance and Industrial Outcomes: The Case of Global Aircraft Engine Manufacturing," paper for the 52nd Annual Meeting of the Industrial Relations Research Association, Boston, 2000; author interview with James Parent; UTC Form 10-K, 1998, 1999.

predicted that the combination of layoffs and job transfers could save the company $100 million to $150 million a year starting in 2001.[41]

The IAM protested that the company's unilateral declaration violated an important clause in the 1998 labor agreement—Letter 22 Workplace Guarantees and Subcontracting—which bound Pratt to discuss any plans to remove work with the IAM and to give the union an opportunity to match the cost savings that might accrue to the company from such a move. The letter read in part:

> The Company will make every effort to preserve the work presently and normally manufactured by employees covered by Article 2 of this Agreement. Therefore, it is not the intent of the Company to use subcontractors for the purpose of reducing or transferring work that is presently and normally manufactured by employees in the bargaining unit nor place such work in Maine or Georgia. . . .[42]

As news of the North Haven closing spread, Gary Daly, age 48 with 20 years of service at Pratt, typified workers' reactions. The company is "making record profits, and all they want is cheap labor, to bust the union" he noted. "We've got mortgages and families and are trying to send our kids to school. What are we going to do, flip burgers?" John Amato, a five-year Pratt worker, added, "I'm 25 and by the time I'm 40, there's going to be nothing left in Connecticut. They are going for cheap labor, that's all they want."[43]

Federal Courts Intervene

Faced with the possible loss of an important source of new work, on September 16, 1999, the IAM went to Federal Court to challenge the restructuring plan. The union argued that the proposed cuts violated the 1998 labor agreement, which obligated management to make reasonable efforts to keep work historically performed in Connecticut in the state at least until the contract expired in 2001. Stunning UTC, the United States District Court issued an injunction blocking the company's move until the case was heard. On February 18, 2000, citing specific clauses in the collective bargaining agreement, Judge Janet Hall ruled,

---

[41] Matthew Lubanko, "Plan Wins Friends on Wall Street," *Hartford Courant,* 13 August (1999), D1.

[42] *Agreement Between Aeronautical Industrial District Lodge 91, I.A.M.A.W., AFL-CIO and Affiliated Locals and Pratt & Whitney* (1998), p. 126. Barbara Nagy, "Pratt Braces For Upheaval," *Hartford Courant,* 13 August (1999), 1; Dan Haar and Stacy Wong, "Shift: Connecticut's Gain Comes With Pain," *Hartford Courant,* 13 August (1999), 1.

[43] Robin Stansbury and Matthew Kauffman, "Local Businesses React," *Hartford Courant,* 13 August (1999), D1; Patricia Seremet, "Shock Turns to Anger," *Hartford Courant,* 13 August (1999), D1.

"Pratt made, in fact, no effort to preserve the parts repair work presently and normally manufactured by bargaining unit employees." IAM members were jubilant when Judge Hall ruled:

> Pratt's object was profit maximization, with no effort made to preserve the work in question. Its decision was driven by a desire solely to lower costs, in order to be more competitive and gain more business, all of which is rational and reasonable from a business perspective, absent Pratt's contractual obligation to the Union.

Pratt appealed the ruling and on October 26, 2000 the United States Court of Appeals for the Second Circuit upheld Judge Hall's decision preventing UTC from moving the engine-repair work for the life of the contract.[44]

READY FOR A FIGHT

Buoyed by their court victory, District 91's leaders prepared for what they felt would be bruising contract negotiations in the fall of 2001. Unionists expected that Pratt would demand the removal of the job-security language. Eager to head off another round of concessionary bargaining and determined to preserve existing jobs, unionists established a broad-based jobs-preservation campaign under the banner "Grow Jobs in Connecticut." One component of the campaign was a report that District 91 commissioned on deindustrialization in Connecticut. The Chicago-based Center for Labor & Community Research (CLCR) prepared an analysis of the projected financial and job losses in Connecticut if UTC curtailed manufacturing in the state, which became the centerpiece for an educational campaign with union members, the state legislature, church and community groups, and other trade unions.

CLCR determined that curtailed manufacturing would mean an end to 11,300 Connecticut UTC jobs—6,100 production jobs and 5,200 support jobs. A "ripple effect" cut of almost 21,000 additional jobs would be caused by the decreased wages and spending power UTC's layoffs provoked. Thus, total job loss could reach 32,400. CLCR reported that jobs in retail trade (3,763), business services (3,608), health services (1,648), wholesale trade (1,034), and construction (1,024) would be the most severely

---

[44] Court Brief, United States District Court, District of Connecticut. Civil Action No. 3:99-CV-1827 (JCH). Aeronautical Indus. Dist. Lodge 91 of the Int'l Ass'n of Machinists and Aerospace Workers, AFL-CIO Plaintiff, v. United Technologies Corp., Pratt & Whitney Defendant (18 February 2000).

impacted. Estimated costs for two years following the cessation of manufacturing included.[45]

- The loss of $304 million in local, state, and federal tax revenue along with an additional $119 million worth of expenditures to cover increased unemployment compensation. The two-year total cost to government would be $423 million.
- Two years after job loss—based on Connecticut wage figures—a terminated production worker with a new job would earn 76 percent of his former income. Consideration was given to the fact that laid-off workers could receive severance wages and that many workers might receive some portion of their pension.
- Based on March 2001 labor market information, it was estimated that 20 percent of Pratt & Whitney and Hamilton Sundstrand workers (2,285 people) would remain unemployed for at least 26 weeks and that 4.6 percent (521 people) would be unemployed after one year. Among the ripple-effect workers, 699 people would be unemployed for at least one year. Thus, 1,220 people would be unemployed for at least one year.

THE DECEMBER 2001 STRIKE

The company's 2001 contract offer contained a 10 percent pay raise and a $1,000 signing bonus. But, as anticipated, no job-security provisions were included. Instead, the proposed contract called for the immediate move out of state of 500 East Hartford jobs, with vague promises to bring in new work. At the strike-vote meeting, Gary Allen, IAM's national aerospace coordinator, told several thousand workers, "This is your defining moment as a union. You've got to send a message." East Hartford local president Mike Stone added, "We can either die on the vine or fight to grow jobs in the state of Connecticut. Nothing is won without sacrifice. It is our time to sacrifice."

On the picket line 15-year Pratt worker Greg Adorno asked, "What's the point of giving somebody a 10 percent raise if they're not going to be here to benefit

---

[45] Ken Blum, Social Cost Analysis of the Impact of Closing UTC's Aircraft Engine and Parts Plants in Connecticut (Chicago, 2001). For a discussion of employment multipliers and their calculation, see Dean Baker and Thea Lee, Employment Multipliers in the U.S. Economy, Working Paper No. 107 (Washington, DC, 1993). This study utilized an input-output model developed by the U.S. Forest Service called Implan. The model produced multipliers showing sales, indirect business taxes, and jobs for all industries that produce inputs for the aircraft and missile engines and parts plants, and also industries producing goods and services consumed by UTC workers. The Center for Labor & Community Research was founded in 1982 as the Midwest Center for Labor Research and has been involved in research and worker/community organizing campaigns to stop deindustrialization and preserve working-class communities. It can be reached at www.clcr.org

from it?" For IAM District 91 chief negotiator James Parent, the issues were cut-and-dry, especially when 63 percent of Pratt's membership had been lost over the previous 10 years. "We were at a point at the end of negotiations where we were close. It's not an issue of money. It's an issue of whether the jobs are going to be here. What good is a good package if you don't have a job?" Howard Haberern, with 34 years at Pratt, added, "We're saying, leave the work in Connecticut. That's the crux of the whole thing."[46] The IAM's national website reported,

> This is a strike to protect America's defense industrial base. This is a strike to keep good paying jobs and decent retirements available to the people of Connecticut. We seek a contract that keeps Pratt & Whitney successful and that keeps our members working. The company has illegally refused to provide information on subcontracted work inside the plants and on work they plan to send to outside vendors or overseas.

The union refused to abrogate the language it had used in Federal Court to block Pratt's earlier restructuring efforts. On the strike website, Allen remarked, "The time has come to stand up and fight to save the best industrial jobs in Connecticut. IAM members and the people in our communities take this fight very seriously and we are committed to win."[47] Comments from the picket line reflected the strike's very high stakes. "I'm striking for the younger people," said 54-year-old Mary Hurlburt. "They need a younger generation coming in to build these engines."[48]

Ten days into the strike, on December 13, 2001 workers ratified a new contract by a 75 percent affirmative vote of the 4,000 votes cast. Pratt's prestrike wage offer remained unchanged. However, in an extremely important victory, Pratt agreed in writing to produce a new engine in Connecticut and all existing work remained subject to the court-tested Workplace Guarantee contract language. As a symbol of their commitment to "Grow Connecticut," Pratt agreed to start their first joint Union/Company Apprenticeship Program. In addition, the company agreed to participate in the High Performance Work Organization training program at the IAM's New Technology Center in Maryland.[49]

---

[46] Barbara Nagy, "Union Votes to Strike at Pratt," *Hartford Courant,* 3 December (2001), 1; John Moran and Barbara Nagy, "Job Security the Issue for Pratt Strikers," *Hartford Courant,* 4 December (2001), 1.

[47] www.goiam.org/news

[48] Barbara Nagy, "Pratt Negotiations May Resume Soon," *Hartford Courant,* 5 December (2001), 1.

[49] Barbara Nagy and John Moran, "Strike is Over at Pratt," *Hartford Courant,* 14 December (2001), 1.

CLOSING THOUGHTS

In Connecticut, at the start of 2004, there were roughly the same number of jobs as in 1998, 1.64 million. However, the low wages of most service employment and part-time employment, the bulk of the jobs since the mid-1990s that replaced manufacturing, contributed to a 14 percent drop in median family income in Connecticut between 1990 and 2000. For all manufacturing, the average weekly wage in 2003 was $1,116.19; in services it was $876. Newspaper headlines like these capture the overall state of Connecticut's labor market: "Forecast for Connecticut Employment Cut Back in Regional Economic Report; Interest Up, Jobs Outlook Down," Kenneth Gosselin, *Hartford Courant*, November 11, 2004; "Office Depot to Cut About 100 Call Center Jobs in Connecticut," Maria Garriga, *New Haven Register*, November 2, 2004; "Connecticut Suffers Job Setback as 4,200 Positions Are Lost in June," *Connecticut Post*, Rob Varnon, July 20, 2004; "Economists Predict Job Growth Won't Last," *Associated Press Wire*, Laura Walsh, August 25, 2004; "State Loses 2,200 Jobs: Hits 6-Year Low as Nation Gains," *Hartford Courant*, Michael Remez, April 23, 2004; "It's Not Just the Jobs Lost, But the Pay in the New Ones," *New York Times*, Edmund Andrews, August 9, 2004; "Connecticut's Economy 'Very Fragile' Governor States," *Hartford Courant*, Mark Pazniokas, July 28, 2004. Connecticut Governor Jodi Rell got it right when in July 2004 she remarked, "The bottom line is it's all about jobs. It's jobs. It's jobs. It's jobs."[50]

As the evidence in this chapter demonstrates, in the drive to maximize production and increase shareholder value, worker empowerment, and team building played second violin to the first chair of reduced production costs. The delicate underpinnings of plant-level trust were increasingly threatened by the wherewithal of corporations like Pratt to unilaterally shift production to gain even the slightest competitive advantages. Workers and their unions were squeezed between a rock and a hard place: They were condemned as backward thinkers should they refuse to consider management-proposed changes to things like seniority provisions and job classifications; yet they were equally doomed when they acceded only to have managers "pick their brains" and transfer the work anyway to plants in less expensive parts of the world as Pratt & Whitney attempted.[51]

In 2003 the AFL-CIO's Industrial Union Council issued a report titled "Revitalizing American Manufacturing." Its first two sentences say it all. "American manufacturing is in a deep crisis. From 2000 to 2002 the country lost manufacturing jobs every month, the longest such stretch of monthly job losses since the Great Depression." The report noted that: "The crisis is

---

[50] Mark Pazniokas, "Connecticut's Economy 'Very Fragile' Governor States," *Hartford Courant*, 28 July 2004, 1.

[51] Edmund Andrews, "It's Not Just the Jobs Lost, But the Pay in the New Ones," *NYT*, 9 August, 2004, C1.

undermining the livelihoods of America's working families, and if it persists, it could have serious consequences for the nation's economy as a whole."[52] In Connecticut, the unemployment rate in several old industrial cities, including Bridgeport, East Hartford, and Waterbury nearly doubled the statewide average of 4.6 percent in June 2004.

From 2000 to 2004 Connecticut's manufacturing employment fell from 343,682 to 274,625; over the same period service employment fell to 908,725 from 925,389. Over these years, 3,462 jobs were lost in primary metals (–25 percent), 8,689 jobs were lost in industrial machinery (–20 percent), 32,263 jobs were lost in transportation equipment (–49 percent), and 17,278 jobs were lost in measuring and control instruments (–44 percent). Which sectors grew? The "winners," by jobs added, were health services, 19,437 (11 percent); educational services, 6,962 (7 percent); and social services, 5,101 (11 percent). Connecticut also lost nearly 16 percent of its engineering jobs (–16,500) between 1999 and 2004.

The implications for the middle-class wage structure in the United States are disturbing. This is the case because it is manufacturing that generated the highly-skilled, well-paid work that led to additional employment opportunities in small, family-owned machine shops like those scattered across Connecticut: neighborhood restaurants, local construction companies, banks, financial services, and real estate brokers. Manufacturing exports bring revenue into the state; economists refer to this as the "multiplier effect." When these jobs disappear, the opposite effect takes over and the erosion of well-paying work continues to cause social dislocation and economic misery in the Connecticut River Valley.

What happened to the aircraft engine and engine parts and components industry reflected several disturbing trends for workers and communities that mirrored the socioeconomic downturns faced by defense workers in the late twentieth century. Ann Markusen and Laura Powers concluded that a majority of laid-off defense workers "did not, on average, experience rapid re-employment at wages comparable or better" than their lost jobs. A sizable minority experienced a drop in earnings of 50 percent or more, which suggests "many defense workers did not become re-employed in jobs that capitalized on their existing skills." With the wherewithal to manufacture around the globe, Pratt, GE and other companies were able to play-off unions, communities, and nations for "sweetheart" financial deals in return for jobs.[53]

---

[52] AFL-CIO Industrial Union Department, "Revitalizing American Manufacturing," www.aflcio.org/manufacturing

[53] Laura Powers and Ann Markusen, *A Just Transition? Lessons from Defense Worker Adjustment in the 1990s,* Economic Policy Institute Technical Paper No. 237 (1999), Washington DC, 3, 25; author interview with Jeff Crosby, union president at GE Lynn, Winter, 1998.

Over the years the state and municipal governments did little to protect the remainder of their state and city's manufacturing jobs. In the late 1980s and early 1990s, while manufacturers exited Connecticut and Massachusetts, the mayors of Hartford and Springfield engaged in a newspaper advertisement war, each mayor trying to entice manufacturers from the other's city to their state. While the Connecticut legislature funded programs to encourage business research in biotechnology and medical devices, these programs did very little to help displaced aerospace workers.

The stories I heard during my September 2004 conversation with three Pratt & Whitney workers confirmed the pessimistic newspaper headlines that appear earlier in this section. All three men had been laid off at least once since 2001. Two men had just been recalled to work in Middletown, while the other one hoped for a recall soon. Each one had a personal story of the economic hardships the layoffs caused. But, despite the constant insecurity associated with working at Pratt, they each wanted to be recalled because there were no jobs available paying even nearly what they earned there. One worker drove a soda delivery truck in Greater New Haven 55 to 60 hours a week. The second, with several years of experience as an aircraft engine mechanic, found part-time jobs at Home Depot and Wal-Mart. He then "got lucky" and found full-time work at a newly opened Bed, Bath and Beyond store. But, once the store settled into a routine, his hours were cut back. The third person took a job selling clothing in a department store at 50 percent of his former hourly wage and averaged 25 hours a week. These men, in their late 30s and early 40s, always have worked. They suffered from the physical stress and anxiety associated with steep employment and income loss and the pressures associated with losing their family's medical insurance. They stopped going out to eat, curtailed going to the movies, and made the television and car last a little longer.

It is no geographical accident that highly skilled jet engine and aerospace production took place in Connecticut for well over 50 years. The Connecticut River Valley's fertile skill base provided the engineering and precision production skills required for this sector to grow and prosper.[54] But when ultramodern plants were built elsewhere and fewer investments were made in Connecticut, management produced the self-fulfilling prophecy that Connecticut's factories were no longer productive enough.

Economist Mary O'Sullivan described innovation as the process through which productive resources are developed and utilized to generate higher quality and lower cost products than had previously been available.[55] At the enterprise level, strategic decisions are made that determine the performance of the firm.

[54] B. Almeida, "Linking Institutions of Governance."
[55] Mary O'Sullivan, "The Innovative Enterprise and Corporate Governance," *Cambridge Journal of Economics*, 24 (2000a): 393-416.

These decisions have effects on the economy as a whole. A work-removal strategy generates high near-term returns for shareholders, as UTC's stock performance and handsome executive rewards indicate. However, the communities that were home to these corporations and industrial sectors in the prosperous times are left to suffer years of falling living standards and sharp population losses, a trend clearly visible in the Connecticut River Valley. In its degenerative phase, the Connecticut River Valley productive system faced a challenge from Japan based on production and innovation principles that were, in many ways, the keys to the region's earlier success. And the valley faced a challenge from the globalizing activities of U.S. corporations like Pratt & Whitney and American Bosch. They used world markets to outsource production and, as the demands of shareholders mobilized on a global scale, focused their managers' attention on short-term gain based on downsizing, deskilling, plant closures, cutbacks in research and development, and the neglect of investment in physical and human capital.[56]

It remains the case that the exigencies of global capitalism foster and impose decisions that are made far removed from individual factory floors, and void of a collective workers' voice. Thus, absent a consistent, concerted, and coordinated international labor voice, global production giants have the capacity to exercise significant bargaining leverage over their worldwide workforce and the power to worsen wages and working conditions for growing numbers of manufacturing workers as we have seen in Connecticut. The best hope for workers and their unions is to forge national and international bonds similar to the reach forged by global corporations. Plant closures and deindustrialization cannot be contested one factory at a time; but this is easier said than done.[57]

In closing, consider the remarks made in 2000 by UTC chairman George David before the Council on Foreign Relations. In discussing employment, he stated that Americans "don't want the jobs at the bottom of the economy, we want the jobs at the top, the issue is how to get there." Noting that UTC employed 201,000 people in 1990, and 148,000 in 2000—with an announced additional 10 percent cut coming—David urged corporations to "guard against

---

[56] Robert Forrant and Frank Wilkinson, "Globalisation and Degenerative Production Systems: The Case of the Connecticut River Valley," a paper presented at the conference Clusters, Industrial Districts and Firms: The Challenge of Globalization, Modena, Italy, September 12-13, 2003.

[57] Suzanne Konzelmann and Robert Forrant, "Creative Work Systems in Destructive Markets," in Brendan Burchell, Simon Deakin, Jonathan Michie, and Jill Rubery, eds., *Systems of Production: Markets, Organizations and Performance* (New York, Routledge, 2003): 129-158. For a discussion of a local union's corporate strategy, Andrew Jonas, "Investigating the Local-Global Paradox: Corporate Strategy, Union Local Autonomy, and Community Action in Chicago," in Andrew Herod, ed., *Organizing the Landscape: Geographical Perspectives on Labor Unionism* (Minneapolis, University of Minnesota Press, 1998): 325-350.

displacement" and to "establish and adhere to standards of performance and conduct internationally that are fair to employees everywhere."[58] At the time of David's talk, Pratt & Whitney machinist John Cloutier worked every day with the idea in the back of his mind "how much longer will I have this job." With gallows humor, unionist Ted Durkin expressed a similar feeling. "The old ethic that many companies had that their workforces really mattered is long gone. Now, when you leave the plant on Friday not laid off, you feel like you had a great week!" David's "fairness standard" was lost on both men.

---

[58] George David, "The Opportunity to Expand Skills and the Knowledge Base," 15 March, 2000. Speech before the Council on Foreign Relations, City News Publishing Company Vital Speeches, 66, No. 14, 439.

CHAPTER 8

Staggering Job Loss,
a Shrinking Revenue Base,
and Grinding Decline

It was there that the sleight-of-hand lawyers proved that the demands lacked
all validity for the simple reason that the company did not have, never had
had, and never would have any workers in its service because they were
all hired on a temporary and occasional basis. . . . and by a decision of
the court it was established and set down in solemn decree that the workers
did not exist.

— Gabriel Garcia-Marquez, *One Hundred Years of Solitude*

FROM BEEHIVE TO CITY OF HOMES

To review, in the 1980s a dramatic wave of lay-offs and plant closings among the
Connecticut River Valley's largest machine-tool and metalworking manufacturers led to rapid industrial decline and massive dislocation for several thousands
of the region's best-paid workers. The people who did the work and the trade
unions that represented them became extinct. Compounding the situation, there
were nearly two decades of hapless efforts by various local and state governments
to overcome employment loss and build some sort of sustainable economy.
Springfield, Massachusetts, the hardest hit city, fell into serious disrepair. Corrupt
officials exacerbated the problem and caused residents, already cynical about
their government, to become even more disenchanted with city leaders. Its
once-powerful agglomeration of skills and innovative firms depleted, Springfield
staggered, nearly bankrupt, into the new century.[1]

Even New England's vaunted education and training system, which once
satisfied employers' skills demands, couldn't turn the tide of economic failure.
In an earlier era firms sought out the Connecticut River Valley for its abundance

---

[1] Robert Forrant and Erin Flynn, "Seizing Agglomeration's Potential: The Greater-
Springfield Massachusetts Metalworking Sector in Transition, 1986-1996," *Regional Studies,*
32 (1998): 209-223.

of "high skills and scientific workers." Firms settled in the Connecticut River Valley because

> . . . areas like New England have a large number of firms which change their products and production processes frequently. Change means restructuring, learning new methods, testing, and experimenting. While a company which produces a large volume of output using a well-defined and unchanging production process looks to site its plants in low cost areas with little regard for distance from headquarters, companies which are changing and developing usually must keep a close watch on production. The combination of first, the need for specialized skills and, second, the changing nature of a firm's need for resources helps keep industrial agglomerations together.[2]

Springfield and the valley's deindustrialization story opens a window on how agglomeration gone bad affected hundreds of industrial cities. When managers at the American Bosch, Pratt & Whitney, and Jones & Lamson stopped investing in their skill base and searched for cheaper skills outside the region and the nation, the region's "innovation agglomeration" atrophied.

Recent historical studies of the textile, machinery, metalworking, and plastics industries reveal that a systematic learning process among enterprises and institutions strengthens skills and builds a regional economy's capacity for innovation. Prosperous "learning regions" depended on workers applying their intelligence at work. This facilitated the life-long learning required for successful knowledge-intensive production.[3] This proposition held true in Greater Springfield for nearly two centuries as new machine tools and knowledge sharing advantaged firms. Skilled workers exchanged their expertise; the idea was to "accept the best

[2] John S. Hekman, "The Future of High Technology Industry in New England: A Case Study of Computers," New England Economic Review (January/February 1980): 5-17, 6-7; John S. Hekman and John S. Strong, "The Evolution of New England Industry," New England Economic Review (March/April 1981): 35-46, 36.

[3] Richard Florida, "Toward the Learning Region," Futures (1995): 527-536. For historical studies on the importance of skill and collaboration, see Cristiano Antonelli and Roberto Marchionatti, "Technological and Organisational Change in a Process of Industrial Rejuvenation: The Case of the Italian Cotton Textile Industry," Cambridge Journal of Economics, 22 (1998): 1-18; Axel Wieandt, "'Innovation and the Creation, Development and Destruction of Markets in the World Machine Tool Industry," Small Business Economics, 6 (1994): 421-437; Vittorio Capecchi, "In Search of Flexibility: The Bologna Metalworking Industry, 1900-1992," in Charles Sabel and Jonathan Zeitlin, eds., World of Possibilities: Flexibility and Mass Production in Western Industrialization (New York: Cambridge University Press, 1997): 381-418; Philip Scranton, Endless Novelty: Specialty Production and American Industrialization, 1865-1925 (Princeton, NJ: Princeton University Press, 1997). For empirical studies of present-day regional industrial clusters and how firms and regions develop skills competencies, see the special issue of Regional Studies, "Regional Networking, Collective Learning and Innovation in High Technology SMEs in Europe," 33 (1999); Andrew Herod, "From a Geography of Labor to a Labor Geography: Labor's Spatial Fix and the Geography of Capitalism," Antipode, 29 (1997): 1-31.

and use it to the shop's betterment."[4] In the early 1950s the President' Council of Economic Advisers warned President Truman that New England firms were turning away from their historical strengths: skill development, technological innovation, and the diffusion of new production methods.[5] By 1968 even the Armory succumbed in the wake of defense-spending cuts, and in response, Springfield's Chamber of Commerce changed the city's nickname from the "Industrial Beehive" to the "City of Homes."[6] The scale of decline is evidenced in Table 8.1, which lists the major layoffs and closings in Hampden County between 1982 and 1990. The search for the next cheap place to get things made supplanted the valley's golden age of skill; metal fatigue had set in.[7]

In 1982 organized labor demanded that the Massachusetts legislature adopt plant closing legislation aimed at stopping the exit of jobs. Governor Michael Dukakis established a 38-member Commission on the Future of Mature Industries made up of leaders from business, labor, government, and academia and charged it with developing "an industrial policy to move the state toward a truly balanced economy . . . in terms of its industrial mix and in its distribution of benefits to the Commonwealth's regions and citizens."[8] Three issues overshadowed the Commission's work: the types of extra assistance, if any, workers caught in closings should receive; the proper economic-development role for state government in distressed regions; and whether firms should be required to give their employees and the state prenotification of layoffs and closings. While the

[4]Quote from the superintendent of the Osborn Manufacturing Company in Patrick Malone, "Little kinks and devices at the Springfield Armory, 1892-1918," *Journal of the Society for Industrial Archeology,* 14 (1988): 59-76, 64.

[5]Merrit Roe Smith, *Harpers Ferry Armory and the New Technology: The Challenge of Change* (Ithaca: Cornell University Press, 1977), 104-105.

[6]For a more detailed look at skills, see Michael Best and Robert Forrant, "Community-based Careers and Economic Virtue: Arming, Disarming, and Rearming the Springfield, Western Massachusetts Metalworking Region," in Michael B. Arthur and Denise M. Rousseau, eds., *The Boundaryless Career: A New Employment Principle for a New Organizational Era* (New York: Oxford University Press, 1996): 314-330.

[7]Robert Forrant, *Plant Closing and Major Layoffs in Springfield, Massachusetts* (Springfield, MA: Machine Action Project, 1986); Robert Forrant and Erin Flynn, "Seizing Agglomeration's Potential," *Regional Studies,* 32 (1998): 209-221; David Lampe, *The Massachusetts Miracle: High Technology and Economic Revitalization* (Cambridge, MA: MIT Press, 1988). Lynn E. Browne and Steven Sass, "The Transition From a Mill-Based to a Knowledge-Based Economy: New England, 1940-2000," in Peter Temin, ed., *Engines of Enterprise: An Economic History of New England* (Cambridge, MA: Harvard University Press, 2000): 201-249; Susan Rosegrant and David R. Lampe, *Route 128: Lessons from Boston's High-Tech Community* (New York: Basic Books, 1992); Michael Best and Robert Forrant, "Creating Industrial Capacity: Pentagon-led vs. Production-led Industrial Policies," in Jonathan Michie and John Grieve Smith, eds., *Creating Industrial Capacity: Toward Full Employment* (New York: Oxford University Press, 1996): 225-254.

[8]Judith Leff, "United Technologies and the Closing of the American Bosch," Harvard Business School Case Study, May 1986, 6.

Table 8.1. Layoffs and Closings in Springfield-Area Metalworking, 1982-1990

Company	Status	No. of jobs eliminated	Closure dates	Years in city	Peak employment since 1960
American Bosch	Closed	1,500	2/86	80	1800
Chapman Valve	Closed	250	6/86	100+	2700
Columbia Bicycle	Closed	250	6/88	80+	1000
Kidder Stacy	Closed	90	9/89	100+	325
Northeast Wire	Closed	35	1990	22	125
Oxford Precision	Closed	60	9/86	40	120
Package Machinery	Closed	400	9/88	100+	950
Plainville Casting	Closed	65	4/87	65	75
Portage Casting	Closed	60	8/86	36	100
Rafferty Steel	Closed	50	11/85	40	—
Rexnord Roller Chain	Closed	200	6/89	100+	675
Springfield Foundry	Closed	75	4/86	100+	285
Van Norman	Closed	275	10/83	90	1200
Van Valkenberg Plating	Closed	40	7/86	100+	135
Wico Prestolite	Closed	250	3/82	80	675
Atlas Copco	Layoffs	565	1980s	70+	1000
Easco Hand Tool	Layoffs	2,000	1980s	75+	2200
Storms Drop Forge	Layoffs	125	1980s	60+	250

Commission deliberated, 200 more firms closed and 18,000 additional workers lost their jobs.[9] In the end, the Commission produced weak, voluntary notification language that encouraged employers to give workers 90 days notice of shutdowns. A new Industrial Services Program (ISP) worked with unions and firms to avert closings, provide retraining if a closing occurred, and help specific communities affected by a large number of closures.[10]

AMERICAN BOSCH AND SPRINGFIELD: INTERTWINED HISTORIES OF PROSPERITY AND DECLINE

In December 2004 a fire destroyed the former American Bosch plant. The morning after the fire, managers at Danaher Tool (formerly Moore Drop Forge and EASCO Hand Tool), one of Bosch's North End neighbors and one of the few remaining metalworking firms in Springfield, announced its closing. Anxious to see the factory's ruins, and anticipating that several ex-Bosch workers would be too, I drove to the fire scene. At the destroyed building, it felt like I was attending a friend's wake. Still standing was the once white, now soot-stained front wall of the original factory building with the year 1911, signifying when the factory opened in the city, still visible. Around me stood nearly 100 former Bosch workers, each person eager to exchange stories about the old days. Memories flooded back as I walked down Main Street to the far corner of the building and peered through the rubble into the area of the factory where I had worked. I thought about workmates who showed up early every day, started their coffee pots and argued about the relative merits of the Boston Red Sox and the New York Yankees or the Boston Bruins and the New York Rangers (hockey mattered then). People sold donuts and newspapers to raise money for their children's college tuition or a local charity. Small-time gamblers sold betting tickets on the weekly football games.

The fire finalized the historical disconnect between several generations of relative working-class prosperity and the new, harsh reality represented by Springfield's dysfunctional urban center, its decaying neighborhood housing stock, and its slim hopes for an economic turnaround after years of neglect and irresponsible governance. At numerous intervals over 200 years, working people flocked to Springfield for the well-paying jobs they could find there; in 2004 young people voted with their feet and moved on if they could.

Just a few months before the fire, the Massachusetts legislature and Governor Mitt Romney took the unusual step of creating a Finance Control Board—chaired by the Commonwealth's Department of Revenue Commissioner Alan

---

[9]J. Leff, "United Technologies and the Closing of the American Bosch," 6.

[10]J. Leff, "United Technologies and the Closing of the American Bosch," 6; Governor's Commission on the Future of Mature Industries, *Final Report* (Commonwealth of Massachusetts, 1984).

LeBovidge—"to initiate and implement extraordinary remedies to achieve a long-term solution" to the city's money mess. By the time of the December fire, the Control Board had tightened its hold over the city's spending decisions. For the Control Board, the way forward seemed to come at the expense of teachers, school cafeteria workers, firefighters, policemen, and other city workers. Springfield needed to shrink its level of public services and focus on spending curbs.[11]

Recall that in his history of Massachusetts industry, Orra Stone called Springfield "a beehive of diversified production. " A 1941 Work Projects Administration study pointed out that

> Springfield's products have been for the most part the essentials of other industries, the machines, the tools, and units that turn the wheels of industry the world over. Because of this inter-relationship and the diversification of her industries, Springfield has suffered less from economic upheaval than single-industry cities of New England.[12]

In the 1950s and1960s Springfield's and most of the region's metalworkers enjoyed relatively good wages, and the city's downtown benefited. However, the wave of industrial closings and the loss of nearly 11,000 manufacturing jobs provoked the near collapse of many of the city's leading financial institutions. Because of the consolidation of manufacturing and financial services, Springfield's leading capitalists "lost ownership and control over capital," and one after another downtown's local banks and department stores closed. To add to the problem, several overly ambitious riverfront development projects failed to materialize. Elected officials and local and regional economic-development organizations and agencies spent years covering over the decline while searching for a new scheme that could breathe life.[13] However, in 2004 Springfield, the Bay State's third-largest city, had a $40-million budget deficit; deindustrialization's chickens had come to the empty downtown to roost! Wishful thinking, mismanagement, corruption, a soaring crime rate, and the failure of the region's extensive network of colleges and universities to contribute much time to strategizing over a solution to economic decline had turned even the most profound Springfield optimists into doomsayers.

Once installed, the Control Board focused on a handful of symptoms of distress, but it failed to address the historical relationship between the disappearance of well-paying work and the city's plight. No one in a responsible position discussed how the loss of half of Greater Springfield's manufacturing plants between 1950

[11] Alan LeBovidge, Letter from the Chairperson of the Springfield Finance Control Board to Eric Criss, Secretary, Executive Office of Administration and Finance, September 1, 2004.

[12] Writers' Program of the Works Progress Administration, *Springfield, Massachusetts* (Springfield: City of Springfield, 1941, 57.

[13] Bjorn Claeson, *The System Feeds on Us: An Ethnography of Poor People and Elites in a New England City,* PhD dissertation, Johns Hopkins University, 1996, 48.

and 1987 accompanied by the loss of 43 percent of Hampden County's industrial employment between 1980 and 2000 affected the city's finances. There can be little doubt that the cumulative impact of the closings and layoffs breached the historical continuity of the valley as a world leader in precision metalworking. And it was equally obvious that new high-wage replacement work had not materialized. Yet, from 2004 to 2007, rather than focus at least some of their attention on job creation and economic development, the Finance Control Board's turnaround strategy was predicated on "the containment of personnel costs."[14] Failing to focus on growing the city out of its budget mess, recovery remained unreachable. In April 2007 the Executive Director of the Control Board admitted as much when he reported that the city "faces a $3.2-million budget deficit for the fiscal year starting July 1 and deficits for the following three fiscal years" if it tries to pay back the original loan by 2009 as the enabling legislation required. The deficit required further cuts in city services and/or a series of new tax and revenue-raising measures.[15]

JOBS DO MATTER

There were at least six good reasons why members of the Finance Control Board, local and state economic development officials, and political leaders needed to make connections between employment loss and plant closings and Springfield's fiscal situation. First, blue-collar know-how had been a critical source of the city's and the state's competitive advantage and the basis for many business innovations that brought in wealth from outside the region. Second, well-paid industrial workers paid local and state taxes that helped to fund schools and fueled growth in the retail, real estate, and entertainment sectors. Third, workers' secure employment had allowed them to send their daughters and sons to college and helped to reproduce the state's vaunted skill base. Fourth, a statewide infrastructure of hundreds of small and medium-sized metalworking, plastics, and precision manufacturing firms received lucrative subcontracts from companies outside the region. Fifth, the wages in services lagged well behind manufacturing wages. And sixth, median household income in western Massachusetts' industrial cities dropped well below the state average of $50,502. The numbers in 2005 were: Greenfield, $33,110; Holyoke, $30,441; North Adams, $27,601; Pittsfield, $35,655; Springfield, $30,417.

Springfield's wage figure helps us to understand its present financial condition. Simply put, deindustrialization meant impoverishment for thousands of people. In his ethnographic study of Springfield's poverty-stricken neighborhoods, Bjorn Claeson found that between 1960 and 1990 the number of people

---

[14] *Boston Globe Editorial*, 17 June, 2005, 22.
[15] Dan Ring, "Springfield needs more time to repay loans," *The Republican*, 5 April, 2007.

employed in manufacturing in Springfield declined from approximately 23,000 to 12,000. He concluded that

> The wholesale and retail industry employed roughly the same number of people in Springfield in 1990 as in 1960 (13,563 versus 13,230). The service industry labor market, by contrast, grew during the same period of time; the total number of services in the city increased from 7,659 to 17,524. But, the service and retail jobs that increasingly dominate the labor market pay an average of $7,000 and $17,000 respectively less per year than the average manufacturing job, even accounting for wage reductions in manufacturing. Many people who formerly would have enjoyed stable industrial jobs and comfortable wage lead an existence even more insecure, having been pushed into the city's dangerous informal service economy.[16]

While manufacturing employment fell across Massachusetts and in Hampden County between 2000 and 2004, there was some growth in lower wage services employment and in some engineering and business services categories. The state continued to lose metalworking jobs: employment fell in this category from 197,000 jobs in 2000 to 167,656 jobs in 2004, a 15 percent fall off. Hampden County lost 16 percent of its metalworking employment over the same period and at the end of 2005 there were slightly less than 10,000 jobs in this category, a far cry from the thousands of jobs that existed as late as the early 1980s. Across Massachusetts and in Hampden County in particular these jobs were replaced by employment in several finance categories that paid reasonably well but required an education far different than the one that laid off metalworkers had, or low wage retail and restaurant employment.

As the employment crisis in manufacturing worsened, Springfield's leaders wrongly assumed that Massachusetts' boom in electronics, finance, and bio-technology would right the ship. But, by late 2001 Hampden County's employment stagnated. Even though the Bay State added almost 500,000 service-sector jobs over the 1980s and 1990s, the majority of the well-paying ones were inside the Route 495 beltway, far closer to Boston than to Springfield. According to the *Boston Globe*'s Charles Stein, "The new economy never made it this far outside the Massachusetts Turnpike." Stein summarized, "A lot of middle-class people left for better economic opportunities, while the number of poor people grew steadily over the past two decades. This shift helped make Springfield one of the poorest cities in Massachusetts."[17] Springfield's unemployment rate of 8.5 percent was a lot higher in several of its Hispanic and African American neighborhoods. The public-health infrastructure got smaller. School nurses were fired. Fourteen thousand streetlights were turned

[16] Bjorn Claeson, *The System Feeds on Us*, 49.
[17] Charles Stein, "Almost a Ward of the State," *Boston Globe*, 18 June, 2004, C1.

off for almost two years. Jobs in the police department and schools were cut. Fire stations closed on a rotating basis.[18]

To reiterate, the vaunted service economy produced far too few well-paying, full-time jobs. In Massachusetts, the gap between average manufacturing and services wages did not close appreciably between 1997 and 2003. For the country, "Industries ranked in the bottom fifth for wages and salaries have added 477,000 jobs since January 2004, while industries in the top fifth for wages had no increases at all. . . ."[19] In 2003 three of the largest occupations adding jobs in Massachusetts—cashiers, food preparation, waiters and waitresses—paid average wages below $10 an hour. In the same year, nine of the fifteen largest occupations in the Bay State reported average wages of less than $15 an hour. "Given the high cost of living in Massachusetts this proliferation of low-wage jobs is a major public policy challenge. . . ."[20] In Hampden County, all manufacturing employment fell from 34,301 jobs in 1998 to 28,000 in 2004, while service jobs increased from 86,500 to nearly 96,000. Over that period service-sector wages barely registered over $650 a week, while the remaining manufacturing jobs averaged $850.

Commenting on August 2004 national employment data, *New York Times* business reporter Louis Uchitelle noted that layoffs are "more frequent now in good times and bad, than they were in similar cycles a decade ago." Across the country, the almost 60 percent of laid-off workers who found a new job earned less money, compared with about 50 percent of workers who went through the same experience in the early 1990s. In other words, both the number of new jobs and the wages of jobs continues to moderate, so that even when employment growth occurred, the wealth base eroded. This is what transpired in Springfield. Thus, absent sharp tax increases or an infusion of new revenues from the state or federal government to make up for lost taxes and local spending by workers, essential services—education, youth programs, police and fire protection—suffer, and jobs that depend on disposable income, like restaurants, disappear. Michael Yates confirms these trends: "For a nation as rich as the United States, there are a very large number of low-paying jobs. One of the most interesting data sets in the *The State of Working America* is that for the fraction of jobs which pay an hourly wage rate insufficient to support a family of four at the poverty level of income with full-time, year-round work." One-quarter of all

[18] Robert Forrant and Shaun Barry, "Winners and Losers: High-Tech Employment Deals an Uneven Hand," *Massachusetts Benchmarks,* 4(3), 2001: 12-16; Mark Brenner, "The Economy: A Growing Divide with Uneven Prospects," in Tom Juravich, ed., *The Future of Work in Massachusetts* (Amherst: University of Massachusetts Press, 2007): 11-32.

[19] Edmund Andrews, "It's Not Just the Jobs Lost, But the Pay in the New Ones," *NYT,* 9 August, 2004, C1; Charles Stein, "Wages Don't Figure in Rebound," *BG,* May 5, 2004, 1. Inflation-adjusted average manufacturing wages in the Commonwealth were $1,120 in 1997 and $1,116 in 2003; services wages averaged $747 in 1997 and $876 in 2003.

[20] M. Brenner, "The Economy," 2007.

jobs pay at or below poverty wages; for Blacks, the figure is 30.4 percent and for Hispanic workers 39.8 percent. For Black women the figure is 33.9 percent and for Hispanic women, 45.8 percent.[21]

"A COMATOSE PATIENT ON LIFE SUPPORT": THE FINANCE CONTROL BOARD TAKES CHARGE

This brings us back to Springfield, Massachusetts. Several Springfield business associations, including Future Springfield, the Springfield Taxpayers Association, and Springfield Central, Inc. attempted to lead a business revival of sorts in the 1980s. So-called public–private partnerships were going to save the day. But these partnerships could not stop the decline of the city's central commercial and financial corridor along Main Street between the *Springfield Republican*'s newspaper offices and city hall and the civic center. Two of the city's leading retailers, Forbes and Wallace along with Steigers, vacated their multistory department stores in 1976 and 1994 respectively, no match for the large indoor malls that sprang up along Interstate Route 91.

For years, Springfield's recovery rested on its $110 million riverfront development project, anchored by the new Naismith Memorial Basketball Hall of Fame, and the renovation of its downtown civic center. "Entertainment complexes, riverboat gambling, interactive museums, crafts and arts centers, and riverboat rides" were proposed to supplement activities at the Hall of Fame. In other words, tourism dollars were to spark a revival of sorts. However, the Basketball Hall of Fame never generated the visits that consultants predicted, nor is there any evidence that well-paying jobs materialized along the riverfront. Among its difficulties, the riverfront is cut off from the city's commercial downtown by a six-lane raised highway and railroad tracks. By the early 1990s nearly one-quarter of downtown office buildings were vacant. "The Society of Industrial and Office realtors ranked Greater Springfield as the area with the sixth-highest office vacancy rate in the country."[22]

The collapse persisted through a lengthy period of economic expansion elsewhere in the state. For Springfield, according to Robert Nakosteen, a professor of economics and statistics at the Isenberg School of Management at the University of Massachusetts Amherst, this created a significant structural problem whereby the city could not "depend on its own tax base. All the wealth just moved out of the city." William Ward, head of the Hampden County Regional Employment Board,

[21] Louis Uchitelle, "Layoff Rates at 8.7%, Highest Since 80's," *NYT*, 2 August, 2004, C2; Michael Yates, "A Statistical Portrait of the U.S. Working Class," *Monthly Review*, 56(11), 2005: 12-31.
[22] Bjorn Claeson, *The System Feeds on Us*, 304-305; Marla Goldberg, "Attendance dips, hope rises at Hall," *Sunday Republican*, 17 April, 2005, 1; B. J. Roche, "Under Control?" *CommonWealth*, Summer 2005: 50-60.

noted that as the well-paying work disappeared, the replacement wages for workers fortunate enough to find new jobs lagged well behind their previous pay and benefits.[23] Yet, the city's financial problems were not taken seriously, even in the mid-1990s, when it received a $21-million state loan and sold its municipally owned hospital to a private company to cover budget shortfalls.

Fifteen years later the Finance Control Board (FCB) focused on bringing costs in line with projected city revenues, cutting back on essential services, and reducing personnel costs. For the Control Board, "Some combination of increases in economic productivity, reduction in wages and benefits, and work rule changes must be accomplished if the city is to have annual balanced budgets." In September 2004 FCB Chairman LeBovidge summarized the situation this way: "It is clear that an integral part of the recovery plan for the city of Springfield must include work rule changes, benefits restructuring and take-home pay reductions for municipal workers." In 2004 *The Republican* called the city "a financial basket case."[24] As the crisis worsened, *Republican* reporter Dan Ring wrote, "Although Springfield is the third-largest city in the Commonwealth out of 351 municipalities it has the lowest bond rating, the fourth-lowest income per capita, the second-lowest property values and the highest nonresidential property tax rate in the state."[25]

City officials negotiated a relief package with the Romney administration and the legislature. The governor offered approximately $51 million in interest-free loans to cover the shortfall in the $437-million fiscal year 2004 budget, so long as the city agreed to let a state-appointed control board make future spending decisions. Attached to the proposal was the suspension of collective bargaining for the city's unions.[26] Ken Donnelly, secretary treasurer of the Professional Firefighters of Massachusetts, accused the governor of "trying to break the unions. I haven't seen anything this bad in 32 years." Timothy Collins, president of the Springfield Education Association, said that the control board plan represented "the lowest day of my life when you have a mayor and a governor stripping us of our collective bargaining rights. It's almost un-American. Shame on the governor and shame on the mayor." Ken Poole, who represented Public Works employees, noted that his union had 364 members in 1999 and in mid-2004 just 208 members.

---

[23] Robert Nakosteen quoted in Adam Gorlick, "Springfield Bailout Bill Stalls Due to Union Concerns," Associated Press, 4 June, 2004; Interview with William Ward, March 25, 2005.

[24] Scott Greenberger, "State Eying Municipal Bailout: Springfield Facing $20M Budget Deficit," *BG*, 29 May, 2004, B1; LeBovidge letter to Kriss, 1 September, 2004; *Boston Herald*, "Better Rail Service Would Help Get W. Mass Economy on Track," 26 June, 2004, 18.

[25] Dan Ring, "Finneran Downplays Bankruptcy," *The Republican*, 16 June, 2004, 1.

[26] Trudy Tynan, "With State Aid Promised, Springfield Now Faces the Hard Part," *The Associated Press*, 16 July, 2004; Peter DeMarco and Tyrone Richardson, Bumpy Road is Seen for Springfield," *BG*, 6 June, 2004, B3.

Ultimately, the city received a $52-million interest-free loan to be paid back by 2012. The $52-million figure matched what the city was owed in delinquent property taxes. With the loan came the FCB to take over fiscal management of the city through the summer of 2007. The Board's term was extended to 2009 in mid-2007 when it became apparent that Springfield would not be able to pay the loan back by 2012 as was required in the enabling legislation.[27] And, despite the arguments from union leaders that job cuts and wage freezes would negatively impact the provision of essential protective and educational services and cause more residents to leave the city, the Board instituted a wage freeze. Teachers' previously negotiated pay increases were held back, causing the exodus of nearly 250 teachers during the 2004-2005 academic year.[28] By early 2005 Springfield was being referred to as "a city under siege."[29] In one of its first public statements, the Board informed residents that

> No solution to the city's fiscal crisis can be achieved without a substantial reduction of personnel costs and expenses. It is clear that an integral part of the recovery plan for the city of Springfield must include work rule changes, benefits restructuring and take-home pay reductions for municipal employees.[30]

Eric Kriss, one of Governor Mitt Romney's chief financial advisors, described the Board as "a tool to help the city recover financially" and contended that a turnaround could occur only with the good will and effort of municipal employees. But, with 20 percent of the city's workforce cut between 2002 and 2004, and the private-sector job base continuing to shrink, it was difficult to imagine why city workers would go along with the FCB's plans. Observers also found it difficult to see where any badly needed economic stimulus would come from. This prompted *The Republican* to remind its readers: "While we agree that work rule and benefit changes need to be made regarding city employees, we vigorously oppose the reduction of their wages and think it would be unconscionable to do so." For good measure, the newspaper's editorial added, "The Control Board should be working for a surgical plan to restore the city's finances, not a hatchet job that leaves the city as nothing more than a comatose patient on life support."[31]

[27] Peter Goonan, "Current Tax Collection Bodes Well," *The Repubican,* 3 September, 2004, 1.

[28] Quotes in Adam Gorlick, Springfield Bailout Bill Stalls Due to Union Concerns," *The Associated Press,* 4 June, 2004.

[29] Roselyn Tantraphol, "Springfield: A City Under Siege," *Hartford Courant,* 17 April, 2005, 1.

[30] P. Goonan, 2004, 1.

[31] *The Republican,* "Finance Control Board too Quick on the Draw," 3 September, 2004, 16.

SPRINGFIELD IN 2007:
THREE YEARS OF FINANCE CONTROL BOARD GOVERNANCE

For most of the last two centuries the Connecticut River Valley, with Springfield as its leading city, related to the rest of the country and the world as a stellar manufacturing center, its metalworkers and machinery builders fueling the nation's industrial revolution. In historical succession, industries including textiles, paper, shoes, rifles and handguns, industrial machinery, aircraft engines, and computers generated spectacular wealth and advanced workers' living standards. Metalworking growth stemmed from three related factors: continual innovations in product design and development stimulated by the Springfield Armory; a nucleus of locally-owned, collaborative, machine-tool builders and precision metalworking firms whose expertise provided the region with the first-mover benefits of any technological breakthrough; and the base of skilled workers performing the precision machining required to turn out world-class products.

Springfield and the region were caught up in the accelerated pace of globalization, and the skill base was no longer a sufficient magnet to preserve and grow well-paying work. Once locally owned firms changed hands, their assets were globalized, and the region's ability to shape and reshape its economic future slipped away. Springfield scrambled to save what jobs it could, offering corporations financial inducement to stay or move in, much like Columbus, Mississippi, did when it lured American Bosch there in the mid-1950s. Springfield and nearby Hartford, Connecticut, even engaged in a border war, each city's mayor offering inducements to firms to move employment approximately 30 miles north or south along Route 91. While politicians fiddled, the skill base cultivated up and down the Connecticut River Valley for over a century disappeared. East Hartford and Springfield—once home to major industries—suffered years of falling living standards and sharp population losses.

The original catalyst for economic development in the Connecticut River Valley was the establishment of the Springfield Armory. A central objective of the Armory was the development of precision engineering and its use in gun production. Its willingness to diffuse technical knowledge to its contractors, spread best practice, and its ability to attract and train skilled mechanics laid the foundation of a highly skilled workforce. In turn, this served as a repository of knowledge, the means of incorporating new technical information, and the source of highly innovative new business start-ups. Burgeoning expertise in machine-tool technology provided the basis for a capital-goods sector that interacted with emerging industries, creating a diverse manufacturing base. Both benefited from learning processes within networks of machine builders, small specialist engineering shops, education and training institutions, and final-goods producers. The strong shop-floor skill base, combined with innovative and forward-looking employers, provided the region with a competitive advantage for close to 150 years.

The productive system reached its zenith during the Second World War. The river valley is suffering economically today due to the failure to develop a new "Armory," a new catalyst for sustainable prosperity. No amount of belt tightening, no long-term freeze on teachers' wages, no fanciful notions that tourist attractions will grow a plentiful supply of well-paying jobs can arrest the city and region's slump. Cooperation among the region's trade association, trade unions, educational institutions, and supportive state and federal agencies is essential for meaningful job creation to occur.

The history of the American Bosch and its "precision valley" home during the 1950s and 1960s depicts a fluid period when, in plants that contained skilled workers and work routines not yet highly automated, it may have been possible for richer, more productive union–management shop-floor relationships to mature. But, as work disappeared, the moment slipped away and thereafter only infrequent lip service was paid to organizing a valleywide community campaign against runaway shops and lost jobs. This left the "artificial spatial divides between the workplace and the broader community" intact and strengthened the more unified corporate America, intent on limiting labor's role in economic decision making.[32]

Unionists interested in production questions confronted the perspective of an erstwhile ally like the Industrial Relations Research Association (IRRA): "the management function of initiating, directing, and providing a driving force remains as a basic value in a dynamic, progressive economy."[33] The IRRA's position is similar to the one held by corporate officers in attendance at President Truman's post-Second World War labor–management conference. The excitement generated on America's shop floors by Reuther's 1940 plan to turn the automobile assembly lines of Detroit into airplane factories was forgotten at the national level, yet as the Bosch story indicates, at the plant level, production issues mattered. The excitement that the Reuther plan evoked came from the fact that it represented "counterplanning from the shop floor. Organized and coordinated through the union, veteran machinists and tool-and-die men had a better overall understanding of industry techniques than did any individual corporate manager."[34] The Bosch story helps us shape a more thorough understanding of post-World War II industry decline, and it helps clarify why workers, with a sense of history, opposed employer calls for participation in the 1980s that sounded very much like Local 206's calls for participation in the 1950s and 1960s.

In 1983 economists Thomas Weisskopf, Samuel Bowles, and David Gordon developed an analytical model to help explain lagging U.S. business innovation

[32] Andrew Herod, *Labor Geographies: Workers and the Landscapes of Capitalism* (New York: The Guilford Press, 2001), 268.

[33] L. Reed Tripp, "The Union's Role in Industry—Its Extents and Limits," in Industrial Relations Research Association, *Interpreting the Labor Movement* (1952), 103.

[34] Nelson Lichtenstein, *Walter Reuther: The Most Dangerous Man in Detroit* (New York: Basic Books, 1995), 162.

and productivity since the mid-1960s. They argued that the principal problem was the rapid decline in work intensity after 1966; workers' hearts and minds were disengaged from their labor.[35] Compare this to what Martin Kenney and Richard Florida discovered in Japanese transplant companies: "Perhaps the key element of the Japanese industrial system lies in its ability to harness workers' knowledge as a source of value directly at the point of production."[36]

While Springfield's skilled workers were perceived as a threat to managerial prerogative, according to William Lazonick, in Japan and Germany workers were viewed as "a source of enhanced value creation."[37] By discounting skill and worker input, managers discarded the utilization of the very knowledge base essential for their success. What sense did it make for management to erect barriers against the production knowledge of the 50 men who joined the Bosch 25-year club in the early 1950s? This group's 10 tool-and-die makers and set-up men had 250 years of experience manufacturing diesel components; Perelle's management team had zero. Surely managers could have learned something from these men! After numerous rebuffs, unionists got the point and turned to strikes and job actions to block management's efficiency, speed-up, production rationalization and cost-cutting strategies.

Bosch unionists' insistence on linking selling price and market share to quality offered an alternative management vision, albeit one that required an investment in the workforce and a willingness by managers like Perelle to make room for the tacit production knowledge that workers possessed. In an early 1950s editorial entitled "Quality is an Investment," the *Labor Bulletin* acknowledged that "we live in a highly competitive world, and product quality and selling price must be attractive enough to solicit business." The editorial noted, "Actually, the quality and selling price go hand in hand, like ham and eggs, toast and butter, etc. How could you possibly maintain a harmonious relationship between the two if some irresponsible people cause parts to be machined over and over again, thus throwing the actual selling price to a lower level than the actual cost?" Quality work, the union concluded, was essential to safeguard jobs and the city's economic future.[38]

Unionists articulated an axiom not fully appreciated by U.S. managers until well into the late 1970s. Unionists knew full well that quality production was an essential ingredient of job security and offered a running critique of management's

---

[35] Thomas Weisskopf, Samuel Bowles, and David Gordon, "Hearts and Minds: A Social Model of U.S. Productivity Growth," *Brookings Papers on Economic Activity*, 1983 (no. 2): 381-450: 382-383, 422.

[36] Martin Kenney and Richard Florida, *Beyond Mass Production: The Japanese System and Its Transfer to the U.S.* (New York: Oxford University Press, 1993), 39.

[37] William Lazonick, *Competitive Advantage on the Shop Floor* (Cambridge: Harvard University Press, 1990), 290-292.

[38] *LB*, September, 1952.

quality strategy that was remarkably similar to that being offered in Japan by such highly celebrated quality-improvement champions as W. Edwards Deming and J. W. Juran. While one could argue that Bosch unionists had little real interest in solving production problems and were acting mainly to impede management change efforts, a close examination of the historical record reveals a more complex interpretation and shows how corporate–union animus after World War II prevented managers from acknowledging any positive union overtures toward the construction of shopfloor problem-solving partnerships. Ironically, such problem-solving arrangements conformed closely to the strategy employed by American Bosch's ablest competitor and Springfield primogenitor, Robert Bosch, GmBH, and the union representing Robert Bosch workers. Robert Bosch recognized the importance of skilled labor and, through the works councils in its plants drew upon the knowledge of the workforce to wrest the automotive and agricultural diesel markets rather easily away from its U.S. rival in the 1960s.

After 1971 labor relations remained contentious on three issues: the timing of set-ups; the modification of the piecework incentive system through the use of pre-determined time standards; and the proper role for workers in the resolution of production-related problems. Management continued to argue that labor costs needed to be dramatically lowered if the plant was to be competitive in the global economy; in other words, survival of the Springfield factory was contingent on workers' providing the necessary "pound of flesh," something unionists were never willing to give. These were the wrong arguments to be having. While many Bosch workers were highly skilled, they were not allowed to apply their skills toward in-plant decisions. The irony is that ARMA's competitors in Germany and Japan pursued improvement strategies with their workers. Inside Toyota, labor and management did not fight about incentive times on machine-tool set-ups, rather they worked to reduce the time required to do them. German metalworking firms did not simply reorganize production by the use of computers and labor-saving equipment; instead, they embraced existing tacit shop-floor knowledge to maximize their technology investments.[39]

---

[39] For a discussion of what competitor firms were up to, see Taiichi Ohno, *The Toyota Production System: Beyond Large Scale Production* (Cambridge: Progress Press, 1988); Margaret Hilton, "Shared Training: Learning from Germany," *Monthly Labor Review* (March 1991): 33-37; David Marsden, "A Phoenix from the Ashes of Apprenticeship? Vocational Training in Britain," *International Contributions to Labour Studies*, 5 (1995): 87-114; "In the Japanese system," Ohno writes, "operators acquire a broad spectrum of production skills and participate in building up a total system in the production plant. In this way, the individual can find value in working," 14. The purpose here is not to debate Japanese-style management and its effects on unions and workers, or to treat lightly the literature on the subject, but to suggest what competitor countries were doing on their factory floors. By and large, U.S. companies took Bosch's overtly confrontational approach, not the team-building and problem-solving orientation employed in Japan.

When, in the late 1950s, Perelle realized that he needed the plant's skill base, he never signaled workers that their knowledge was important. Instead, he established a technology committee without one union representative, and with Ahab-like determination, searched high and low for workers with skill that he could pay less money to or a technology substitute for labor. The failure of management in thousands of manufacturing facilities to recognize and accept workers' interest in honest participation contributed to the calcification of labor relations, helped cause lagging productivity growth, and eventually enabled the devastation of manufacturing cities like East Hartford, Connecticut; Springfield, Massachusetts; and Springfield, Vermont—cities that had relied for years on the historical skill, shrewdness, and tacit knowledge of hard-working people. Bosch workers were neither stupid nor blind; but after about 1970 they became selectively deaf and dumb, and used their guile only to do whatever was minimally required to get through an 8-hour shift.

Managers resisted workers' efforts to democratize their workplaces and engage in shopfloor decision making. Similarly, the Finance Control Board took away residents' voice in helping to rebuild their city. Eighteen months into the Control Board's rule, unions representing teachers, police, and firefighters fought through the courts to get their negotiated pay increases restored. A 23-year-old forklift operator expressed the feelings of many residents: "Just get it over with. To know your city is going broke—it's time to move out of here. There's no opportunity here."[40] Labor leaders believed that Governor Romney was more interested in imposing conservative fiscal measures and policies on the city to bolster his national political stature, than in solving the problems Springfield confronted. Cost-cutting ideas included charging fees for trash removal, closing libraries, selling the municipal golf course, and transferring city employees to the state employees' health care plan. Tim Collins, president of the Springfield Education Association and an outspoken critic of the Control Board, charged

> These political leaders have starved this city into this situation, so they could put forward their Draconian agenda. And the leadership of the Legislature is letting the city fail because they want to give Romney a black eye as he runs for president.[41]

In July 2007, after three years of the Control Board's existence, and after the Democrat, Deval Patrick, was elected governor and put several new members on the Board, for the first time the Board talked openly about how it might stimulate economic development. Calls were made for the colleges and universities in the region to lend their expertise to the monumental task of finding several new engines of prosperity for the valley, ones that might match the skills and innovation that had previously propelled the regional economy forward.

[40] Quoted in Stephanie Ebbert, "Springfield Edges Toward Fiscal Abyss," *BG*, 17 January, 2006.
[41] Collins quoted in S. Ebbert, "Springfield Edges Toward Fiscal Abyss," *BG*, 17 January, 2006.

References

BOOKS AND ARTICLES

Adler, W. M. 2000. *Mollie's Job: A Story of Life and Work on the Global Assembly Line,* New York, Scribner.

Alexander, A. J. 1994. "Adaptation to Change in the US Machine Tool Industry," in Hong W. Tan and Haruo Shimada Kingsbury, Eds., *Troubled Industries in the United States and Japan,* New York, Palgrave, 321-367.

Almeida, B. 2002. "Good Jobs Flying Away: The U.S. Jet Engine Industry," in W. Lazonick and M. O'Sullivan, Eds., *Corporate Governance and Sustainable Prosperity: Industrial Innovation, International Competition and Intergenerational Dependence,* New York, Palgrave, 104-140.

Altman, D. 2002. "Nation's Unemployment Rate Rises to 5.8%," *New York Times,* 5 January, B1.

American Machinist. 1964. "Numerical Control: The Second Decade," Special Report No. 559, October 26.

Andrews, E. 2004. "It's Not Just the Jobs Lost, But the Pay in the New Ones," *New York Times,* August 9, C1.

Antonelli, C. and R. Marchionatti, R. 1998. "Technological and Organisational Change in a Process of Industrial Rejuvenation: The Case of the Italian Cotton Textile Industry," *Cambridge Journal of Economics,* 22, 1-18.

Applebaum, E. and Batt, R. 1994. *The New American Workplace: Transforming Work Systems in the United States,* Ithaca, ILR Press.

Arnold, A. J. 1999. "Innovation, Deskilling and Profitability in the British Machine-Tools Industry: Albert Herbert 1887-1927," *Journal of Industrial History,* 2, 50-71.

Artman, C. 1930. *The Industrial Structure of New England: Part One of the Commercial Survey of New England,* Washington, D.C., U.S. Department of Commerce.

Ashburn, A. 1990. "The Machine Tool Industry: The Crumbling Foundation," in D. Hicks, Ed., *Is New Technology Enough? Making and Remaking U.S. Basic Industries.* Washington, D.C.: American Enterprise Institute for Public Policy Research, 19-85.

Association for Manufacturing Technology. 1996a. *The Economic Handbook of the Machine Tool Industry 1996-1997,* McLean, VA, Association of Manufacturing Technology.

Association for Manufacturing Technology. 1996b. *1995 Machine-Tool Scorecard,* McLean, VA, Association of Manufacturing Technology.

Atkins, R. M. 1952. "A Program for Relocating the New Plant," *Harvard Business Review,* 30, November-December, 113-118.

Babson, S. 1991. *Building the Union: Skilled Workers and Anglo-Gaelic Immigrants in the Rise of the UAW,* New Brunswick, Rutgers University Press.

Backman, J. 1962. *The Economics of the Electrical Manufacturing Industry*, New York, New York University Press.
Barber, R. and Scott, R. 1995. *Jobs on the Wing: Trading Away the Future of the U.S. Aerospace Industry*, Washington, D.C., Economic Policy Institute.
Barnard, J. 1986. "Rebirth of the United Automobile Workers: The General Motors Tool and Diemakers' Strike of 1939," *Labor History*, 27, 165-187.
Bernstein, A. 1998. "What Price Peace: GM Lost a Lot to the UAW, and Labor Relations are Still Bad," *Business Week*, August 10, 24.
Bernstein, A. 1999. "Welch's march to the South," *Business Week*, December, 6, 74.
Bernstein, M. 1994. "Understanding American Economic Decline: The Contours of the Late-Twentieth-Century Experience," in Michael A. Berstein and David E. Adler, Eds., *Understanding American Economic Decline*, New York, Cambridge University Press, 1994, 3-33.
Best, M. 2001. *The New Competitive Advantage: The Renewal of American Industry*, New York, Oxford University Press.
Best, M. 1990. *The New Competition*, Cambridge, Harvard University Press.
Best, M. and Forrant, R. 1998. "Community-Based Careers and Economic Virtue: Arming, Disarming, and Rearming the Springfield, Western Massachusetts Metalworking Region," in M. Arthur and D. Rousseau, Eds., *The Boundaryless Career*, Cambridge, England, Oxford University Press, 314-330.
Bluestone, B. and Harrison, B. 1982. *The Deindustrialization of America*, New York, Basic Books.
Bluestone, B. and Harrison, B. 1988. *The Great U-Turn: Corporate Restructuring and the Polarizing of America*, New York, Basic Books.
Bolz, R. 1954. "A Successful Partnership," *Automation*, September 1, 1954, 13.
Bombardieri, M. 2002. "Richer, Poorer," *The Boston Globe*, 5 May, B1.
Bonislawski, M. 1992. *The Anti-Communist Movement and Industrial Unionism: IUE vs. UE*, University of Massachusetts Boston Master of Arts Thesis.
Boucher, N. 1994. "A Natural History of the Connecticut Valley Metal Trade," *Regional Review* Winter, 6-12.
Bradsher, K. 1998b. "General Motors Plans to Build New, Efficient Assembly Plants," *The New York* Times, August 6, 1.
Brenner, M. 2007. "The Economy: A Growing Divide with Uneven Prospects," in Tom Juravich, Ed., *The Future of Work in Massachusetts*, Amherst, University of Massachusetts Press, 2007, 11-32.
Brody, D. 1980. *Workers in Industrial America: Essays on the Twentieth Century Struggle*, New York, Oxford University Press.
Brody, D. 1993. *In Labor's Cause: Main Themes on the History of the American Worker*, New York, Oxford University Press.
Broehl, W. 1959. *Precision Valley: The Machine Tool Companies of Springfield*, Vermont, Englewood Cliffs, NJ, Prentice-Hall.
Brown, E. C. 1939. "The New Collective Bargaining in Mass Production: Methods, Results, Problems," *Journal of Political Economy*, 47, 30-66.
Browne, L. and Sass, S. 2000. "The Transition From a Mill-Based to a Knowledge-Based Economy: New England, 1940-2000," in P. Temin, Ed., *Engines of Enterprise: An Economic History of New England*, Cambridge, MA, Harvard University Press, 201-249.

Capecchi, V. 1997. "In Search of Flexibility: The Bologna Metalworking Industry, 1900-1992," in C. Sabel and J. Zeitlin, Eds., *World of Possibilities: Flexibility and Mass Production in Western Industrialization*, New York, Cambridge University Press, 381-418.

Cappelli, P., Bassi, L., Katz, H., Knoke, D., Osterman, P. and Useem, M. 1997. *Change at Work*, New York, Oxford University Press.

Chokki, T. 1986. "A History of the Machine Tool Industry in Japan," in M. Fransman, Ed., *Machinery and Economic Development*, New York, St. Martin's, 124-152.

Claeson, B. 1996. *The System Feeds on Us: An Ethnography of Poor People And Elites in a New England City*, PhD dissertation, Johns Hopkins University, 1996.

Cobb, J. 1988. "Beyond Planters and Industrialists: A New Perspective on the New South," *Journal of Southern History*, 54, 1988, 45-68.

Cobb, J. 1993. *The Selling of the South: The Southern Crusade for Industrial Development*, Urbana, University of Illinois Press, second edition.

Collins, C., Leondar-Wright, B. and Sklar, H. 1999. *Shifting Fortunes: The Perils of the Growing American Wealth Gap*, Boston, United for a Fair Economy.

Collis, David. 1988a. *Kingsbury Machine Tool Corporation, Harvard Business School case study no. 9-388-110*, Boston, Harvard Business School.

Collis, David. 1988b. "The Machine Tool Industry and Industrial Policy, 1955-1982," in A. M. Spence and H. Hazards, Eds., *International Competitiveness*, New York, Harper Business.

Committee on the Machine Tool Industry. 1983. *The U.S. Machine Tool Industry and the Defense Industrial Base*, Washington, D.C., National Academy Press.

Commonwealth of Massachusetts. 1913. *A Directory of Massachusetts Manufacturers*, Boston, MA.

Commonwealth of Massachusetts. 1993. *Choosing to Compete: A Statewide Strategy for Job Creation and Economic Growth*, Boston, Executive Office of Economic Affairs.

Cope, K. 1994. *Makers of American Machinists' Tools*, Mendham, NJ, Astragal Press.

Corcoran, William. 1990. "The Machine Tool Industry Under Fire," in D. Losman and Shu-Jan Liang, Eds., *The Promise of American Industry*, New York, Quorum Books, 227-248.

Cowie, J. 1999. *Capital Moves: RCA's 70-year Question for Cheap Labor*, Ithaca, Cornell University Press, 1999.

Craypo, C. 1984. "The Deindustrialization of a Factory Town: Plant Closings and Phasedowns in South Bend, Indiana, 1954-1983," in Donald Kennedy, Ed., *Labor and Reindustrialization: Workers and Corporate Change*, University Park, PA, The Pennsylvania State University Press, 27-67.

Critical Technologies Institute. 1994. *The Decline of the U.S. Machine Tool Industry and Prospects for its Sustainable Recovery*, two volumes, Santa Monica, CA, Rand.

Cumbler, J. 1989. *A Social History of Economic Decline: Business, Politics and Work in Trenton*, New Brunswick, Rutgers University Press.

D'Amoto, D. J. 1985. *Springfield-350 Years: A Pictorial History*, Virginia, The Donning Company.

De Caux, L. 1970. *Labor Radical*, Boston, Beacon Press.

Deyrup, F. 1948. *Arms Makers of the Connecticut Valley*, Northampton, MA, Smith College Studies in History.

DiFilippo, Anthony. 1986. *Military Spending and Industrial Decline: A Study of the American Machine Tool Industry,* New York, Greenwood Press.

Doty, W. 1952. "The Southern Picture," *The Spectator,* August, 44-45.

Dudley, K. M. 1994. *The End of the Line: Lost Jobs, New Lives in Postindustrial America,* Chicago, University of Chicago Press.

Eckley, R. S. 1991. *Global Competition in Capital Goods: An American Perspective,* New York, Quorum Books.

Fairris, D. 1997. *Shopfloor Matters: Labor-Management Relations in Twentieth-Century American Manufacturing,* London, Routledge.

Field, B. 1946. *Piper Tompkins,* New York, Doubleday & Co., Inc., 1946.

Flint, A. and Dedman, B. 2002. "Urban Renaissance Eludes State's Mid-sized Cities," *Boston Globe,* June 23, 1.

Florida R. 1996. "Regional Creative Destruction: Production Organization, Globalization, and the Economic Transformation of the Midwest," *Economic Geography,* 72, 315-335.

Floyd, J. S. Jr. 1952. *Effects of Taxation on Industrial Location,* Chapel Hill, The University of North Carolina Press.

Flynn, E. K. 2001. *Expediting Organizational Transformation in the Small Firm Sector: Lessons from the Metalworking Industry,* Ph.D. diss., Massachusetts Institute of Technology.

Forrant, R. 1994. *Skill Was Never Enough: American Bosch, Local 206 and the Decline of Metalworking in Springfield, Massachusetts, 1900-1970,* University of Massachusetts at Amherst, unpublished Ph.D. Dissertation.

Forrant, R. 1996. "Skilled Workers and Union Organization in Springfield: The American Bosch Story," *Historical Journal of Massachusetts, 24*(1).

Forrant, R. 2000. "Between a Rock and a Hard Place: U.S. Industrial Unions, Shop Floor Participation and the Lean, Mean Global Economy," *Cambridge Journal of Economics,* 24, 751-769.

Forrant, R. 2001. "'Neither a sleepy village nor a coarse factory town': Skill in the Greater Springfield Massachusetts Industrial Economy 1800-1990," *Journal of Industrial History,* 4, 24-47.

Forrant, R. 2002. "Good Jobs and the Cutting Edge," in W. Lazonick and M. O'Sullivan, Eds., *Corporate Governance and Sustainable Prosperity: Industrial Innovation, International Competition and Intergenerational Dependence,* New York, Palgrave, 78-103.

Forrant, R. 2002. "Too Many Bends in the River: The Decline of the Connecticut River Valley Machine Tool Industry," *Journal of Industrial History,* 5(2), 71-91.

Forrant, R. 2002. "The Global Machine Tool Industry," in Malcolm Warner, Ed., *International Encyclopedia of Business and Management,* London, International Thompson Publishing, 2309-2316.

Forrant, R. and Barry, S. 2001. "Winners and Losers: High-Tech Employment Deals an Uneven Hand," *Massachusetts Benchmarks,* Summer, 12-16.

Forrant, R. and Flynn, E. 1998. "Seizing Agglomeration's Potential: the Greater Springfield Massachusetts Metalworking District in Transition, 1986-1996," *Regional Studies,* 32, 209-222.

Forrant, R. and Wilkinson, F. 2003. "Globalisation and Degenerative Production Systems: The Case of the Connecticut River Valley," a paper presented at the conference Clusters, Industrial Districts and Firms: The Challenge of Globalization, Modena, Italy, September 12-13.

Fortune, 1959. "Charles Perelle's Spacemanship," 59(1).

Friedlander, P. 1975. *The Emergence of a UAW Local, 1936-1939: A Study of Class and Culture*, Pittsburgh, University of Pittsburgh Press.

Frisch, M. 1972. *Town into City: Springfield Massachusetts and the Meaning of Community, 1840-1880*, Cambridge, Harvard University Press.

Fuchs, V. 1962. *Changes in the Location of Manufacturing in the United States Since 1929*, New Haven, Yale University Press.

Gabriele, M. 1988. "Goldman, Building a Machine Tool Empire," *Metalworking News*, August 15, 1.

Gibb, George S. 1950. *The Saco-Lowell Shops: Textile Machinery Building in New England 1813-1949*, New York, Russell and Russell.

Glasmeier, A. 2000. *Manufacturing Time: Global Competition in the Watch Industry, 1795-2000*, New York, Guilford.

Glover, J. and Cornell, W. 1941. *The Development of American Industries*, New York, Prentice-Hall.

Gordon, D. M. 1994. "Chickens Home to Roost: From Prosperity to Stagnation in the Postwar U.S. Economy," in M. Bernstein and D. Adler, Eds., *Understanding American Economic Decline*, New York, Cambridge University Press, 34-76.

Gormally, L. 1990. "Van Norman: A Jewel of a Company," *Springfield Journal*, 15(14), 4-5.

Graham, L. 1995. *On the Line at Subaru-Isuzu: The Japanese Model and the American Worker*, Ithaca, ILR Press.

Green, M. 1876. *Springfield Memories: Odds and Ends of Anecdote and Early Doings*, Springfield, Whitney and Adams.

Greider, W. 1997. *One World Ready or Not: The Manic Logic of Global Capitalism*, New York, Simon & Schuster.

Halpern, M. 1988. *UAW Politics in the Cold War Era*, Albany, State University of New York Press.

Hansen, F. 1998. "Compensation in the New Economy," *Compensation and Benefits Review*, January/February, 7-15.

Harrison, B. 1994. *Lean and Mean: The Changing Landscape of Corporate Power in the Age of Flexibility*, New York, Basic Books.

Harrison, B. and Bluestone, B. 1988. *The Great U-Turn: Corporate Restructuring and the Polarizing of America*, New York, Basic Books.

Hartford, W. 1990. *Working People of Holyoke: Class and Ethnicity in a Massachusetts Mill Town*, New Brunswick, Rutgers University Press.

Harvey, D. and Swyngedouw, E. 1993. "Industrial Restructuring, Community Disempowerment and Grass-Roots Resistance, in T. Hayter and D. Harvey, Eds., *The Factor & The City*, London, Mansell Publishing, 11-25.

Hayter, T. and Harvey, D. (Eds.). 1993. *The Factory & The City: The Story of the Cowley Automobile Works in Oxford*, London, Mansell.

Hekman, J. S. 1980. "The Future of High Technology Industry in New England: A Case Study of Computers," *New England Economic Review*, January/February 1980, 5-17.

Hekman, J. S. and John S. Strong, J. S. 1981. "The Evolution of New England Industry," *New England Economic Review*, March/April, 35-46.

Herod, A. 1997. "From a Geography of Labor to a Labor Geography: Labor's Spatial Fix and the Geography of Capitalism," *Antipode*, 29, 1-31.

Herod, A. 1998. *Organizing the Landscape: Geographical Perspectives on Labor Unionism*, Minneapolis, University of Minnesota Press, 1998.

Herod, A. 2001. *Labor Geographies: Workers and the Landscapes of Capitalism*, New York, The Guilford Press.

Herzenberg, S., Alic, J. and Wial, H. 1998. *New Rules for a New Economy: Employment and Opportunity in Postindustrial America*, Ithaca, Cornell University Press.

Hicks, Donald. 1986. *Automation Technology and Industrial Renewal: Adjustment Dynamics in the U.S. Metalworking Sector*, Washington, D.C., American Enterprise Institute for Public Policy Research.

Hilton, M. 1991. "Shared Training: Learning from Germany," *Monthly Labor Review* March, 33-37.

Holland, M. 1989. *When the Machine Stopped: A Cautionary Tale From Industrial America*, Boston, Harvard Business School Press.

Hounshell, D. 1984. *From the American System to Mass Production, 1800-1932*, Baltimore, Johns Hopkins University Press.

International Labour Organization. 1997. *World Labour Report: Industrial Relations, Democracy and Social Stability, 1997-1998*, Geneva, International Labour Office.

Japan Society for the Promotion of the Machine Industry. 1994. *On the Symbiosis of the Machine Industry*, 29.

Japan Society for the Promotion of the Machine Industry. 1996. *Machinery Industry Continues to Recover*, 30.

Jonas, A. 1998. "Investigating the Local-Global Paradox: Corporate Strategy, Union Local Autonomy, and Community Action in Chicago," in Andrew Herod, Ed., *Organizing the Landscape: Geographical Perspectives on Labor Unionism*, Minneapolis, University of Minnesota Press, 325-350.

Jones, B. 1997. *Forcing the Factory of the Future: Cybernation and Societal Institutions*, Cambridge, Cambridge University Press.

Jones, O. 1997. "Changing the Balance? Taylorism, TQM, and Work Organisation," *New Technology, Work and Employment*, 12, 13-24.

Kapstein, E. 1996. "Workers and the World Economy," *Foreign Affairs*, 75, 16-37.

Kennedy, J. F. 1954. "New England and the South: The Struggle for Industry," *The Atlantic Monthly*, January, 33.

Kenney, M., and Florida, R. 1993. *Beyond Mass Production: The Japanese System and its Transfer to the U.S.*, New York, Oxford University Press.

Khermouch, G. 1990. "Vermont USA Shifts Focus, Turns Profit," *Metalworking News*, September 3, 6.

Keil, R. 1998. *Los Angeles: Globalization, Urbanization and Social Struggles*, New York, Academic Press.

King, M. 1884. *King's Handbook of Springfield, Massachusetts: A Series of Monographs Historical and Descriptive*, Springfield, James D. Gill.

Kirsch, M. H. 1998. *In the Wake of the Giant: Multinational Restructuring and Uneven Development in a New England Community*, New York, State University of New York Press.

Kochan, T., Lansbury, R. and MacDuffie, J. P. 1997. *After Lean Production: Evolving Employment Practices in the World Auto Industry*, Ithaca, Cornell University Press.

Koizumi, K. 2002. "In Search of Wakon: The Cultural Dynamics of the Rise of Manufacturing Technology in Postwar Japan," *Technology and Culture*, 43, 29-49.

Konzelmann, S. and Forrant, R. 2003. "Creative Work Systems in Destructive Markets," in Brendan Burchell, Simon Deakin, Jonathan Michie and Jill Rubery, Eds., *Systems of Production: Markets, Organizations and Performance,* New York, Routledge, 129-158.

Lampe, D. 1988. *The Massachusetts Miracle: High Technology and Economic Revitalization,* Cambridge, The MIT Press.

Lazonick, W. 1990. *Competitive Advantage on the Shop Floor,* Cambridge, Harvard University Press.

Lazonick, W. and O'Sullivan, M. 2002. "Maximizing Shareholder Value: A New Ideology for Corporate Governance," in W. Lazonick and M. O'Sullivan, Eds., *Corporate Governance and Sustainable Prosperity: Industrial Innovation, International Competition and Intergenerational Dependence,* New York, Palgrave, 2002, 11-36.

Leahey, P. 1985. "Skilled Labor and the Rise of the Modern Corporation: The Case of the Electrical Industry," *Labor History,* 27, 31-53.

Leff, J, 1986. *United Technologies and the Closing of the American Bosch,* Harvard Business School Case Study 9-386-174.

Lichtenstein, N. 1980. "Auto Worker Militancy and the Structure of Factory Life, 1937-1955," *Journal of American History,* 67, 335-353.

Lichtenstein, N. 1982. *Labor's War at Home: The CIO in World War II,* New York, Cambridge University Press.

Lichtenstein, N. 1983. "Conflict Over Workers' Control: The Automobile Industry in World War II," in M. Frisch and D. Walkowitz, Eds., *Working Class America: Essays on Labour, Community and American Society,* Urbana, University of Illinois Press, 284-311.

Lichtenstein, N. 1992. "Reutherism on the Shop Floor: Union Strategy and Shop Floor Conflict in the USA, 1946-1970," in Steven Tolliday and Jonathan Zeitlin, Eds., *Between Fordism and Flexibility,* Providence, RI, Berg Publishing, 121-143.

Lichtenstein, N. 1995. *The Most Dangerous Man in Detroit: Walter Reuther and the Fate of American Labor,* New York, Basic Books.

Lichtenstein, N. and Harris, H. J., Eds. 1993. *Industrial Democracy in America: The Ambiguous Promise,* New York, Cambridge University Press.

Lipietz, A. 1987. *Mirages and Miracles: The Crisis of Global Fordism,* London, Verso.

Lumpkin, K. 1934. *Shutdowns in the Connecticut River Valley,* Northampton, MA, Smith College Studies in History.

Malone, P. 1988. "Little Kinks and Devices at the Springfield Armory, 1892-1918," *Journal of the Society for Industrial Archeology,* 14, no. 1, 59-76.

March, Artemis. 1988. *The U.S. Machine Tool Industry and its Foreign Competitors,* Cambridge, MIT Commission on Industrial Productivity.

Markusen, A. and Yudken, J. 1992. *Dismantling the Cold War Economy,* New York, Basic Books.

Markusen, A. et al., 1991. *The Rise of the Gunbelt,* New York, Oxford University Press.

Marsden, D. 1995. "A Phoenix from the Ashes of Apprenticeship? Vocational Training in Britain," *International Contributions to Labour Studies,* 5, 87-114.

Marvin, P. 1954. "Automatic Machines at Work," *Automation,* 1, August, 34-37.

Massey, D. and Meegan, R. 1982. *The Anatomy of Job Loss: The How, Why and Where of Employment Decline,* London, Methuen and Co.

Mealey, M. 1974. "NC and Computers Build NC," *World Manufacturing,* November, 31-34.

Meredith, R. 1997. "The Brave New World of General Motors," *The New York Times,* October 26, section 3, 1.

Meyer, D. 1998. "Formation of Advanced Technology Districts: New England Textile Machinery and Firearms," *Economic Geography,* Extra Issue, 31-45.

Meyer, J. 1944. "Trade Union Plans for Postwar Reconstruction in the United States," *Social Research,* 11, 491-505.

Meyer, S. 1981. *The Five Dollar Day: Labor Management and Social Control in the Ford Motor Company, 1908-1921,* Albany, State University of New York Press.

Meyer, S. 1988. "Technology and the Workplace: Skilled and Production Workers at Allis-Chalmers, 1900-1941," *Technology and Culture,* 29(4), 839-864.

Meyer, S. 1992. *Stalin Over Wisconsin: The Making and Unmaking of Militant Unionism, 1900-1950,* New Brunswick, Rutgers University Press.

Millman, J. 1998. "Mexico is becoming auto-making hot spot," *Wall Street Journal,* June 23, 17.

Montgomery, D. 1979. *Workers' Control in America: Studies in the History of Work, Technology, and Labor Struggles,* New York, Cambridge University Press.

Moody, K. 1997. *Workers in a Lean World: Unions in the International Economy,* New York, Verso.

Mortimer, W. 1971. *Organize: My Life as A Union Man,* Boston, Beacon Press.

National Machine Tool Builders Association. 1981. *Meeting the Japanese Challenge,* McLean, VA, National Machine Tool Builders Association.

National Research Council. 1983. *The U.S. Machine Tool Industry and the Defense Industrial Base,* Washington, D.C., National Academy Press.

Noble, D. 1986. *Forces of Production: A Social History of Industrial Automation,* New York, Oxford University Press.

North, K. 1997. *Localizing Global Production: Know-how Transfer in International Manufacturing,* Geneva, ILO Press.

O'Brien, F. S. 1968. "The 'Communist Dominated' Unions in the United States Since 1950," *Labor History,* 9, 174-190.

Ohno, T. 1988. *The Toyota Production System: Beyond Large Scale Production,* Cambridge, Productivity Press.

O'Sullivan, M. 2000a. "The Innovative Enterprise and Corporate Governance," *Cambridge Journal of Economics,* 24, 393-416.

O'Sullivan, M. 2000b. "Shareholder Value, Financial Theory and Economic Performance," paper presented at the 52nd Annual Meeting of the Industrial Relations Research Association, Boston: 2000.

Palfrey, 1846. *Statistics of the Condition and Products of Certain Branches of Industry in Massachuetts for the Year Ending April 1, 1945.*

Powers, L. and Markusen, A. 1999. "A Just Transition? Lessons from Defense Worker Adjustment in the 1990s," Washington D.C., Economic Policy Institute Technical Paper No. 237.

Raff, D. 1991. "Ford Welfare Capitalism in its Economic Context," in Sanford Jacoby, Ed., *Masters to Managers,* New York, Columbia University Press.

Reilly, J. 1986. *A History of the Westinghouse Electric Company in Springfield, 1915-1970: The Demise of a Giant,* unpublished paper in the Pioneer Valley Historical Society Westinghouse Papers.

Robinson, I. 1955. *Yankee Toolmaker,* Bridgeport, CT, The Bullard Company.

Roe, J. W. 1916. *English and American Tool Builders,* New York, McGraw-Hill Book Company.

Rolt, L. T. 1965. *A Short History of Machine Tools,* Cambridge, MIT Press.

Rosenberg, N., Ed. 1969. *The American System of Manufacturers: The Report of the Committee on the Machinery of the United States 1855 and Special Reports of George Wallis and Joseph Whitworth,* Edinburgh, Scotland, Edinburgh University Press.

Rosenberg, N. 1963. "Technological Change in the Machine Tool Industry, 1840-1910," *Journal of Economic History,* 23, 414-443.

Rosswurm, S., Ed. 1992. *The CIO's Left-led Unions,* New Brunswick, Rutgers University Press.

Roy, D. 1952. "Quota Restriction and Goldbricking in a Machine Shop," *American Journal of Sociology,* 57, 1952, 427-442.

Roy, D. 1954. "Efficiency and 'The Fix': Informal Intergroup Relations in a Piecework Machine Shop," *American Journal of Sociology,* 60, 1954, 255-266.

Schatz, R. 1977. *American Electrical Workers: Work, Struggles, Aspirations 1930-1950,* Ph.D. diss., University of Pittsburgh, 1977.

Schatz, R. 1979. "Union Pioneers: The Founders of Local Unions at GE and Westinghouse, 1933-1937," *Journal of American History,* 66, 586-602.

Schatz, R. 1983. *The Electrical Workers: A History of Labor at General Electric and Westinghouse, 1923-1960,* Urbana, Ill., University of Illinois Press.

Schiff, G. and Goldfield, N. 1994. "Deming Meets Braverman: Toward a Progressive Analysis of the Continuous Quality Improvement Paradigm," *International Journal of Health Services,* 24(4).

Scott, J. 2002. "In Some Pockets, 90's Boom Was a Bust," *New York Times,* June 17, A16.

Scranton, P. 1997. *Endless Novelty: Specialty Production and American Industrialization, 1865-1925,* Princeton, NJ: Princeton University Press.

Seider, M. 1994. "The CIO in Rural Massachusetts: Sprague Electric and North Adams, 1937-1944," *Historical Journal of Massachusetts,* 22, 51-73.

Shaiken, H. 1987. *Automation and Global Production: Automobile Engine Production in U.S. Mexican Studies.*

Slichter, S. 1941. *Union Policies and Industrial Management,* Washington, D.C.

Smith, M. R. 1977. *Harpers Ferry Armory and the New Technology: The Challenge of Change,* Ithaca, Cornell University Press.

Stanton, R. F. V. 1930. *Accuracy For Seventy Years 1860-1930,* Hartford, CT.

Stone, A. 1929. *The Vermont of Today,* New York, Lewis Historical Publishing Company.

Stone, O. 1930. *History of Massachusetts Industries: Their Inception, Growth and Success,* Boston, S. J. Clarke Publishing Company.

Sum, A. M., Harrington, P. et al., 2002. *The State of the American Dream in Massachusetts, 2002,* Boston, MassINC.

Tagliabue, J. J. 1997. "Buona note, guten tag: Europe's New Workdays," *The New York Times,* October 20, D1.

Tager, J. 1991. "The Massachusetts Miracle," *Historical Journal of Massachusetts,* 19, Summer, 111-132.

Tolliday, S. and Zeitlin, J. 1992. "Shop-Floor Bargaining, Contract Unionism and Job Control: An Anglo-American Perspective," in Steven Tolliday and Jonathan Zeitlin, Eds., *Between Fordism and Flexibility*, Providence, RI, Berg Publishing, 99-120.

Tomb, J. O. 1953. "Should Industry Move South," *Harvard Business Review*, 31, September-October, 83-90.

Trainer, G. A. 1979. *The Metalworking Machinery Industry in New England: An Analysis of Investment Behavior*, master's thesis, Massachusetts Institute of Technology, 1979.

Tripp, L. 1952. "The Union's Role in Industry—Its Extent and Limits," in G. Brooks and M. Derber, Eds., *Interpreting the Labor Movement*, Madison, Industrial Relations Research Association.

Tsuji, M., Ishikawa, M., and Ishikawa, M. 1996. *Technology Transfer and Management in East Asian Machine Tool Industries: Lessons Learned From the Japanese Machine Tool Industry*, Osaka University.

Tull, B. 2000. *The Springfield Armory as Industrial Policy: Interchangeable Parts and the Precision Corridor*, Ph.D. diss., University of Massachusetts Amherst.

Uchitelle, L. 1997, "Global Good Times Meet the Global Glut," *The New York Times*, November 16, D1.

United Technologies. 1985. *Corporation Annual Report*, Hartford, CT.

Van Hosen Taber, M. 1955. *A History of the Cutlery Industry in the Connecticut Valley*, Northampton, MA, Smith College Studies in History.

Wagoner, Harliss. 1968. *The United States Machine Tool Industry From 1900 to 1950*, Cambridge, MIT Press.

Washburn, C. G. 1917. *Industrial Worcester*, Worcester, The Davis Press.

Weaver, F. 2002. *Economic Literacy: Basic Economics With an Attitude*, New York, Rowan & Littlefield.

Weil, F. 1998. "Capitalism and Industrialization in New England, 1815-1845," *The Journal of American History*, 84, 1334-1354.

Weinberg, D. 1996. "A Brief Look at Postwar U.S. Income Inequality," *Current Population Reports*, 60-191.

Weisskopf, T., Bowles, S. and Gordon, D. 1983. "Hearts and Minds: A Social Model of U.S. Productivity Growth," *Brookings Papers on Economic Activity*, no. 2.

Whittlesey, D. 1920. *The Springfield Armory: A Study in Institutional Development*, Chicago, University of Chicago unpublished Ph.D. Dis.

Wieandt, A. 1994. "'Innovation and the Creation, Development and Destruction of Markets in the World Machine Tool Industry," *Small Business Economics*, 6, 421-437.

Woodbury, R. 1972. *Studies in the History of Machine Tools*, Cambridge, MIT Press.

Wypijewski, J. 2001. "GE Brings Bad Things to Life," *The Nation*, February 12, 18-23.

Yates, M. D. 2002. "Economic Crisis and the Crisis of U.S. Labor," *Monthly Review*, 53, 47-55.

Yates, M. D. 2005. "A Statistical Portrait of the U.S. Working Class," *Monthly Review*, 56, November, 12-31.

ARCHIVES AND MANUSCRIPT COLLECTIONS

The largest collection of papers on the history of the United Electrical, Radio and Machine Workers Union is located at the University of Pittsburgh Library. There are hundreds of documents on the history of the union in New England, with several documents detailing organizing efforts in the Connecticut River Valley. For Springfield, the Pioneer Valley Historical Society's library contains well-indexed business history files on many of the city's largest companies and newspaper holdings dating back to the Civil War that are also well-indexed by firm. City Directories date back to approximately 1830 and are very useful in determining such things as worker occupations and numbers of firms in the city. Various state and federal census documents are also in the library and are an important source in understanding the workforce structure. For Bosch and Local 206 the single best source is the extensive holdings at the University of Massachusetts Amherst. The union donated all of its records to the library in the Summer of 1986 when the plant closed. There are thousands of well-organized files with an excellent index covering the history of the local from 1942 forward. The papers are organized in five broad categories, administration, correspondence, company-union relations, publications, and membership. Included in the holdings are individual grievance and arbitration files, membership and dues check-off lists, correspondence with various local and national unions, an almost complete set of union newspapers dating from 1951 to 1970, minutes of various union meetings, and several contracts.

GOVERNMENT DOCUMENTS

Massachusetts Department of Labor and Industries, *Annual Reports, 1938, 1949*
Massachusetts Population Census, 1880, 1930
Springfield City Directory, various years
United States Department of Commerce, *Manufacturing Census, Selected Years, 1890-1987*
United States Population Census, 1880-1950

NEWSPAPERS

American Bosch *Craftsman*
American Bosch *Progress*
American Bosch *Local 206 Bulletin*
Boston Globe (BG)
Commercial Dispatch (CD) Columbus, Mississippi
Hartford Courant
Holyoke Transcript-Telegram (HTT)
New York Times (NYT)
Springfield Daily News (SDN)

Springfield Evening News (SEN)
Springfield Morning Union (SMU)
Springfield Republican (SR)
Springfield Sunday Republican (SSR)
The Republican
United Electrical Workers News (UEN)

Note: The names of Springfield, Massachusetts, newspapers changed numerous times over the years covered in this book. Once a city with many daily and Sunday newspapers, as befits the city's and the region's decline, in 2008 there is one newspaper of record, *The Republican.* In nearby Hartford, Connecticut, there is one newspaper, the *Hartford Courant.*

Index

ABA. *See* American Bosch *listings*
Adamson, Jon, 111
Adorno, Greg, 156
AFL-CIO, 50
Alien Property Custodian (APC), 45-48
Allen, Charles, 65
Allen, Gary, 156
Allis-Chalmers, 90
Almeida, Beth, 144
Alsop, Joseph, 52
Amalgamated Meatcutters, 2
Amato, John, 154
AMBAC Industries, 97
American Bosch (1911-1950)
    Alien Property Custodian's office takes
        control in 1941, 45-48
    apprenticeship program, collaborative
        (1936), 31
    Armory, Springfield, 1
    Athletic Association, 8
    Bosch Local 206, 40-43
    electoral strategy in Springfield, 39
    employment losses/layoffs, 50
    fuel-injection equipment production
        starts in 1938, 36
    International Union of Electrical
        Workers, 53-57
    origins in 1911, 33
    photographs, early, 34-35
    skilled workers and union organization,
        44-45
    starter parts for U.S. vehicle industry,
        produced 50 percent of, 33
    Treasury Department (U.S.) takes
        control in 1941, 45

[Athletic Association]
    unionization starts in 1930s, 36-38
    union locals caught up in internecine
        battles, 50
    United Electrical, Radio and Machine
        Workers, 51-57
    war work boost and post-war decline,
        45-50
    work distribution, 44
    World War I, seized for security
        reasons during, 33, 36
    See also History/growth of industry
        along Connecticut River region;
        Importer of machine tools, U.S. as
        an; Springfield (MA)
American Bosch (1950s-early 1960s)
    contractualism, 80
    cordial relations between workforce
        and management, 79, 80
    cost-improvement program, 84
    denials of plant relocations, 63-64
    Europe, work moves to, 76-77
    grievance system, a dysfunctional,
        89-92
    Kennedy (John F.) talks about plant
        relocations, 71-72
    Labor-Management Production
        Committee, 80, 83, 109
    manufacturing facilities, closing of,
        59-60
    numerically controlled machines, 87-89
    relocations, plant, 60-65
    reorganization of corporate labor
        relations, 82-84
    scrap problem, 84-87

For Product Safety Concerns and Information please contact our
EU representative GPSR@taylorandfrancis.com Taylor & Francis
Verlag GmbH, Kaufingerstraße 24, 80331 München, Germany